CW01376254

This book brings together an interesting set of contributions on the important theme of informality, ranging from cross-border petty trading to informal blue-collar moonlighting, employment and entrepreneurship. The editors stimulate a timely discussion about the nature of informality and encourage readers to think laterally and broadly about the relationship between informality and the formal structures of power and economy.
Sally Nikoline Cummings, University of St Andrews, UK

This book is essential reading not only for those who seek a nuanced understanding of the nature of informal economic practices but also those interested in acquiring a deeper appreciation of this most fascinating of regions, the world that abandoned communism, often without implementing a sustainable alternative. Illuminating and frequently surprising, even for those intimate with the region, this superb collection is destined to become the standard work for those intrigued by these vital economic practices that lie just beneath the surface or out of public view throughout the post-communist world.
Donnacha Ó Beacháin, Dublin City University, Ireland

From illicit taxi drivers in Slovakia to herb traders in Azerbaijan, the diverse and rich ethnographic case studies in this volume provide a vivid and colourful analysis of informal practices and transactions in the post-socialist space. *The Informal Post-Socialist Economy* makes an important contribution to our conceptual understanding of informal practices. Rather than viewing informality as marginal, transitional and lurking in the shadows, in this volume Jeremy Morris and Abel Polese adopt a post-structural approach and have brought together cases studies that finesse a more nuanced understanding of informality. This is achieved by studying informal economic practices through the lens of the socially embedded everyday lived experience of people's lives. In doing so, it achieves a shift in our normative understanding of the nature of informal practices and also challenges the perceived binary between formal and informal economies. The significant in-field experience and interdisciplinary nature of the volume's contributions give the ethnographic case studies great depth, which acts to highlight the tension within informal economic practices between a capitalist individualist logic and a logic of mutuality and reciprocity. This probing and fascinating book will be of great interest to a broad range of scholars and students interested in the economy and politics of post-Socialist states.
Rico Isaacs, Oxford Brookes University, UK

This edited volume is an excellent contribution to our understanding of informality in the context of post-socialist economies. With rich empirical evidence gathered from a vast geography stretching between Central Asia and Eastern Europe, the authors reveal an untold story of capitalist transformation. In their anthropological and ethnographic research, the human condition takes the central place, not frequently misrepresented economic growth figures and business statistics. We read about tragedies and disappointments, as well as hopes of new entrepreneurs within capitalist market developments, all of whom strive to have a small stake in the "winners' world". *Informal Post-Socialist Economy* is a very valuable source for scholars and practitioners.
Gül Berna Özcan, Royal Holloway, University of London, UK

This book has long been overdue because its authors analyse informal economic practices beyond a normative moral perspective by choosing 'composite informants' to make clear that these practices are also highly politicized. An innovative and inspiring form to present ethnographic data!
Bettina Bruns, Leipzig Institute for Regional Geography, Germany

This book assembles an impressive number of case studies on informal economic practices related to employment and work in post-socialist countries. Mainly following a socio-anthropological approach, they provide deep insights into everyday life in these societies. Even more importantly, they offer many (often implicit) challenges to conventional wisdom on post-socialist transition and informality. The book can, thus, be of special value to open-minded social scientists.

Heiko Pleines, Research Centre for East European Studies at the University of Bremen, Germany

This is the first book that really brings out the interface between those two levels and shows how, without the former, we cannot understand the latter. Not only that, it also demonstrates the relevance of informal transactions in post-socialist spaces. It also offers a hands-on overview on how informal mechanisms operate, providing the reader with an understanding of how embedded and important these transactions are, both at the micro and macro levels in post-socialist societies.

Gaudenz Assenza, Director, University for the Future Initiative, Slovakia

This book, edited by Morris and Polese, is a highly successful effort to shed light on an important aspect of post-socialist economies, the informal economy, which influences all spheres of life, from electoral politics to cultural transformations. The ethnographic approach taken in this book, which focuses on individual life stories within a wider context of informal economy, allows the editors to reveal a unique and refreshing perspective on this vital aspect of post-socialist transition.

Mikayel Zolyan, V. Brusov Yerevan State Linguistic University, Armenia

This book is a deep exploration into the nature and diversity of informal economies. The editors have put together contributions from authors with a deep experience in the field, thereby allowing them to go well-beyond normative approaches by engaging with a variety of case studies. They not only demonstrate how little the phenomenon has been explored, especially in post-socialism, but they also, and equally importantly, show how wide informal economies underpin the structure of a society and that informality cannot be circumscribed to the weak or the poor but is a reality affecting the life of all segments a society.

Cui Shoujun, Renmin University of China

This book is a most comprehensive attempt to describe how informality works, its causes and its effects. It provides an interesting account on how "things are getting done" and on the never-ending competition between a state and its citizens. I am confident it will be of use not only to scholars but also to practitioners and anyone interested in public and social policy.

Han Kurbanov, Turkmen Academy of Science, Turkmenistan

The Informal Post-Socialist Economy

From smugglers to entrepreneurs, blue-collar workers and taxi drivers, this book deals with the multitude of characters engaged in informal economic practices in the former socialist regions. Going beyond a conception of informality as opposed to the formal sector, its authors demonstrate the fluid nature of informal transactions straddling the crossroads between illegal, illicit, socially acceptable and symbolically meaningful practices. Their argument is informed by a wide range of case studies, from Central Europe to the Baltics and Central Asia, each of which is constructed around a single informant. Each chapter narrates the story of a composite person or household that was carefully selected or constructed by an author with long-standing ethnographic research experience in the given field site.

Wide in geographical, empirical and theoretical scope, the book uses ethnographic narrative accounts of everyday life to make links between 'ordinary' meanings of informality. Challenging reductively economistic perspectives on cross-border trading, undeclared work and other informal activities, the authors illustrate the wide variety of interpretive meanings that people ascribe to such practices. Alongside 'getting by' and 'getting ahead' in recently marketised societies, these meanings relate to sociality, kinship ties and solidarity, along with more surprising 'political' and moral reasonings.

Jeremy Morris is a Senior Lecturer at the University of Birmingham, UK.

Abel Polese is a Research Fellow at the Institute for International Conflict Resolution and Reconstruction of Dublin City University, Ireland.

Routledge Contemporary Russia and Eastern Europe Series

Liberal Nationalism in Central Europe
Stefan Auer

Civil-Military Relations in Russia and Eastern Europe
David J. Betz

The Extreme Nationalist Threat in Russia
The growing influence of Western Rightist Ideas
Thomas Parland

Economic Development in Tatarstan
Global markets and a Russian Region
Leo McCann

Adapting to Russia's New Labour Market
Gender and employment strategy
Edited by Sarah Ashwin

Building Democracy and Civil Society East of the Elbe
Essays in honour of Edmund Mokrzycki
Edited by Sven Eliaeson

The Telengits of Southern Siberia
Landscape, religion and knowledge in motion
Agnieszka Halemba

The Development of Capitalism in Russia
Simon Clarke

Russian Television Today
Primetime drama and comedy
David MacFadyen

The Rebuilding of Greater Russia
Putin's foreign policy towards the CIS countries
Bertil Nygren

A Russian Factory Enters the Market Economy
Claudio Morrison

Democracy Building and Civil Society in Post-Soviet Armenia
Armine Ishkanian

NATO-Russia Relations in the Twenty-First Century
Aurel Braun

Russian Military Reform
A failed exercise in defence decision making
Carolina Vendil Pallin

The Multilateral Dimension in Russian Foreign Policy
Edited by Elana Wilson Rowe and Stina Torjesen

Russian Nationalism and the National Reassertion of Russia
Edited by Marlène Laruelle

The Caucasus – An Introduction
Frederik Coene

Radical Islam in the Former Soviet Union
Edited by Galina M. Yemelianova

Russia's European Agenda and the Baltic States
Janina Šleivytė

Regional Development in Central and Eastern Europe:
Development processes and policy challenges
Edited by Grzegorz Gorzelak, John Bachtler and Maciej Smętkowski

Russia and Europe
Reaching agreements, digging trenches
Kjell Engelbrekt and Bertil Nygren

Russia's Skinheads
Exploring and rethinking subcultural lives
Hilary Pilkington, Elena Omel'chenko and Al'bina Garifzianova

The Colour Revolutions in the Former Soviet Republics
Successes and failures
Edited by Donnacha Ó Beacháin and Abel Polese

Russian Mass Media and Changing Values
Edited by Arja Rosenholm, Kaarle Nordenstreng and Elena Trubina

The Heritage of Soviet Oriental Studies
Edited by Michael Kemper and Stephan Conermann

Religion and Language in Post-Soviet Russia
Brian P. Bennett

Jewish Women Writers in the Soviet Union
Rina Lapidus

Chinese Migrants in Russia, Central Asia and Eastern Europe
Edited by Felix B. Chang and Sunnie T. Rucker-Chang

Poland's EU Accession
Sergiusz Trzeciak

The Russian Armed Forces in Transition
Economic, geopolitical and institutional uncertainties
Edited by Roger N. McDermott, Bertil Nygren and Carolina Vendil Pallin

The Religious Factor in Russia's Foreign Policy
Alicja Curanović

Postcommunist Film - Russia, Eastern Europe and World Culture
Moving images of postcommunism
Edited by Lars Lyngsgaard Fjord Kristensen

Russian Multinationals
From regional supremacy to global lead
Andrei Panibratov

Russian Anthropology After the Collapse of Communism
Edited by Albert Baiburin, Catriona Kelly and Nikolai Vakhtin

The Post-Soviet Russian Orthodox Church
Politics, culture and Greater Russia
Katja Richters

Lenin's Terror
The ideological origins of early Soviet State violence
James Ryan

Life in Post-Communist Eastern Europe after EU Membership
Edited by Donnacha Ó Beacháin, Vera Sheridan and Sabina Stan

EU – Border Security
Challenges, (mis)perceptions, and responses
Serghei Golunov

Power and Legitimacy - Challenges from Russia
Edited by Per-Arne Bodin, Stefan Hedlund and Elena Namli

Managing Ethnic Diversity in Russia
Edited by Oleh Protsyk and Benedikt Harzl

Believing in Russia – Religious Policy After Communism
Geraldine Fagan

The Changing Russian University
From state to market
Tatiana Maximova-Mentzoni

The Transition to National Armies in the Former Soviet Republics, 1988–2005
Jesse Paul Lehrke

The Fall of the Iron Curtain and the Culture of Europe
Peter I. Barta

Russia After 2012
From Putin to Medvedev to Putin – continuity, change, or revolution?
Edited by J.L. Black and Michael Johns

Business in Post-Communist Russia
Privatisation and the limits of transformation
Mikhail Glazunov

Rural Inequality in Divided Russia
Stephen K. Wegren

Business Leaders and New Varieties of Capitalism in Post-Communist Europe
Edited by Katharina Bluhm, Bernd Martens and Vera Trappmann

Russian Energy and Security up to 2030
Edited by Susanne Oxenstierna and Veli-Pekka Tynkkynen

The Informal Post-Socialist Economy
Embedded practices and livelihoods
Edited by Jeremy Morris and Abel Polese

Russia and East Asia
Informal and gradual integration
Edited by Tsuneo Akaha and Anna Vassilieva

The Making of Modern Georgia, 1918–2012
The first georgian republic and its successors
Edited by Stephen F. Jones

The Informal Post-Socialist Economy

Embedded practices and livelihoods

**Edited by Jeremy Morris
and Abel Polese**

Routledge
Taylor & Francis Group
LONDON AND NEW YORK

First published 2014
by Routledge
2 Park Square, Milton Park, Abingdon, Oxon OX14 4RN
and by Routledge
711 Third Avenue, New York, NY 10017

Routledge is an imprint of the Taylor & Francis Group, an informa business

© 2014 selection and editorial material, Jeremy Morris and Abel Polese; individual chapters, the contributors

The right of Jeremy Morris and Abel Polese to be identified as authors of the editorial material, and of the individual authors as authors of their contributions, has been asserted by them in accordance with sections 77 and 78 of the Copyright, Designs and Patents Act 1988.

All rights reserved. No part of this book may be reprinted or reproduced or utilised in any form or by any electronic, mechanical, or other means, now known or hereafter invented, including photocopying and recording, or in any information storage or retrieval system, without permission in writing from the publishers.

Trademark notice: Product or corporate names may be trademarks or registered trademarks, and are used only for identification and explanation without intent to infringe.

British Library Cataloguing in Publication Data
A catalogue record for this book is available from the British Library

Library of Congress Cataloging in Publication Data
  Morris, Jeremy and Polese, Abel
  The informal post-socialist economy : embedded practices and livelihoods / edited by Jeremy Morris and Abel Polese.
    pages ; cm. — (Routledge contemporary Russia and Eastern Europe series ; 50)
  Includes bibliographical references and index.
  1. Informal sector (Economics)—Former Soviet republics.
  2. Informal sector (Economics)—Russia (Federation) 3. Informal sector (Economics)—Europe, Eastern. 4. Small business—Former Soviet republics. 5. Small business—Russia (Federation) 6. Small business—Europe, Eastern. 7. Post-communism—Economic aspects—Former Soviet republics. 8. Post-communism—Economic aspects—Russia (Federation) 9. Post-communism—Economic aspects—Europe, Eastern. I. Morris, Jeremy, 1974- editor. II. Polese, Abel, editor of compilation. III. Series: Routledge contemporary Russia and Eastern Europe series; 50.
  HD2346.F6154 2014
  330—dc23
  2013025730

ISBN: 978-0-415-85491-7 (hbk)
ISBN: 978-0-203-74054-5 (ebk)

Typeset in Times New Roman
by Swales & Willis Ltd, Exeter, Devon, UK

Contents

List of contributors	xi
Acknowledgments	xiv
Foreword by Catherine Wanner	xvi

Introduction: informality – enduring practices,
entwined livelihoods 1
JEREMY MORRIS AND ABEL POLESE

PART 1
**'Entrepreneurial' informality? Self- and off-the-books
employment** 19

1 The diverse livelihood practices of healthcare workers
   in Ukraine: the case of Sasha and Natasha 21
   COLIN C. WILLIAMS AND OLGA ONOSCHENKO

2 The story of Šarūnas: an *Invisible Citizen* of Lithuania 35
   IDA HARBOE KNUDSEN

3 Moonlighting strangers met on the way: the nexus of
   informality and blue-collar sociality in Russia 51
   JEREMY MORRIS

4 Nannies and informality in Romanian local childcare markets 67
   BORBÁLA KOVÁCS

5 Drinking with Vova: an individual entrepreneur between
   illegality and informality 85
   ABEL POLESE

6 When is an illicit taxi driver more than a taxi driver? Case studies from transit and trucking in post-socialist Slovakia 102
DAVID KARJANEN

PART 2
At home abroad? Transnational informality and the invisible flows of people and goods 119

7 From shuttle trader to businesswomen: the informal bazaar economy in Kyrgyzstan 121
ANNA CIEŚLEWSKA

8 'Business as casual': shuttle trade on the Belarus–Lithuania border 135
OLGA SASUNKEVICH

9 'The glove compartment half-full of letters' – informality and cross-border trade at the edge of the Schengen Area 152
KRISTINE MÜLLER AND JUDITH MIGGELBRINK

10 Informal economy writ large and small: from Azerbaijani herb traders to Moscow shop owners 165
LALE YALÇIN-HECKMANN

Index 187

Contributors

Anna Cieślewska is a Researcher at the Institute of Applied Social Science, the University of Warsaw. Her academic background is in International Development. Since 2006, she has also been working for the Polish NGO sector as a Researcher, implementing various social and research projects in the region of the former Soviet Union, such as Chechnya, Georgia, Armenia, Kyrgyzstan, Tajikistan and others. She is particularly interested in the socio-economic development of Central Asia and Caucasus, the consequences of implementation of development policies into the ex-USSR and Eastern Europe, migration, Islamic doctrine and local traditions in the post-Soviet region, and contemporary aspects of the coexistence of Arab-Muslim civilizations and the West.

Ida Harboe Knudsen is a Post-doctoral Fellow at the Institute for Culture and Society of Aarhus University, Denmark. She wrote her PhD on the topic of changes for Lithuania's small-scale farmers in light of the EU accession at the Max Planck Institute for Social Anthropology. In 2012, she published a book with Anthem Press based on the dissertation. Currently, she is situated in Aarhus and is working on a project financed by the Danish Independent Research Council on invisible citizens, illegal work and shadow economies. She has published on the subjects of agriculture, EU, market and trade, and mafia groups and illegal work.

David Karjanen is Assistant Professor of American Studies and the affiliate faculty with the Center for German and European Studies at the University of Minnesota. He was previously a Post-doctoral Fellow at the Center for Comparative Immigration Studies, UCSD, and a Fulbright Fellow to the Slovak Republic. His research is on the comparative political economy and work systems of Europe and the United States.

Borbála Kovács is currently Visiting Assistant Professor at the Department of Political Science, Central European University. Her research focuses on the impact of family policy provisions on young children's care arrangements, the organisation of childcare in Central and Eastern Europe, Romania in particular, and social politics, from a micro-level perspective. Borbála regularly contributes social policy analyses for the Bucharest-based Median Research Centre think tank's OpenPolitics.ro initiative.

xii *Contributors*

Judith Miggelbrink received her PhD in geography from the University of Leipzig, Germany. She is coordinator of the research unit 'Production of Space: State and Society' at the Leibniz Institute for Regional Geography in Leipzig. She has led several research projects concerning the role of spatiality and territoriality, especially on the effects of borders in everyday life and practices, as well as on indigeneity in a Northern European context.

Jeremy Morris is a Senior Lecturer in Russian at the University of Birmingham, UK. His research interests include new media, informal economy, class, precarity and, more generally, post-socialism. His current research is focused on ethnographic approaches to understanding actually lived experience in the former Soviet Union. He has published widely on material cultures of the working class in Russia, social networks and new media, virtue ethics and lay normativity, and the informal economy.

Kristine Müller is a Social Geographer in Berlin, Germany. Her main research interest lies in the dynamics of social inequality. From 2005 until 2011, she was based at the Leibniz Institute for Regional Development and Structural Planning in Erkner, Germany, where she also contributed to the research project 'Geographies at the edges of the European project'. She recently received her PhD in geography at the University of Potsdam, Germany.

Olga Onoschenko has a PhD from the Management School at the University of Sheffield, UK. Her research explores the nature and extent of informal work in Ukraine. Her main research interest focuses on the informal economy particularly in the post-Soviet countries.

Abel Polese is a Research Fellow at the Institute for International Conflict Resolution and Reconstruction of Dublin City University and Senior Research Fellow at the Institute of Political Science and Governance of Tallinn University. Prior to these, he worked as a Policy Analyst for the European Commission, DG Research and Innovation, and as a Research Fellow for the University of Edinburgh, Dresden Technical University and Odessa National University. With Routledge, he has previously published *The Colour Revolutions in the Former Soviet Union: Successes and Failures*, London and New York: Routledge, 2010 (co-edited with D. Ó Beacháin) and he is a co-editor of *Studies of Transition States and Societies*, an open-access bi-annual journal with focus on the former USSR.

Olga Sasunkevich is a Researcher at the International Research Training Group 'Baltic Borderlands: Shifting Boundaries of Mind and Culture in the Baltic Sea Region' (Greifswald University, Germany). She has studied sociology and gender studies at the European Humanities University in Vilnius, Lithuania, and Media Studies at the Belarusian State University in Minsk. Her research interests include border studies, gender studies, informal economy and post-socialist transformations. Her recent publications are: Place, Gender and Class on Borderlands: Towards a Theoretical Framework of Studying the Border between Belarus and Lithuania, in *Gender Studies and Research* (Lyčiu studijos ir tyrimai), 2011, 52–66.

Colin C. Williams is a Professor of Public Policy in the Management School at the University of Sheffield, UK. His research interests include the informal economy, work organization and the future of work, subjects on which he has published some 20 monographs and 270 journal articles over the past 25 years.

Lale Yalçın-Heckmann studied sociology in the USA and Turkey and anthropology in London (PhD, at LSE). From 2000 to 2009, she was a Senior Researcher working on privatization and agrarian property in Azerbaijan and she led the research group 'Caucasian Boundaries and Citizenship from Below' on the South Caucasus (2006–2009) at the Max Planck Institute for Social Anthropology in Halle/Saale. Since 2010, she has been Docent in Anthropology at the University of Pardubice, Czech Republic, and, since 2012, a member of principal faculty of the international research school ANARCHIE at Max Planck. Her research areas and themes, among others, include Kurds in Turkey and the Caucasus, migrants and Islam in Europe, gender and kinship, property and rural economy in Azerbaijan, citizenship, migration, ethnicity, informal economy and political anthropology, especially with reference to the Caucasus.

Acknowledgements

Academic works are rarely the result of a single individual; more often they are the result of synergies consolidated over several years that are interwoven through personal and professional relationships. Friendships and children are born; the story of books becomes also the story of some people's lives.

This book springs out of a fortunate series of casual encounters that could have led to a completely different outcome. Abel's interest in informal economies is to be credited to an invitation by Denis Carter and Michaela Benson (to which the author is grateful for their guidance throughout the submission process) to a special issue of *Anthropology in Action*, which prompted him to reflect on the phenomenon of informal payments in which he became embedded during his fieldwork in Ukraine. Such interest became the starting point of a Marie Curie International Outgoing Fellowship focusing on informal economies in Turkey and Ukraine. During the two years spent doing fieldwork and the time spent processing the final data an unpayable debt was accrued towards all those helping in the field. In particular, in Ukraine Aleksandr Prigarin and Viktor Stepanenko were vital to the understanding of the local meaning of informality. In Turkey much gratitude goes to Erhan Dogan for his friendship and constant support and Gunay Goksu Ozdogan for her invitation to join the MURCIR research team. The fundamentals of this book and of our collaboration were thanks to Colin Williams (even if he might not be aware of it). Colin responded to a call for a paper by Abel in 2008 and offered vital support over the years, which led to a special issue of the *International Journal of Sociology and Social Policy* co-edited with Peter Rodgers for which Jeremy wrote one of the articles.

How we came to all this is merely by chance, since we both applied to present at the 2011 BASEES conference and ended up in the same panel, becoming aware of one another's existence. The idea of a book was tested at the Commission for Urban Anthropology 2011 conference in Corinth and, thanks to the encouragement of some colleagues (among whom we want to thank Italo Pardo, Giuliana Prato, Marcello Mollica and Manos Spyridakis) the idea of the book was further shaped.

Aware of how long academic publishing may take and how quickly we were able to put this book together, we cannot be more grateful to our authors, many of whom have had the patience to put up with all our comments, suggestions and criticisms while succeeding in producing chapters in a relatively short amount of time. We are also grateful to all those who have allowed us to reflect on the concept of the book and further shape our ideas, which were presented in several parts of the world: from the Aleksanteri Institute (thanks to Katalin Miklossy) to the OSCE Academy in Bishkek (thanks to Maksim Ryabkov), the University of Sussex (thanks to Margaret Elizabeth Sleeboom-Faulkner), the University of Azores (thanks to Carlos Amaral), and the University of Fribourg (thanks to Christian Giordano and Nicholas Hayoz).

In the course of the project, many people have contributed in different ways to its success and we would like to thank: Andrei Melville, Leon Kosals, Borish Zhelezov, Oxana Kharitanova, Mariya Eremenko, Anton Sobolev and Irina Soboleva (Moscow Higher School of Economics); Donnacha Ó Beacháin and John Doyle (Dublin City University); Françoise Companjen (Free University of Amsterdam); Mariane Mesnil (Free University of Brussels); Uwe Backes (Hannah Arendt Institute in Dresden); Tanya Richardson (Wilfred Laurey University); Rico Isaacs (Oxford Brookes University); Cathy Wanner (Penn State University); Magda Craciun (University of Pardubice); Gaudenz Assenza (Palacky University); Mikheil Zolyan (Yerevan); George Welton and David Jijelava (GeoWel Research); Shujun Cuj (Renmin University); Mathias Rauch; Fredrik Coene (European Commission); Chris Hann (Max Planck Institute for Social Anthropology); Deema Kaneff (University of Birmingham); Sally Cummings and Rick Fawn (University of St Andrews); Heiko Pleines (Forschungstelle Osteuropa, Bremen); Denis Volkov (Levada Centre, Moscow); Robert Kevilhan (USAID). We would also like to thank all those who have read this book and written their endorsements.

We also owe a deep debt of gratitude to our institutions, which have been always supportive towards our work; in Tallinn our thanks go to Raivo Vetik, Anu Toots, George Sootla, Tiiu Pohl, Aet Annist, Maria Jäärats, Eva Sermann, Peeter Müürsepp, and Aimar Ventsel.

This publication was supported by several grants and we credit the Marie Curie scheme (grants no: IOF-219691, IRSES-295232, IRSES-318961, ITN-316825) for providing the funding for some of the research and meetings that were necessary to prepare this volume.

Finally, we would like to thank Peter Sowden from Routledge for always being ready to answer all our questions and his capacity to be friendly and professional at the same time.

Foreword

Catherine Wanner

Professor of History and Cultural Anthropology, The Pennsylvania State University

Several decades ago, European and other Western societies came under an anthropological lens and were studied for their exotic and paradoxical qualities too. This shift to make the familiar seem strange, the known seem new, takes on an added and much needed dimension in the book you are about to read. The editors have collected vivid portraits of how individuals experience economic life in post-socialist Eastern European societies. Testifying louder and more forcefully than an abstract argument, these essays illustrate the value of subjecting to critical ethnographic study something as taken for granted as "superior," natural and omnipresent as capitalism.

When talented ethnographers undertake such a critical gaze in societies that have been "transitioning" from socialism to capitalism for 20 years, the familiar does indeed become strange and the known is recast anew. Novel dimensions and unforeseen zones of capitalism emerge for which we struggle to find categories, labels and models of analysis, revealing the extent to which we have normalized the assumptions that underlie our understandings – and judgments – of capitalist economic practices and dynamics. These keen observers offer us ethnographic portraits of individuals who, once thrust into a different economic system, find themselves functioning in a "grey economy," a "second economy" and other betwixt and between zones where jobs cannot be located squarely in the public sector nor can private companies be defined as something separate and distinct from state-run enterprises. These spheres of economic activity, when subject to ethnographic analysis, appear not only interdependent but interpenetrating as well.

One of the main arguments of this book is that the informal sector has not been given the scholarly attention it deserves. It should not be dismissed as an unfortunate byproduct of the transition, a temporary vestige of the harmful, deforming effects of socialism. Rather, these authors suggest that many of the informal practices they have observed in Eastern Europe are not only produced by capitalist dynamics of wealth production and distribution, but also sustained by them. In other words, it is the very structure and workings of capitalism, laid bare on the ruins of socialism, that actually allow for the embedding of informal practices within the formal sector. As such, capitalist wage–labor practices and the variety of other income-generating strategies that are in play in the formal sector in formerly socialist societies are not only interdependent, but even predicated upon, a far more improvised, transitory and fluctuating set of informal practices that are operative at all levels of the economy. In summary then, this book prompts us to reconsider just how productive it is to categorize economic practices as being part of the formal sector, that is, an economic sphere subject to state regulation, as opposed to the informal sector, ostensibly a sphere beyond the long arm of the state. These ethnographic essays illustrate the myriad ways in which these distinctions and classifications of economic practices do not hold up when even the state itself, in the form of regulatory agencies and law enforcement, operates across sectors with great ease and frequency.

This book also offers a second challenge concerning established thinking on how the informal sector operates. It has become conventional wisdom in Western societies to assume that informal economic practices thrive in the shadows among the most socially marginalized individuals. Yet, in these essays we see highly skilled doctors, successful businessmen, and energetic and promising young entrepreneurs all making wide use of informal practices. Indeed, one of the factors that make self-employment so attractive in these societies is the range of informal possibilities it offers to generate profit alongside formal, declared transactions designed to do the same.

One is also prompted to rethink exchange and the motives for entering into reciprocal relationships of exchange and the trust that underlies them. Does one choose an exchange partner primarily based on economic or social motives? These essays marshal ethnographic evidence to argue that the motivations for exchange are constantly shifting along a continuum of considerations that include economic pressures, social ties, and work obligations. It is far more productive, therefore, to analyze the contours of context that make certain motives, be they economic or social, take precedence at particular moments, rather than flat declarations of cause and effect.

The "thick descriptions" of economic life in the former Soviet Bloc contained in these essays give us a better understanding of why it is more useful to focus on the range of practices individuals have available to them at a particular moment and the circumstances that shape that range of choices, rather than their access to formal or informal sectors to earn money. Such dualisms miss the point that capitalist practices can be made to bend to accommodate individual will. They are constantly adapting to the moral obligations associated with certain social relationships as well as to the specific political mandates in which provisioning activities are obliged to function.

The focus on practices and the zones in which they are embedded, rather than established understandings of zones, allow these authors to document the hybrid forms of economic practice and new concepts that govern economic life in this region. By committing to fully describing these practices, many of these authors have used native terms for which there are no English language equivalents. For example, such practices are rendered as *kompromat* (Russian for compromising information used to threaten a person into cooperation or collusion), *blat* (Russian for functional connections embedded in social networks to draw upon for favors), and *poplatok* versus *uplatok* (Slovakian to delineate a bribe as something different from a fee paid between acquaintances and even to kin for protective services). The widespread use of such concepts in a multitude of settings suggests the extent to which bribes are seen as something qualitatively different from a variety of established fee structures, ranging from gifts to payments that can be used to circumvent legal and other restrictions. Yet such payments are frequently without the obvious and pervasive moral condemnation attached to bribery. Further complicating the picture is that a payment can appear to others outside the transaction as a bribe, although those involved can view it as an entirely morally acceptable form of cooperation because of the economic, social or kin obligations that are attached. This means that "illicit" flows of money to some are simple transactions among partners to others.

Moreover, the possibility for massive outmigration after the collapse of socialist regimes means that social and economic networks now straddle state borders. Goods, ideas and people are circulating with ever growing intensity, which often locates informal economic practices in multiple states at once. Even if a state attempted to regulate these forms of trade and exchange, it would at times be difficult to know which state would be responsible for doing so as the movement of people and goods is often either circular or multidirectional. A trader in Bishkek, for example, can buy goods from a Chinese merchant, bring the goods to Russia for resale, where she buys foodstuffs that she takes back to Kyrgyzstan for resale to, among others, the Chinese traders who sold her goods in the first place.

China is hardly the only border crossed. The EU border is also considered a resource for shuttle traders in the western regions of the former Soviet Union. Cross-border trade there offers other possibilities and allows individuals to earn a living thanks to manipulation and violation of border regulations designed to "secure" the border. In essence, borders have become opportunities every bit as much as they are impediments to trade of all kinds.

And finally, the ethnographically vivid descriptions of the working lives of individuals living through this transition and yet still trying to fulfill their dreams and provide for their children and for the next generation more broadly underscore the real cost of the predatory tendencies of capitalism. In the same breath, these portraits are a testimony to the resilience of the human spirit. The tenacity with which these individuals invent and reinvent themselves to create and recreate a means of earning a living so as to sew and resew the fraying of their lives together is truly impressive. Rather than marveling at human survival skills, we should read these essays for their instructional value. Not only do these portraits help us to see the roots of injustice, and how individuals try to recapture their dignity, but they also suggest myriad possibilities for finding solutions that neither lie squarely within "capitalism" nor in "socialism," but rather in some innovative selection of aspects of each system that still leaves a space for the human will to improvise. Having detailed the persistence of diverse economic practices in play in formerly socialist societies, the feasibility of alternative trajectories for economic development beyond market hegemony becomes apparent. The reader of these essays is called upon to begin to imagine what those possibilities might be.

Catherine Wanner is a Professor of History and Cultural Anthropology at The Pennsylvania State University. She received her doctorate in cultural anthropology from Columbia University. She is the author of *Burden of Dreams: History and Identity in Post-Soviet Ukraine* (1998), *Communities of the Converted: Ukrainians and Global Evangelism* (2007), which won four prizes and was named a Choice Outstanding Academic Title. She is a co-editor of *Religion, Morality and Community in Post-Soviet Societies* (2008) and editor of *State Secularism and Lived Religion in Soviet Russia and Ukraine* (2012). She is currently writing a book on Soviet policies of secularization and the transformation of religious life in the former Soviet Union after World War II.

Introduction

Informality – enduring practices, entwined livelihoods

Jeremy Morris and Abel Polese

Informality is here to stay. News of Greek pensioners resorting to barter, the hoarding of currency under proverbial mattresses from Portugal to Estonia, the rush to purchase gold bullion, and the economic necessity, for many EU citizens, of combining cash-in-hand work with taxed employment in order to exploit a Byzantine system of means-tested benefits, are signs, not only of the current economic crisis, but also the perennial question of the sovereignty of the state in terms of legitimizing economic activity and the right to a claim of the productive activities of its citizens. Cue the wry smiles from post-socialist citizens: 'We've seen this before – banking expropriation (a 'tax') in Cyprus – only ten per cent of deposits lost! Get used to it. Cash is here to stay,' said one of our Russian informants on the crisis *du jour* as we completed this book.[1]

The ubiquity of informality, and the mistake of seeing it as purely a 'transition' phenomenon – something that institutionally-deficient Eastern European countries are plagued by, are two key issues this book addresses. Informality is not receding, and if anything, looking to its persistence and the social and economic role it plays in post-socialist societies – the way it is 'embedded' socially and in the formal economy – could serve as a possible mapping of the futures of many developed countries' economies for which the current economic crisis is arguably a mere foretaste of lasting change. Now systemic crisis and a neoliberal near-consensus among elites has brought the firepower of 'shock therapy' and the small-state agenda back home, with cynical proposals that 'there is no alternative'. After all, the ex-socialist countries became 'laboratories for experiments' in neoliberal policies prior to the current assault on social democracy in the West (Merrien and Mendy 2010: 44). In a less clinical metaphor, the East became the firing range upon which the western international financial organizations, staffed in the main by US and UK educated economists, sought to test out their big guns of monetarism, deregulation, privatization and the retreat of the social state. One of the results of this ideologically-driven transition in post-socialist states since the 1990s has been an increase in informal economic activities and relations, something few economists considered fully at the time of policy implementation.

And so, international institutions with development and state-building policies turn to measuring the informal economy, still seeing it as somehow separate from the formal: it is termed 'black', 'grey', shadow, etc. This is problematic not least because in some post-socialist states the bureaucratically-accounted for and taxed share is barely 50 per cent of wealth. At the same time, statistical estimates of informality are open to criticism – after all, how do you measure a shadow as it recoils from the clutches of researchers armed with surveys and the like? Economists look at electricity consumption and try to measure the gap between expected consumption given GDP and what is actually consumed. This is then offered as a proxy for the level of informality. This is in turn criticized by other economists as underestimating informality (Andrews *et al.* 2011), as so many activities can take place without impacting electricity consumption – most of the examples in this book included. The informal economy in scholarship then becomes the *non-observed economy in national accounts* but continues to elude quantitative probing. There is perhaps only one certainty about informality in the region that we can glean from reviewing the attempts to quantify it: it has increased markedly since the end of the socialist period, and certainly since 2000, and it is at the very least a fifth of GDP in the westernmost states (Slovakia in our example), and perhaps 40 per cent or more in Russia, Ukraine, the Caucasus and Central Asia (Schneider *et al.* 2010). However, the admission by economists of the 'severe form of non-robustness' (Andrews *et al.* 2011: 11) of even these figures leads us to the premise of this book: to examine and, however incompletely, understand embedded and enduring phenomena such as informality, you need an embedded methodology.

The inadequacy of even micro-survey approaches in contributing to quantifying, let alone understanding, the workings of informality (Schneider 2002: 33) led us to the idea for a cluster of ethnographies on informality. From Slovakia to Azerbaijan, this book takes individual composite or representative cases – 'the Ukrainian doctors', for example – to apprehend the moments of informality in post-socialist citizens' lives from the inside out. The classic ethnography presents empirical material based on the articulated experience of people in concrete times and places (Denzin 1997). When it comes to activities that are sometimes illegal or at least rule-breaking (e.g. pilfering from work to gain materials for self-provisioning, taking under-the-table payments for optometry tests), ethnography is well placed to capture the 'slices, glimpses and specimens' (ibid: 247) of non-formal economic activity that other methodologies cannot. At its best, ethnography can work out of these concrete moments of informality to larger scales of meaning. The editors of this volume have not been prescriptive in how authors achieve this – some choose to remain largely within the classic frame of the ethnography where informants and their interpretations speak for themselves. Other authors choose to engage directly with the literature on informality (discussed in the next section), or other literatures, such as state-society relations, transnationalism and the political economy of multi-state entities such as the EU, or the classic anthropological concerns of kinship, the rural, and reciprocity proper. Perhaps most importantly though, these case studies of informality are diachronically integrated – all represent what is happening in the second decade of this century, more than 20 years after the end of the Soviet Union. Much intensive research on informality emerged from fieldwork carried out by anthropologists in the immediate period after the collapse of the Soviet Union. The current volume, in however modest a way, can hopefully engage in a dialogue with that literature as much as with theoretical concerns.

Informal–formal mutualism – the imbricated scales on a butterfly's wing

At the highest level of generalization, informal economic practices are defined as activities that are not 'regulated, monitored or controlled directly or indirectly by the state' (Routh 2011: 211).[2] Since Hart's investigation of economic activity outside the 'organized labour force' in Ghana in 1973 and the resultant coining of the term 'informal economy', scholars from various disciplines have investigated the nature of informal transactions and practices. Anthropological researchers in particular have produced a rich literature on mutuality, reciprocity, kinship and other networks of support. Recently the informality of economic activities in particular has come into sharp focus as a key concern in understanding precarity and post-socialism, especially within geography (Özcan 2010; Round *et al.* 2008). Following Hart's approach, a dual-economy thesis was initially proposed whereby unregulated practices existed in parallel to the formal organized and regulated practices. Over time, informality came to be identified with undesirable economic transactions – i.e. it prevented capital formation and put incomes beyond the range of taxation, and was also thought to be typified by exploitative employment conditions. 'Formalization' became seen as the solution to the problem of the dual-economy division and numerous domestic policy and international programmes, the latter associated with the IMF and World Bank, were framed to promote this outcome. A final problem is the binary thinking that such a label as 'informal' reproduced. One can talk of informal only as long as there is a formal sector (Hart 2005). However, the informal sector encompasses nearly two thirds (1.8 billion) of a global working population of some three billion (see Jütting and Laiglesia 2009). Such increasing awareness on the role and size of the informal economy in the world has prompted a growing number of national governments, not only in the global south but, and even more importantly, in the EU and the Western world in general, to move from an approach seeking to eradicate the undeclared economy to a more pragmatic approach seeking to formalize undeclared work and revenues.

A different kind of dualism can be seen in understandings of informality in socialist and post-socialist states in the (former) Soviet Union and Eastern Europe. Informal economic activities were defined as those not reflected in official reporting. These were, first, constituted by households reliant on subsistence production and redistribution, including informal work on private land plots, informal credit relationships, and mutual aid, and second, a shadow economy where enterprises actively hid their revenues from the tax authorities of the state. The latter entails non-registration of enterprises or some parts of enterprises, double-book-keeping and informal contracts of employment. Clearly, the first set of practices was viewed as more dominant in the socialist era, and the second set of practices coming to the fore since 1989/91. However, as Verdery summarizes, under socialism 'a huge repertoire of strategies for obtaining consumer good and services' (1996: 27) constituted a vast 'second' economy – including moonlighting in second, unofficial roles, barter, favour-exchange, stealing or utilization of enterprise resources by employees, to name but a few practices. This was a rich inheritance for post-socialist countries and when mixed with mass impoverishment due to more, or frequently, less, successful economic reform, and large-scale unemployment, there was fertile ground for even more growth in informality of all kinds.

In the late 1980s, just as socialist societies were about to start tasting marketizing reforms and 'shock therapy', the dualist view of formal versus informal in capitalist societies came to be challenged by the structuralist position of Portes, Castells and others who argued that under the 'competitive pressure of the global market "formal" firms engage in "informal" practices to reduce their cost of production' (Routh 2011: 211–12). With this came the realization that the formal and informal are strongly entwined. This line of thinking was further developed by Castells and Portes (1989) who argue that this inter-relation is fundamentally the result of neoliberal globalization processes. Furthermore, Christensen offered a further critique of the dualist perspective, showing that formality is linked to Westphalian notions of sovereignty where the state has the ultimate right to regulate economic activities in order to perform its distributive role (Christensen 2006: 36–7). The state is the jealous arbiter of legitimacy in regulating economic activity (Guha-Khasnobis *et al.* 2006: 3–4); therefore, whatever activity, for whatever reason, that takes place outside state oversight or regulation would be 'informal'. Thus, the sometimes undifferentiated treatment of practices as diverse as painting a neighbour's fence for a pack of beers, and large-scale tax fraud by multi-national companies are treated as 'informality'. Finally, Routh identifies the inadequate range of structural and dualist purviews of informality, seeing the former as neglecting the ongoing importance of subsistence and own account activities, and the latter as failing to account for the linkages between sectors (2011). Both these criticisms are important in understanding informality in post-socialism, which is characterized by a mix of these informality contexts – and the scholarship of which overlaps with literatures on corruption. The chapters in this book reflect a long line of such 'embedding' literature from economic anthropology and critical human geography, from Harding and Jenkins (1989) to Gibson-Graham (2008) that has attempted to bridge theories of informality by proposing a continuum or spectrum model where it is imperative to describe the 'real life' of informality. In turn this model acknowledges that it is then often impossible to separate out the formal from the informal (Routh 2011: 217); they are, in the post-socialist context at least, symbiotic – often to the degree that mutualism (in the sense of mutually 'benefiting', a concept borrowed from biology) results.[3] One explicit treatment of the spectrum view is given visual form in the chapter by Williams and Onoschenko on Ukrainian healthcare providers. They see an informal/formal spectrum of activities overlapping rather like the iridescent scales of a butterfly's wings when seen under a microscope, the colour of which is constantly changing depending of the direction of the light source (see Figure 1).

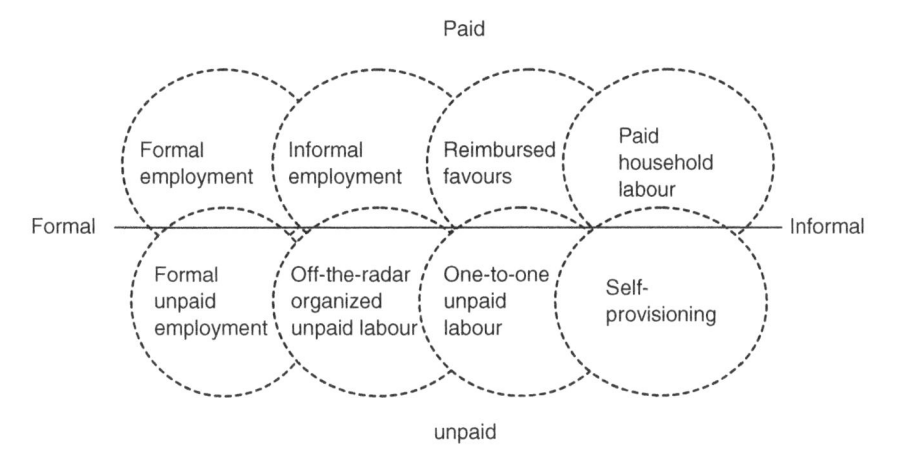

```
                              Paid

           Formal    Informal    Reimbursed   Paid
           employment employment favours      household
                                              labour
Formal ─────────────────────────────────────────────── Informal
           Formal    Off-the-radar One-to-one
           unpaid    organized     unpaid     Self-
           employment unpaid labour labour    provisioning

                              unpaid
```

Figure 1 A classificatory schema of labour practices

Source: Williams and Onoschenko in Chapter 1.

As in the chapter on informal payments to healthcare workers in Ukraine, many of our authors' investigations of informality are prompted by the ongoing contested, as well as profoundly ordinary, socially anchoring, and often rational/practical understandings of informal transactions in post-socialist countries, many of which are deemed to have reached a high level of marketized economic development (and have been accepted into the EU on this basis) but whose citizens still rely on informal practices to a significant degree.[4] Despite the relatively high level of human development in these countries, informality is even explained in some cases by a compensatory, welfare logic, when formal support for poorest citizens is absent, as in the Ukrainian doctors' case, where, as in similar research (Morris and Polese 2014; Polese 2008) treatment payments are often differentiated according to need and non-economic considerations.

Informality: another 'vestige' of socialist-era practices?

Informal and diverse practices have always been at the forefront of anthropological (post-socialist or otherwise) thinking about the 'economy', with extra-market activities given as much attention as market ones. However, some of the recent sociologically-grounded work on post-socialist informality persists in seeing socialist and post-socialist economies, and formality and informality as dichotomous, with informality as a marginal 'problem', separable from the 'important' formal economy. To its credit, recent work in geography and other disciplines has highlighted that informal work, incomes and transactions, may be just as important as a normative understanding of 'work' or employment (Williams and Round 2007; Morris 2012).

The perspective of formal/informal dichotomy reflects a wider unspoken normative bias in non-anthropological approaches to post-socialism that takes one of two approaches. It either, especially at the macro-economic perspective, ignores the importance and persistence of informality, or, where it is acknowledged, it becomes another category of socialist practice which is predicted to wither away as 'market economy' institutions (such as flat income tax regimes, labour flexibility) are adopted by former socialist countries. In extreme cases, Russian transition is painted macro-economically as largely successful, the informal economy is invisible in analysis, except when misinterpreted evidence (Aage 2005) of its widespread nature can be used to buttress the dubious argument that informal incomes cushion financial crises. In a recent paper Anders Åslund makes the confident assertion that in Russia the virtual economy (here he is mainly referring to non-monetary payments between firms) will 'disappear' as the obstacles to free enterprise and globalization are swept away (2004: 400), and that 'corruption', i.e. the informal payments that continue to be part and parcel of the functioning of state and private enterprise in post-socialist societies, will 'subside' with economic growth (ibid: 416). Even Ledeneva's (1998, 2009) sensitive and grounded qualitative overviews, which show how informal practices inherited from Soviet times are monetized and provide the oil that lubricates a whole society, are framed firmly within a 'modernization' teleology. Informality, whether economic or political is a 'trap' (Ledeneva 2013) preventing institutional development along normative lines.

We would argue that these and similar conceptualizations of informality as one of a number of barriers to post-socialist societies' 'normal' development towards market capitalism and democratic governance are part of a continuing 'transitological' approach to studying post-socialist countries (Bunce 1995, Gans-Morse 2004), variously rehashed as developmental and modernization theory, but always having a normative framework and hinging on a teleological view of 'transition' towards 'democratization' and an Anglo-American vision of post-Fordist market institutions. Whether the scope is economic or political, the transition business in scholarship is like a satellite navigation system confronted with a car driver who refuses to respond to directions, instead taking turns at random. As Carothers summarizes, 'no small amount of democratic teleology is implicit in the transition paradigm, no matter how much its adherents have denied it' (2002: 4). Similarly, a fundamental weakness in these approaches is a lack of attention paid to the underlying conditions in transitional countries: 'institutional legacies, ethnic make-up, sociocultural traditions, or other "structural" features' (ibid: 5). This is a frequent blind spot in analyses of social and economic change or continuity in post-socialist spaces, and allows institutionalist-focused scholarship to implicitly or explicitly suggest that informality, along with all the other economic and social 'backwardness' of Eurasia, should be considered transitional.[5] In a recent intervention, Tatjana Thelen takes to task anthropologists too for a similar 'neo-institutionalist' and economistic bias (2011). As socialism (rather obviously) downplayed the importance of private property and property rights as a motor for economic and social development, many scholars see the failure of socialism as rooted in its institutions (ibid: 46). Thelen argues that 'the tendency to view socialist economies as deficient reinforced the focus on informal exchange networks as instrumental, a means of overcoming shortages' (48). Informality and the importance of social network relations, though in no way socialist-specific phenomena, became marked as somehow representative of the 'difference' of these societies and impediments to the development of non-personalized, marketized economic relations in the post-socialist period.

This leads us to view informality within a much wider frame of analysis on post-socialism. Informality becomes an emblematic issue related to the 'deficit' model of understanding East European cultures and societies, as outlined by Burawoy (2001), Thelen (2011), and Verdery (1996), who criticize how purportedly interpretive analyses are so often framed in terms what the region 'lacks' and can be provided with by the importation of western models. Our position then reflects a long line of 'embedding' literature on economic anthropology from Harding and Jenkins (1989) to Gibson-Graham (2008) and on corruption and morality (Pardo 1996, 2004; Torsello 2011, Wanner 2005). This is prompted by practical and grounded understandings of informal transactions in post-socialist countries, whose citizens still rely on informal practices to a significant degree in everyday life even in their dealings with both the state's representatives and other private citizens – whether entrepreneurs, doctors, customs officers, metalworkers or children's nannies. The lay interpretation of informality and the moral reasoning this entails, illustrates the fruitful intersection of the robust theoretical work on corruption and deviance more generally as 'normative' conditions of lay reasoning and legitimization (Haller and Shore, 2005; Polese and Rodgers 2011; Pardo 2004: 39–40; Prato 2004). Informality can thus be seen within a wider context of 'de-othering' the study of the post-socialist space. While more pervasive and significant to household reproduction and social and economic life generally, informality should be seen contributing to a construction of post-socialism as a variant of our current modernity (see Thelen 2011 for this argument applied to the study of socialist societies). As argued at the outset of this introduction, this is a version of modernity that the West needs to take note of, as we stand on the cusp of centrifugal economic and social forces at the heart of the formalization project of the EU *acquis*.

Understanding post-socialist informality as multi-faceted, socially-embedded

Some see the persistence of informality in post-socialist states as evidence of a lack of hegemony of capitalist relations in these spaces (Williams *et al.* 2011). Like them, we see informality as a useful conceptual tool in moving beyond a 'varieties of capitalism' approach to transitional societies. The contributing authors to this book capture well the heterogeneity of informal economy activities justifying the rejection of a sectoral approach and the dualist model that remains in labels such as 'shadow', 'black', etc. Some aspects of informality do resemble informal reciprocal relations from a previous era – Soviet-era *blat*-type practices in healthcare and trade/entrepreneurialism, the thirst for unobtainable commodity items in informal trade, some blue-collar practices that are partly parasitic on the formal enterprise. On the other hand, in each of these cases and others we also perceive informality as tied closely to emerging forms of marketized relations and the particular role (or non-role) of the state. The simultaneous relation of informality to the emergence of the market and the continuing existence of social, cultural and economic norms of the previous period, are particularly noticeable in most chapters, from Slovakia to Russia and Azerbaijan. Similarly, informality is never merely a corollary of the inadequate income from formal employment. Nevertheless, as an interpretive category, that understanding of informality also has its place in the collection: blue-collar workers in Russia and Ukrainian doctors 'moonlight', although the meaning of that English term has much more extra-economic significance in these cases, with social, moral, even political, reasoning featuring strongly. Similarly, our contributors rightly do not view informality through the narrow lens of an alternative to the formal. Even for the most marginal citizens studied in this volume, such as those in Russia, Azerbaijan, Kyrgyzstan, Lithuania and Belarus, informality is tactical, in the Certeau-esque sense – embedded in social life rather than part of a rationalist economic reasoning; informality is often about 'poaching' opportunities and utilizing the rules, and the gaps therein, of the formal. This is most noticeable (in both developed and less-developed states) for the marginal industrial working class and the new 'lumpen' lower middle class (see Harboe's chapter on Lithuania). However, Polese's Ukraine chapter also shows how a relative 'winner' of transition, the small entrepreneur, exploits the available short-circuits in the bureaucratic state's inadequate governance. Most of the time then, to recall Scott's seminal work (1985), or Verdery's phrasing on socialist practices, informality is part of a 'repertoire' of strategies and tactics which include engagement with the formal on some level as well. The case of the Romanian nanny in Kovács' chapter – with a token bank cleaning job but the majority of income in care work – is perhaps the best example of this complex strategy used by individuals.

Thus the overall approach of this book is avowedly 'post-structural', rejecting purely structural explanations (global capitalism and neoliberal reform), at the same time as avoiding dualist sectoral approaches, in favour of an interpretive and analytical understanding of informal economy. This incorporates all activities, from cross-border petty trading, informal blue-collar moonlighting to employment and entrepreneurship (medical, trade and business) that are not part of the 'formal' economy but which are variously parasitic, symbiotic with, or 'embedded' within formal economic, state and global, frames of relations such as the legal-private enterprise, the health service, revenue and customs agencies, transnational trades and service, etc.

Finally, while the image of state withdrawal appears to loom large in discussions of informality, here too the reality is far more complex. As Thelen points out, much of the surviving and coping literature in anthropological work on post-socialism relies on an adoption of the notion of state withdrawal 'despite its one-dimensionality and the diversity of reconfigurations in the private and public spheres, which were inadequately understood' (2011: 50). Based on the evidence in this volume, it is clear that for the economic and socially marginal, changes in state society relations, in particular the loss of social wages in blue-collar work, the loss of pensions, and other social guarantees, do provide a push factor for informality. However, even for those at the margins of society economically, or geographically, as in the case of border trade, there are competing explanations and interpretations of informal practices. For many, informality is often connected to sociality, kinship relations, and a continuity of everyday life tactics that precede the present crisis. While state withdrawal remains a powerful metaphor for scholars and ordinary people alike in their grappling with the meaning of post-socialism, our authors show numerous examples of informality as evidence of ordinary people choosing their *own* distance, even withdrawal (see Harboe's Lithuania chapter) from state–society relations as much as practically possible. This, again, must be seen as one of a number of informal strategies. This view, in turn, must be informed by research informants' responses to neoliberal reforms in their relevant states. What appear as entrepreneurial strategies as a response to injustice and the institution of neocapitalist relations (Kideckel 2008) require further investigation; they are often interpreted through the literature on governmentality, whereby subjects are hailed by an individualizing, self-making ideology that requires them to remould themselves according to the ultra-flexible employment and economic requirements of neoliberalism. But what of those informants in this volume that illustrate a form of entrepreneurial resourcefulness that is at least partly outside the formal economy, certainly opposed to incorporation within state structures, and most significantly, embedded within social and economic relations of reciprocity and mutuality that are difficult to recuperate within a capitalist accumulative logic? It is to be hoped that the present volume provides a modest starting point for scholars to begin to address such questions. By undertaking such investigations, scholars of post-socialism will be best situated to challenge modernization theories and their claims of convergence, whether or not they adopt the language of transition. Post-socialist informality may therefore have an important role to play in reinforcing the relevance of a multiple modernities perspective as developed after Eisenstadt (2000) and as a re-framing of debates as diverse as those around globalization, transnationalism, and substantive, versus formal, economic models of social behaviour. The last binary is at present encapsulated in the debate on the extent of the expansion of neoliberal ideological orthodoxy, tempered by intimations of a swing of a transformational pendulum away from homo economicus and towards more 'embedded' forms of economics: human, diverse and 'real-world' (Hart *et al.* 2010, Gibson-Graham 2008, Fullbrook 2007).

Book overview and chapter summaries

The book is composed of ten case studies, each focusing in depth on a facet of informal economy in eight post-socialist states. However, the focus of this study is significantly wider: five chapters present evidence on transnational informal practices, some of which straddle borders within the former Soviet Union (e.g. Azerbaijan–Russia, Kyrgyzstan–Russia), others which take place between new EU states and those that remain outside (Belarus–Lithuania, Ukraine–Poland). Two further chapters present less familiar examples of transnational informality:

that between Central Asia and other regions of the global south and East Asia (Kyrgyzstan–India/China), and between two EU states (Lithuania–Sweden). All the authors are scholars with significant in-country research experience and long-term commitments to field-work there. Not all are ethnographers; the editors see a diversity of disciplinary backgrounds as contributing to the value of this volume. Thus, some chapters present a more sustained in-depth ethnographic account of informal practices in a locale and beyond, focusing on interpretations by informants and their interactions. Others structure their research differently, presenting us with a contextual account of informality as it appears in national statistics and the domestic discourse of political economy as well as directly confronting state–society relations through their case studies (notably, Polese and Harboe). Regardless of these differences a consistency in the chapters lies in the focus of analysis in the construction of an extended case study or studies. This is in the form of composite ethnographies, usually one or two individuals and their narratives which form a condensed representation of the many informants and respondents encountered in the course of the researcher's fieldwork. In a few cases we have a single individual – the small entrepreneur and businessman in Polese's chapter on Ukraine, combining many interactions within this social milieu by the researcher, and the 'invisible' cash-in-hand itinerant tradesman in Harboe's Lithuania/Sweden. In other cases we are presented with a small number of real informants or composite clusters, such as members of a loose blue-collar social network, as in Morris's chapter on regional Russia, or a kinship group, as in the case of the traders from a single village region in Azerbaijan in Yalçın-Heckmann's chapter. The common basis of all chapters comprises ethnographic interviews and interactions complemented either by participant observation or by survey data collected by the authors over recent years. The final paragraphs to this Introduction provide short summaries of the chapters in the order in which they appear in the volume.

Part 1: 'Entrepreneurial' informality? Self- and off-the-books employment

Williams and Onoschenko, in a chapter on a married couple working in healthcare in Ukraine, set about challenging the 'formalization' thesis. They do this by looking at the diverse economic informality of the two informants: one is a doctor, the other an optometrist. The formalization thesis should be most obvious among middle-class professionals, but on the contrary, the level of this couple's engagement with informal practices is wide and ongoing, primarily due to the poor level of remuneration for public sector workers. This presents a profound challenge to the notion that transition societies should see a decrease in the provision of services informally as barriers to the (legal) registration of business and trade, etc., are removed after socialism. Taking a 'total social organisation of labour' approach, the authors aim to transcend the formal/informal economy dualism and to understand the heterogeneity of labour practices whether paid or unpaid; they exhaustively employ a full spectrum analysis of their informants' practices, including the socially differentiated, under-the-table payments, they receive, some of which depend upon their social and moral interpretation of patient's needs. Their informants' informality in some respects constitutes an unregistered medical practice, justifying the label informal self-employment. The authors also detail their informants' unpaid charity-type work, similarly unregistered, and even find space to discuss their domestic labour, kinship reciprocity and household 'economy'.

In contrast to the relative 'success' of the Ukrainian doctors, Harboe reveals the growth of what can only be described as a 'lumpen' lower middle class, disillusioned with the neoliberal economic reform of the Baltic states now 'safely' within the death-like embrace of EU monetary and fiscal policy; these citizens are on the way to becoming invisible and at the same time as appearing to be politically (or perhaps generationally and culturally) disengaged, their recourse to informal practices, such as seasonal construction in Scandinavia, reflects a rejection of neoliberal reform. Ironically, this informality – avoiding taxes and all mechanisms of the state's bureaucracy, means the 'invisible citizen' increasingly comes to resemble an entrepreneurial self which rational-actor models would see as normative. However, this entrepreneurialism is argued to be more tactical than articulating an urge for 'self improvement' or material gain. Harboe makes the claim that the invisibles' retreat into the shadow economy is a response to the shift to increasingly exploitative labour relations and a general repudiation of the new political-economic settlement in the Baltics, a point Morris's chapter also makes.

Morris's chapter on blue-collar workers in Russia takes up Harboe's themes of entrepreneurialism and retreat from formal employment. He examines how blue-collar workers use connections and skills gained in formal employment in their 'moonlighting' jobs – without which they could not provide an adequate standard of living for their households. A dense web of class-based loyalties allow for informal employment to develop to the extent that it begins to resemble a formal enterprise (in this case a double-glazing manufacture). However, such 'entrepreneurialism', either individually or within a social network, is better understood in terms of providing autonomy, and self-sustaining sociality as much as economic and self-interested rationality. For blue collars, a broad suite of informal practices comprise a 'social gestalt' some of which is unconnected to the formal opportunities of manufacturing (self-provisioning, DIY-cultures and mutual aid), other facets of which are highly imbricated with industrial skills and enterprises within the formal economy (unregistered employment and moonlighting). Informality and sociality are intimate bedfellows: the persistence of post-Fordist social networks of labour supports a resilient informal economy; informality persists both 'because of' and 'in spite of' neoliberal reform.

Kovács provides a contrast to the masculine world of cutters, fitters and welders in Morris's case with a chapter on the intersection of care and money in Hungarian-speaking Romania. Paid childcare brings non-kin together around a core repertoire of practices through which women 'do family'– a social benefit for the informally employed that is at least as important as monetary gain. This chapter is a welcome contribution to scholarship on Romania which so often focuses on unregistered self-employment in subsistence agriculture rather than informal *waged* work. Here a patchwork of formal/informal employment emerges, where a 'token' cleaning job in the formal banking sector is retained despite the more lucrative unregistered nannying. The former is a way of leveraging contacts – out of the precarity of formality, informal opportunities emerge. But the material benefits derived from informal work have symbolic meanings at least as important as escaping poverty. One such symbolic benefit is the possibility to exercise an equality of sorts with the new middle class – the parents of the cared for. Autonomy, self-respect, class and affective reciprocal relations coalesce in nannying employment.

Polese's chapter on a businessman in Ukraine acknowledges the quasi-legality and contested nature of all state–business interactions in this troubled post-Soviet state. Here leverage concerns the relative level of 'dirt' that each interactant (whether entrepreneur, bureaucrat, intermediary or fixer) has on each other. This, Polese reflects, is not very far from the Soviet institution of *kompromat* that eased manipulation of political leaders and people in general. 'In a state with absurd rules every citizen is guilty' and the understanding of the licit may coincide with illegal practices of bribery and customs duty evasion. The entrepreneur is as much a tactician of social relationships as he is of economic ones. In a lively chapter in the form of a dialogue between composite informant and researcher, the businessman emerges as a battler against the 'system' of bureaucratic traps and snares that serve as a vast rent-collecting machinery for denizens of the state apparatus, especially the customs and excise. The equally Byzantine parallel world of informal business practices as 'normality' leads Polese to question the notion of post-socialist transition.

Karjanen on Slovakia continues the focus on the parallelism of the private sector and informality, looking at the flexibility of firms and their employees as they perform one and the same role – logistics and delivery – within the formal and then informal sphere. Karjanen posits that informal arrangements between companies show the hybrid nature of marketized relations. Informalization begets hyper flexibility, as in previous chapters showing the importance of local responses to neoliberalism. Off-the-books elements provide a competitive advantage but also reflect a commoditization of favour exchanges that are inherited from the socialist period. Mutual aid infects forms that might be read as purely economic – such as gypsy cab services that ferry pensioners to hospital. Similarly, Karjanen observes the continuing importance of kinship relations in building trust and sustaining informal practices. As in Polese's chapter, the normative understanding of bribery is challenged. Illicit cigarette smuggling provides capital for a legitimate cleaning company. Finally, the chapter engages with the question of substantivist/economistic perspectives on informality and observes how motivations to engage with informality may shift along a continuum for informants.

Part 2: At home abroad? Transnational informality and the invisible flows of people and goods

Borders, as spaces of various forms of entrepreneurial activities, offer many examples of informal entrepreneurial activities, but Cieślewska, writing on the vast bazaar of Dordoy in Kyrgyzstan, traces the important heritage of the Soviet-era shuttle trade: the small-scale illicit import of coveted consumer goods, as it has evolved into the semi-formal wholesale business of global-scale trade. At the same time, the Dordoy is a symbol of the dissolved multicultural microcosms of the Soviet Union. On the one hand clothes traders are trapped in poverty by informality in the anonymous tomblike shipping containers that serve as almost unregulated shops. While this underpins the marketized relations of Kyrgyz society, informants remain sceptical about their positioning within 'capitalism'. They resolutely see themselves through a different, socialist-era lens of non-accumulative, reciprocal relations with others, even as some of them emerge from drudgery to command real capital and establish semi-licit but unregistered enterprises manufacturing clothing. They are uncomfortably 'balanced' between the formal and the informal, a positioning possible only due to the Dordoy as a unique space outside, yet at the heart of the formal Kyrgyz economy.

In Sasunkevich's chapter on arbitrage she observes an intensification of cross-border trade between Belarus and the Schengen Zone, represented by Lithuania. The border is understood as a resource, but one tempered by historical traces of kinship and traditional social relations in space. Cross-border petty trade is not a professional, but rather an additional and occasional economic practice in which people get involved not because of necessity but rather due to certain favourable circumstances determined by their personal and family stories as well as by the specificities of the border region. Ethno-religious links with Lithuanian Catholics provide an intergenerational and intergroup continuity of experience of people in the Belarusian town. Informality is a living memory that continues but which also changes. A renewed shuttle trade emerges after the visa regime is relaxed due to these ethno-religious links; there is a shift from 'trading for necessity' to opportunistic trading. This opportunity-trading – recalling Certeau-esque tactics – is bound up with social convention in a highly complex way that defies easy interpretation. The space of the trans-border bus is examined as a key site of solidarity between women traders, and perhaps even the implicated male driver. 'Business as casual', but tactical and socially embedded, is the conclusion of this chapter.

Müller and Miggelbrink writing on the Poland–Ukraine border take a representative male small-scale cross-border trader as their focus. Like the Belarus–Lithuania border, this became a Schengen Area border in 2007. In contrast to the previous chapter, this study reveals how the restrictions, opportunities and unpredictable nature of this 'new' border are negotiated by an informant who needs to earn a living from it. This chapter, like Polese's, focuses more on questions of cross-border trade activities as part of a response to an 'unfair' or 'incapable' state that provokes a circumvention of its laws and rules. As a result, cross-border trade is widely accepted as an unavoidable and legitimate way to cope with economic precarity. The trade draws attention to the widening gap between those 'inside' Schengen and those 'outside', who are subject to the 'assemblage' of the border (Walters 2002). Despite new visa politics impeding cross-border flows of people (in contrast to Sasunkevich's chapter), informal cross-border trade is still regarded as part of the normality of life in the border area. Nevertheless, informal practices have become more hazardous and difficult due to EU policies aimed at creating a 'secure' environment. Consequently, not only border crossing itself has become more intricate and expensive, but cross-border trade is increasingly being criminalized, thus requiring new adaptations of practices in order to 'make the border'.

Yalçın-Heckmann's chapter provides a unique insight into two kinds of transnational trade of varying degrees of informality between Azerbaijan and Russia: the tomato and fresh herb trade. It is tempting to see continuities between the socialist-era and contemporary semi-formal market economic and transnational relations and networks, 20 years after the dissolution of the Soviet Union. However, it is equally important to focus on new and emerging structures and relations around the contemporary post-socialist markets. While economic discourses and policies in Azerbaijan ignore petty trade among Azerbaijanis abroad, migration of Azerbaijanis (perhaps a third of the population have been directly engaged in this practice) makes the denial of the economic, social and political significance and consequences of petty trade abroad puzzling to say the least. The meaning of transnational space is shaped by contested, ambivalent and competitive meanings for community, petty trade, informality and the market. The 'illusion of simultaneity' (Werbner forthcoming) of shared socialities, cultural intimacies and 'rupture', felt in visits to home and in relations with kin, play both an important role in this case, given the differential access to economic sources and opportunities in markets in Russia and Azerbaijan. Yalçın-Heckmann's case studies reveal a cleavage between trades that emerge from informality to be more or less formalized by 'rules and regulations' (the tomato trade) and those that remain dominated by Azerbaijani 'socialities and networks' (the herb trade). In the latter the livelihoods of airport workers, customs officers, security personnel, the Russian and Azeri mafia, as well as school teachers in Azerbaijan, are all implicated in this 'illegal' trade to some extent. The irony of this trade is that it offers a threshold to criminalization, of accepting criminal behaviour for the sake of profit, even if earnings are for socially and morally acceptable 'licit' goals in the home community.

As can be seen from the short chapter summaries above, this book presents ethnographies of informal economic practice along a continuum, from 'unemployed' factory workers who steal and resell petrol, to hospital doctors' under-the-table brown envelopes for treatment. The contributors shed light on the full spectrum of embedded 'informality' that confronts the denizen of the post-socialist space and is an open secret.

Drawing from ethnographic accounts of very different places in different societies, the chapters of this book show that no one is excluded from informal practices, which are used regardless of the economic status of a citizen or country. In turn, the editors and contributors alike use the case studies presented to highlight the importance of the more fundamental questions of whether persistent informalization heralds the emergence of a more socially 'embedded' economy (Dale 2010), or whether such practices are merely the micro-level evidence of a retrenchment of marketized social relations in post-socialist societies.

Notes

1 The Cyprus bail-in may come to be seen as a turning point in terms of the growth in informality in the EU states. Now that (as of Spring 2013) expropriation of small deposits is seen as a political expedient that governments as well as the EU and IMF are willing to try (even if it ultimately failed in this case), citizens will likely increasingly resort to non-banking cash payments. The final rescue of Cyprus in March 2013 was notable for the lack of democratic legitimacy in its imposition by the Troika after the domestic parliament rejected the initial proposal. When citizens develop a sense of impoverishing economic policy as a foreign imposition, it isn't difficult to understand the growth of tax evasion or informality as part of a *moral and normative* response to injustice. Something our authors bring out in their chapters.
2 Much of the tracing of the development of theoretical conceptualizations of informality in this opening section is indebted to the overview by Routh (2011).
3 By beneficial we do not refer to advantage for individuals involved, simply that informal practices benefit the formal 'sector' and vice versa. In the former case, this observation arises out of the structural view of informality as part of global capitalism. The latter case is more indicative of the significance of post-socialist studies such as those in this volume which indicate that important aspects of informal practices arise and are sustained by their contact/imbrication with the formal.
4 We would not necessarily subscribe to the accepted economic consensus that post-socialist societies are characterized by substantively more informal activities, merely that informality in the West is less the focus of scholarship, embedded in a more complex way within the formal. For example, in the UK context, as intimated in the opening of this introduction, no one has seriously investigated the huge levels of informal employment that occur as a result of the system of tax-credits that accrue to low-income workers who work a minimum 16 hours-a-week (the incentive is for people to declare 16 hours only and receive the rest as cash-in-hand from a conniving employer who also gains from this arrangement). Similarly, the reported levels of VAT avoidance through cash payments for services in trades, is intuitively too low. Interestingly, estimates of informality in Western countries are often the subject of *greater* uncertainty than in the countries that are the subject of this book. So, for the UK, the difference in the estimate of informality as a share of GDP differs between National Accounts figures and academic research by an order of magnitude. Finally, and perhaps most surprisingly, some economists measure tax evasion (often disaggregated from the informal) as actually higher in a number of EU countries (and not just places like Greece) than in post-socialist ones. When such estimates are excluded from measurements of informality, one is forced to ask whether the focus on informality is not a reflection of policies focusing on the actions of the marginal and poor while ignoring bigger questions about the action of elites (tax avoidance and evasion).
5 In a parallel to our suspicion of the vocabulary of transition, Mkandawire argues that in scholarship on development in Africa (and by extension central Asia, part of the post-socialist world), 'neo-patrimonialism' is a convenient peg on which to hang any various failings in political and economic development, including informal economy. In fact the term really tells us very little 'except perhaps that capitalist relations in their idealized form are not pervasive in Africa' (1998). For a similar position on Central Asia, see Rico Isaacs (2013).

References

Aage, H. (2005) 'The Triumph of Capitalism in Russia and Eastern Europe and its Western Apologetics', *Socialism and Democracy* 19(2): 3–36.

Andrews, D., Caldera Sánchez, A. and Johansson, A. (2011) 'Towards a Better Understanding of the Informal Economy', *OECD Economics Department Working Papers*, No. 873, OECD Publishing. Online. Available: <http://dx.doi.org/10.1787/5kgb1mf88x28-en> (accessed 31 March 2013).

Åslund, A. (2004) 'Russia's Economic Transformation under Putin', *Eurasian Geography and Economics* 45(6): 397–420.

Bunce, V. (1995) 'Should Transitologists Be Grounded?', *Slavic Review* 54(1): 111–27.

Burawoy, M. (2001) 'Neoclassical Sociology: From the End of Communism to the End of Classes', *American Journal of Sociology* 106(4): 1099–120.

Carothers, T. (2002) 'The End of the Transition Paradigm', *Journal of Democracy* 13(1): 5–21.

Castells, M. and Portes, A. (1989) 'World Underneath: The Origins, Dynamics, and Effects of the Informal Economy', in Portes, A., Castells, M. and Benton, L. A. (eds), *The Informal Economy – Studies in Advanced and Less Developed Countries*, Baltimore and London: Johns Hopkins University Press, pp. 11–37.

Christensen, R. K. (2006) 'The Global Path: Soft Law and Non-Sovereigns Formalizing the Potency of the Informal Sector', in Guha-Khasnobis, B., Kanbur, R. and Ostrom, E. (eds), *Linking the Formal and Informal Economy Concepts and Policies*, Oxford University Press, pp. 36–55.

Dale, G. (2010) *Karl Polanyi: The Limits of the Market*, Cambridge and Malden: Polity.

Denzin, N. (1997) *Interpretive Ethnography: Ethnographic Practices for the 21st Century*, Thousand Oaks, London, New Delhi: Sage.

Eisenstadt, S.N. (2000) 'Multiple Modernities', *Daedalus* 129: 1–29.

Fullbrook, E. (ed.) (2007) *Real World Economics: A Post-Autistic Economics Reader*, London and New York: Anthem Press.

Gans-Morse, J. (2004) 'Searching for Transitologists: Contemporary Theories of Post-Communist Transitions and the Myth of a Dominant Paradigm', *Post-Soviet Affairs* 20(4): 320–49.

Gibson-Graham, J. K. (2008) 'Diverse Economies: Performative Practices for "Other Worlds"', *Progress in Human Geography,* 32(5): 613–32.

Guha-Khasnobis, B., Kanbur, B. and Ostrom, E. (2006) 'Beyond Formality and Informality', in Guha-Khasnobis, B., Kanbur, R. and Ostrom, E. (eds), *Linking the Formal and Informal Economy Concepts and Policies*, Oxford University Press. pp. 1–18.

Haller, D. and Shore, C. (eds) (2005) *Corruption: Anthropological Perspectives*, London: Pluto Press.

Harding, P. and Jenkins, R. (1989) *The Myth of the Hidden Economy: Towards a New Understanding of Informal Economic Activity*, Milton Keynes: Open University Press.

Hart, K. (1973) 'Informal Income Opportunities and Urban Employment in Ghana', *Journal of Modern African Studies*, 11(1): 61–89.

—— (2005) 'Formal bureaucracy and the emergent forms of the informal economy', Research Paper, UNU-WIDER, United Nations University (UNU) 2005/11. Online. Available: <http://hdl.handle.net/10419/63313> (accessed 31 March 2013).

Hart, K., Laville, J-L. and Cattani A. (eds) (2010) *The Human Economy: A Citizen's Guide*, Cambridge and Malden: Polity.

Isaacs, R. (2013) 'Bringing the "Formal" Back in: Nur Otan, Informal Networks, and the Countering of Elite Instability in Kazakhstan', Europe-Asia Studies 65(6): 1055–1079.

Jütting, J.P. and Laiglesia, J.R. (2009) 'Employment, Poverty Reduction and Development: what's new?', in Jütting, J. P. and Laiglesia, J. R. (eds), *Is Informal Normal? Towards More and Better Jobs in Developing Countries*, Paris: OECD, pp. 112–39.

Kideckel, D. (2008) *Getting by in Postsocialist Romania: Labor, the Body, and Working-class Culture*, Indiana University Press.

Ledeneva, A. (1998) *Russia's Economy of Favors:* Blat*, Networking and Informal Exchange*, Cambridge: Cambridge University Press.

—— (2009) 'From Russia with Blat: Can Informal Networks Help Modernize Russia?', *Social Research: An International Quarterly* 76(1): 257–88.
—— (2013) *Can Russia Modernise: Sistema, Power Networks and Informal Governance*, Cambridge: Cambridge University Press.
Llanes, M. and Barbour, A. (2007), *Self-employed and Micro-entrepreneurs: Informal Trading and the Journey Towards Formalisation*, London: Community Links.
Merrien, F-X. and Mendy, A. (2010) 'International Organisations', in Hart, K., Laville, J-L. and Cattani, A. (eds), *The Human Economy: A Citizen's Guide*, Cambridge and Malden: Polity, pp. 39–50.
Mkandawire, T. (1998) 'Thinking about Developmental States in Africa', African Economic Research Consortium. African Development in the 21st Century. United Nations University.
Morris, J. (2012) 'Unruly Entrepreneurs: Russian Worker Responses to Insecure Formal Employment', *Global Labour Journal* 3(2): 217–36. Online. Available: <http://digitalcommons.mcmaster.ca/globallabour/vol3/iss2/2> (accessed 31 March 2013).
Morris, J. and Polese, A. (2014) 'Informal Health and Education Sector Payments in Russian and Ukrainian Cities: Structuring Welfare from Below', *European Urban and Regional Studies*, forthcoming.
Özcan, G.B. (2010) *Building States and Markets: Enterprise Development in Central Asia*, Palgrave Macmillan.
Pardo, I. (1996) *Managing Existences in Naples: Morality, Action and Structure*, Cambridge: Cambridge University Press.
—— (ed.) (2004) *Between Morality and the Law: Corruption, Anthropology and Comparative Society*, Aldershot: Ashgate.
Polese, A. (2008) '"If I Receive it, it is a Gift; if I Demand it, then it is a Bribe"': on the Local Meaning of Economic Transactions in Post-Soviet Ukraine', *Anthropology in Action* 15(3): 47–60.
Polese, A. and Rodgers, P. (2011) 'Surviving Post-Socialism: The Role of Informal Economic Practices', *International Journal of Sociology and Social Policy* 31(11/12): 612–18.
Prato, G. (2004) 'The Devil is not as Wicked as People Believe, Neither is the Albanian: Corruption between Moral Discourses and National Identity', in Pardo, I. (ed.) *Between Morality and the Law: Corruption, Anthropology and Comparative Society*, Aldershot: Ashgate.
Round, J., Williams, C. C. and Rodgers, P. (2008) 'Everyday Tactics and Spaces of Power: the Role of Informal Economies in Post-Soviet Ukraine', *Social & Cultural Geography* 9(2): 171–85.
Routh, S. (2011) 'Building Informal Workers Agenda: Imagining "Informal Employment" in Conceptual Resolution of "Informality"', *Global Labour Journal* 2(3): 208–27. Online. Available:<http://digitalcommons.mcmaster.ca/globallabour/vol2/iss3/3>(accessed 31 March 2013).
Schneider, F. (2002) 'Size and Measurement of the Informal Economy in 110 Countries around the World', Paper presented at Workshop of Australian National Tax Centre, ANU, Canberra, Australia, 17 July. Online. Available: <http://rru.worldbank.org/Documents/PapersLinks/informal_economy.pdf> (accessed 31 March 2013).
Schneider, F., Buehn, A. and Montenegro, C. E. (2010) 'Shadow Economies all over the World: New Estimates for 162 Countries from 1999 to 2007', *World Bank Policy Research Paper 5356*.
Scott, J. C. (1985) *Weapons of the Weak: Everyday Forms of Peasant Resistance*, New Haven and London: Yale University Press.

Thelen, T. (2011) 'Shortage, Fuzzy Property and other Dead Ends in the Anthropological Analysis of (Post)socialism', *Critique of Anthropology* 31(1): 43–61.

Torsello, D. (2011) 'The Ethnography of Corruption: Research Themes in Political Anthropology' QoG Working Paper Series 2011: 2 March.

Verdery, K. (1996) *What Was Socialism, and What Comes Next?*, Princeton, NJ; Chichester, West Sussex: Princeton University Press.

Walters, W. (2002) 'Mapping Schengenland: Denaturalizing the Border', *Environment and Planning D: Society and Space* 20 (5): 561–80.

Wanner, C. (2005) 'Money, Morality and New Forms of Exchange in Ukraine', *Ethnos* 71(4): 515–37.

Werbner, P. (forthcoming) 'Migration and Transnational Studies: Between Simultaneity and Rupture', in Qayson, A. and Daswani, G. (eds), *Blackwell Reader in Migration and Transnational Studies*, Oxford: Blackwell.

Williams, C.C. and Round, J. (2007) 'Beyond Negative Depictions of Informal Employment: Some Lessons from Moscow', *Urban Studies*, 44(12): 321–38.

Williams, C.C., Nadin, S. and Rodgers, P. (2011) 'Beyond a "varieties of capitalism" approach in Central and Eastern Europe: Some lessons from Ukraine' Employee Relations 33(4): 413–27.

Part 1
'Entrepreneurial' informality? Self- and off-the-books employment

1 The diverse livelihood practices of healthcare workers in Ukraine

The case of Sasha and Natasha

Colin C. Williams and Olga Onoschenko

Introduction

Every society has to produce, distribute and allocate the goods and services its citizens require. All societies, in consequence, have an economy of some type. Economies, however, can be organized in various ways. To depict how an economy is structured, three modes of delivering goods and services have been commonly differentiated, namely the 'market' (private sector), the 'state' (public sector) and the 'community' (informal or third) sector (Giddens 1998; Gough 2000; Polanyi 1944; Thompson *et al.* 1991), even if different labels are sometimes attached to these realms. Based on this tripartite depiction of economies, a widespread consensus exists regarding the trajectory of economic development in post-Soviet spaces. First, it is believed that goods and services are being increasingly produced and delivered through the formal (market and state) economy rather than through the community or informal sphere (i.e., known as the 'formalization' thesis) and, second, that this formal production and delivery of goods and services is increasingly occurring through the market sector, known as the 'marketization' thesis.

To start to examine this, this chapter examines the lives of Sasha and Natasha. If this transition towards the formal market economy is going to be seen anywhere, it will find expression in this couple. Both have formal jobs as doctors in the Ukrainian health service and, as a dual-career family, should be deeply embedded in the formal market system, earning income which they then use to purchase the goods and services they need. As this chapter will show, however, once one scratches the surface of this composite family's daily life and begins to unravel the livelihood practices they pursue in order to both get-by and get-ahead, one starts to recognize that the transition to the formal market economy is much shallower than at first thought and that they engage in a diversity of economic practices, of which work in the formal market economy is just one amongst many.

To show this, therefore, this chapter is structured as follows. In the first section, we will evaluate critically the shortcomings of the conventional dual economies depiction of economies and, following this, the second section will present a conceptual framework to capture the multifarious economic practices in post-Soviet spaces, namely the 'total social organization of labour' (TSOL) approach. Following this, the third section will then examine the livelihood practices pursued by Sasha and Natasha through this lens, examining the plurality of labour practices that they employ to secure their livelihood. The outcome will be a mapping of the diversity of economic practices that this family uses to secure a livelihood in contemporary Ukraine so as to demonstrate the shallow permeation of the formal market economy and the persistence of diverse economic practices in contemporary Ukraine so as to open up the future to other possibilities than the hegemony of the formal market economy.

Blurring the formal/informal economy dichotomy: from dual to diverse economies

The starting point of this chapter is a recognition that the depiction of the formal economy as strong, extensive and growing, and the discrete and different informal economy as weak, marginal and declining, exemplifies what Derrida (1967) terms a hierarchical binary mode of thought. This formal/informal economy dualism, that is, is first of all grounded in a conceptualization of two opposing economies which are stable, bounded and constituted via negation and, secondly, the resultant separate economies are read hierarchically in a manner that bestows the superordinate (the formal economy) with positive attributes and as growing, whilst the subordinate or subservient 'other' (the informal economy) is endowed with negativity and as dwindling. The outcome is twofold. On the one hand, a relationship of opposition and exclusion is established between the two realms, rather than a representation of similarity and mixture. On the other hand, the resultant dichotomy becomes imbued with a normative discourse of 'progress' in which the extensive superordinate 'us' (the formal economy) becomes privileged over the separate, much weaker and residual subordinate 'other' (the informal economy). As Latouche (1993) recognizes, the informal economy becomes represented as primitive, stagnant, marginal, residual, weak, existing only in the margins and scattered across the economic landscape, whilst the separate and distinct formal economy is constructed as systematic, naturally expansive and extensive.

Since the turn of the millennium, however, a small stream of thought has emerged composed of a loose coupling of an array of post-structuralist, post-development, post-colonial and critical scholars, or what Gibson-Graham (2008), who are two authors writing as one, have termed a 'diverse economies' school of thought. This has begun to contest not only this hierarchical binary reading of the formal and informal economies as separate hostile spheres but also the privileging of the formal over the informal (e.g. Chowdhury 2007; Escobar 2001; Gibson-Graham 1996, 2006, 2008; Gibson-Graham and Ruccio 2001; Latouche 1993; Leyshon 2005; Smith and Stenning 2006; Williams 2002, 2003, 2004, 2005, 2006, 2009; Williams and Round 2007). The aim in doing this has been to try to recover recognition and re-valuing of the plethora of economic practices in contemporary societies and to challenge the assumption that formalization and marketization are totalizing trajectories of economic development.

Livelihood practices: the 'total social organization of labour' approach

Perhaps the most prominent and promising attempt to achieve this so far is the 'total social organization of labour' (TSOL) approach of Glucksmann (2005: 28) who reads 'the economy as a "multiplex" combination of modes, rather than as a dualism'. In her TSOL approach, and as Taylor (2004) displays, a spectrum of labour practices is constructed ranging from formal to informal and this spectrum is then cross-cut by whether the labour is paid or unpaid (Glucksmann 1995, 2000, 2005, 2009). Here, therefore, the intention is to use this TSOL conceptual framework in order to transcend the formal/informal economy dualism and to understand the heterogeneous labour practices in economies, but with one modification. Rather than portray labour as either paid or unpaid, a further spectrum is constructed ranging from wholly monetized, through gift-giving and in-kind labour reciprocity, to wholly non-monetized labour.

As Figure 1 displays, the result is that a seamless array of labour practices are depicted first along a spectrum from relatively formal to more informal labour practices and second, and cross-cutting this, along a further spectrum from wholly non-monetized, through gift exchange and in-kind labour, to wholly monetized labour practices. Hatched circles are deliberately employed to display how although it is possible to name various labour practices along these continua, they are all part of a borderless continua of labour practices, rather than separate kinds, which overlap and merge into one another as one moves along both the formal/informal spectrum of the x-axis and the paid/unpaid spectrum of the y-axis. The consequence is that the borderless fluidity between different labour practices is captured and it is clearly shown how the multiple practices are not discrete but seamlessly entwined and conjoined.

In consequence, rather than adopt a simple dichotomous depiction of labour as being either formal and informal, eight broad and overlapping labour practices are identified, each possessing a range of different varieties and each merging at their borders with the various other practices surrounding them. Below, we consider the prevalence and nature of each of these economic practices by examining the coping practices employed by Sasha and Natasha in their daily lives.

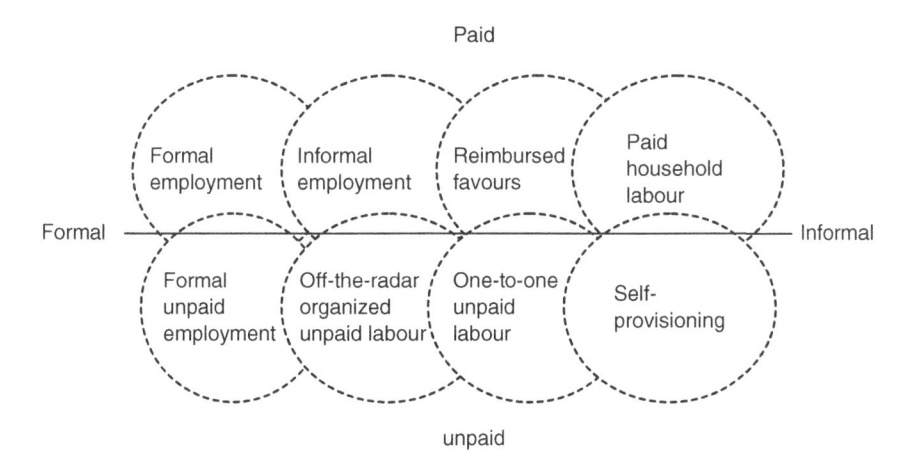

Figure 1 A classificatory schema of labour practices

Livelihood practices: a case study of Sasha and Natasha

Formal employment

Formal employment refers to paid work registered by the state for tax, social security and labour law purposes. Within this formal sphere, three types of formal labour, namely in the private, public and third sectors are conventionally distinguished. However, given that private sector organizations are increasingly pursuing a triple bottom line, whilst public and third sector organizations are also pursuing profit (albeit in order to reinvest so as to achieve wider social and environmental objectives), a blurring of these three varieties of formal employment is occurring. There is also a blurring of the boundaries between formal employment and other labour practices, including formal unpaid labour and informal employment.

This can be clearly seen in the case of Sasha and Natasha. Both are doctors in the Ukrainian health service which, as Lekhan *et al.* (2004) point out, has undergone a radical transformation since the collapse of the Soviet Union. Sasha and Natasha are both employed full-time in the health service. Sasha is a paediatrician at a maternity hospital examining newborns and providing treatment, earning an official salary of 2,000 hryvnias ($250). Natasha, meanwhile, is an ophthalmologist and has two official part-time jobs at public outpatient hospitals where she has both *priom* (surgery hours) and *cherguvannia* (accident & emergency of hours). Both perceive their salaries as insufficient for a decent quality of life. Whilst the price of foodstuffs is relatively low mainly due to lower quality control (1 litre of milk costs approximately $1, a loaf of bread $0.8, a BigMac $2), imported consumer goods, such as clothing or cars are more expensive than in Western Europe due to import taxes.

In order to earn enough, Sasha and Natasha have not turned to the small but burgeoning private healthcare sector. In part, this is because doctors in the private sector receive only 10–15 per cent higher salaries compared with the public sector (Lekhan, 2010: 68). Another factor is that Sasha at least is able to work overtime. As a full-time doctor, he is employed for 40 hours per week for which he earns what he calls a 'single rate'. However, if he works extra hours, he receives one and a half or double wage rates. Indeed, Natasha jokes:

> If you work on single rate, you have nothing to eat. If you work on double rate, you have no time to eat.

At the time of the interview in 2010, Sasha was doing as much overtime as he could, not least because he had heard of forthcoming changes in the healthcare system and was fearful he might be made redundant. At the time, each health administrative area had at least one children's clinic and a separate adult clinic responsible for outpatient care, an in-patient hospital (including for emergency services), a maternity hospital and some specialized hospitals (for treatment of tuberculosis, etc.). Each healthcare area was divided into districts, with each district assigned one or two paediatricians and physicians, spending part of the day doing surgeries in policlinics and the other part of the day visiting patients at home unable to come and who ask to be seen by a doctor at home. At the time of writing, in 2012, Sasha and Natasha were perhaps right to be fearful. In 2011, it was announced that children and adult clinics would be merged, and that there would no longer be separate paediatricians and physicians in each district, but instead just one general practitioner (GP). For Sasha and Natasha, however, it was not just overtime which was important for securing a better livelihood.

Informal employment

Informal employment refers to paid activities unregistered by, or hidden from, the state for tax, social security and labour law purposes (Williams 2009). Such employment ranges from wholly undeclared employment (either as a waged worker or self-employed person) to under-declared formal employment where formal employees receive an additional undeclared wage from their formal employer alongside their formal declared wage (envelope wage) or the formal self-employed do not declare various portions of their earnings.

When asked about whether they were paid an envelope wage, Sasha and Natasha both asserted that although this practice was rife in many walks of Ukrainian life, it did not really apply to them working in the public sector healthcare system. However, they told a different story when it came to wholly undeclared employment. First of all, Sasha did not just work overtime in his formal employment to boost his wage but, more lucratively, engaged in what might be termed informal self-employment and this was currently by far the most important source of income for the household. In his formal job at the maternity hospital, he did many home visits. As he put it,

> 2,500 hryvnias isn't enough to survive. I have to earn money on the side. When I visited mothers and their babies at home, I started charging $5 per call out. One time the mother of one of the patients asked me, how much money she owes for a visit. I said: 'fifty', meaning fifty hryvnias. She brought me $50. Since then, I've raised the fee. I now charge €20 for one-off home call outs. Some clients though pay me a fixed amount per month, €100. For this, I visit the baby regularly until they are one year old and the parents can call me 24 hours seven days a week if the baby is unwell.

When asked whether he wanted to formalize this activity such as by starting up a formal private sector medical practice, he replied:

> If I want to register a private medic, I would need a *cabinet* [doctor's consulting room]. And it is not easy to open a *cabinet* in our country: a lot of papers need to be signed requiring bribes to officials . . . You need to find a place, to get approvals from *sanstanciya* [the sanitation centre], *oblzdravotdel* [the regional healthcare department], formalize everything . . . this would require too much money. Being registered is just not profitable. It would mean dozens of inspectors all taking money from me.

For Sasha, therefore, there is no need to register as a private medic. Natasha, meanwhile, and in addition to her two part-time formal jobs as an ophthalmologist at public outpatient hospitals, is also an undeclared waged employee at an optician's where she conducts eye tests. When asked about this, she says

> My two part-time jobs are in state hospitals. Everybody is officially registered there. As for my secondary activity – it is preferable for me not to be registered as I do not have to pay taxes. My employer is absolutely happy with this – he employs three people, but pays taxes only for one.

Together, this informal employment of Sasha and Natasha generates income worth twice as much as their formal jobs, giving them a comfortable existence.

Reimbursed favours

Reimbursed favours involve the provision of one-to-one help to either kin living outside the household, friends, neighbours or acquaintances where monetary payment is exchanged. Profit, nevertheless, is not always the primary or sole intention of the customer or the supplier. Reimbursed favours exist on a continuum ranging from those conducted for distant social relations or anonymous customers more for profit-oriented reasons to those undertaken for closer social relations where the profit-motive is largely absent and the rationales involve redistribution and consolidating social relationships, with many combinations in between. In Soviet times, such paid favours were separate from *blat*, which Ledeneva (2006: 1) defines as 'the use of personal networks for obtaining goods and services in short supply and for circumventing formal procedures'. In the post-Soviet era, however, where shortages are not so much the problem, *blat* has become monetized in the sense that one pays for favours rendered by one's social networks. It is therefore closely related to reimbursed favours.

For Sasha, such payments for favours are an integral part of his formal occupation. As he comments:

> In the maternity hospital obstetricians usually receive 2,000–3,000 hryvias in cash for each delivery. From this amount they give 20 hryvnias to a nurse and 100 hryvnias to a paediatrician [Sasha's job].

To the remark that such informal payments might be considered a bribe and could be prosecuted, he responded:

> Nobody fights this 'corruption' in hospitals. The state cannot provide doctors with an adequate salary but doctors need to survive. If the informal earnings of healthcare workers were prosecuted, everybody would leave. Therefore the state turns a blind eye.

Sasha sees nothing wrong with taking such gratuities. For him, these payments are not 'bribes' but are gifts from the patient that say 'thank you'. As he explains:

Have you ever visited a doctor in a public hospital who refused to treat you without being paid or extorted money from you? . . . I do not consider that money given as a bribe; it is gift of gratitude by the patient.

Indeed, Polese (2008) stated that cash payments to doctors in Ukraine are perceived more as gratitude rather than corruption. This is the case when the state fails to fulfil its functions, insufficiently rewarding public workers. As Polese (2008: 53) puts it: 'If I receive it, it is a gift. If I demand it, then it is a bribe'. Natasha, meanwhile, does not receive much income in the form of cash-in-hand payments from the patients:

Sometimes I bring home a bunch of bananas, sometimes 30 hryvnias or several chocolate boxes and there are also days when I receive nothing. My speciality is 'unprofitable'. There are much more desirable specialties like dermatologists. They are well paid informally and at the same time the risks are minimal. Anaesthesiology is also very profitable, however the responsibility is huge and only people with brains can choose this specialty.

The types of reimbursed favours so far discussed tend to be quite close to forms of informal employment even if 'profit' is not always the motive on the part of either the purchaser of the service and/or the supplier.

Other types of paid favour, however, are even more social- and less profit-oriented. An example is giving out false 'medical certificates' such as signing off a person as ill when they are not or confirming that they are fit and should be offered a job when this might not be the case. Issuing fraudulent medical certificates is illegal and Sasha does not engage in such a practice, except for closer acquaintances, friends, family and neighbours. When doing so, he does not take payments from close family but the more distant the relationship becomes, the greater the payment he takes. However, he does not do this for strangers whom he does not know well.

Beyond these paid favours for close social relations by Sasha, Natasha sometimes provides eye tests for a token payment. However, the only people she provides such tests for are very close social relations and some elderly people that she does not believe, by the clothes they wear, are able to afford to pay the market rates.

Paid household labour

Sometimes family members are paid by other family members within their household for conducting tasks. In Ukraine, the only time this tends to happen is when the exchange is inter-generational. Sasha and Natasha do not have children so there is no payment to a child for doing chores, such as to help them learn the value of money.

Indeed, the only time that they had engaged in such labour was over a three-month period when Natasha's aunt had lived with them. She had been made redundant at the time and had moved to Mykolayiv in search of work. When she first arrived, she had little money so Sasha and Natasha had provided her with accommodation in return for her doing the everyday housework that needed to be done. This was because she did not want to accept 'charity' and wanted to pay for her stay with them. Realizing that she had little money, they came to an agreement that if she did the housework, she would not have to pay for her stay with them. She had been happy with this arrangement. This, therefore, had been an instance where in-kind labour had been used to reimburse them for the provision of the accommodation, which is a common practice since it avoids any connotation of 'charity' being involved.

Formal unpaid employment

In post-Soviet spaces, people often work unpaid for a trial period when offered a formal job. When conducted in the private sector, this often takes the form of an unpaid internship. Sasha and Natasha had experienced such a form of labour themselves earlier in their careers and also made use of such 'free labour' themselves.

Earlier in her career, when hoping to become an eye surgeon, Natasha had worked on an unpaid internship in the offices of a senior eye surgeon, a competitive position which she had only managed to get after her uncle had used his social networks and friendship with the surgeon to secure her a place. Once she started, the eye surgeon had offered her a paid traineeship but wanted a significant amount of money from her, which she did not possess, in order to secure the traineeship. She had therefore foregone the opportunity, something which she still bitterly regretted not being able to take up.

In more recent years, Sasha had also made use of unpaid internships. Many young people wanted to become doctors and needed to gain work experience in order to help them secure a place on medical degrees. Sasha offered unpaid work placements to young people during the summer months in order that they might gain such work experience. For him, it was an opportunity to get some 'free labour' in order to be able to organize his busy schedule and appointments and at the same time, to accumulate some favours owed from those he employed and their families. Last year, for example, he had employed the son of a woman who distributed the vouchers for the local sanatorium, and had been able to secure places at the sanatorium for several of his clients, for whom he was able to charge an extra fee for securing them a place. Whenever feasible, therefore, he used these unpaid internships as a means of developing his social networks and access to facilities which would otherwise not be available to him.

By far the most popular form of unpaid formal labour in Ukraine, however, is in community-based groups, in the form of what is more commonly deemed to be 'formal volunteering'. Outside of their formal employment, both Sasha and Natasha are very active in terms of engaging in formal volunteering. Both enjoy the hobby of cycling during the weekends when they are not working, and were the president and treasurer of the local cycling club. In addition, both have a keen interest in environmental issues and are members of various environmental groups in the locality, which variously campaign for the preservation of older buildings, green spaces in the city and lower carbon consumption. In addition, and more related to her employment, Natasha is a member of a charity that seeks to improve the conditions of the visually impaired in Mykolayiv. Sasha, similarly, helps coordinate a bereavement self-help group for parents who have lost their new-born children.

Off-the-radar unpaid labour in groups

Sometimes those engaged in unpaid labour in community-based groups might do so illegitimately or informally, such as when caring for children in a community-based group but without the required licences to act as child carer, or when operating a sporting group, community fund-raising or music event without the necessary licences. Many people assume that the current legal responsibilities only apply, such as when caring for others' children, if paid and that if unpaid, they were not applicable.

It might be considered that engaging in unpaid endeavour in community-based groups on an 'off-the-radar' basis is rare. However, Sasha and Natasha show that this is not the case. Many of the young parents that Sasha meets have little money and cannot always purchase the clothes and other goods (e.g. cots, prams, milk sterilizing equipment) that they need. Sasha operates a 'used goods' operation whereby parents who no longer need these goods for themselves can donate them to him and he then distributes them to other families who need them. At first, this started when a couple asked him if he knew anybody who needed some new-born baby clothes and he had taken them and given them to another family. Over the years, this operation had grown such that he was now engaged in quite a large-scale operation passing on 'second-hand' goods to other families and/or acting as a 'broker' between families giving them their respective telephone numbers. Sasha believed that this should be perhaps registered as a charity, given the growing size of the operation, but he had not yet done so.

Similarly, each year, the cycling club organized an event to raise money which involved a music festival where food and drink was sold. However, they seldom applied for all of the necessary licences required to put on this event. By putting it on in the grounds of the hospital, paying his bosses a small fee for doing so, he had avoided the absolute necessity of doing so, since the various inspectors tended to leave events that took place in the hospital grounds alone. However, he fully understood that this annual event officially requires music licences, fire and safety licences and so forth, which he did not seek to acquire due to the time it would take and the number of small-scale 'bribes' he would have to pay. For him, the logic was that it would no longer make charity events worthwhile due to the level of organization required and the little money which would be made once one had paid everybody what they required.

One-to-one unpaid labour

Another form of labour involves the provision of one-to-one unpaid labour either on a one-way or reciprocal basis by or for kin living outside the household, friends, neighbours or acquaintances. For Sasha and Natasha, the only time that they engage in such one-to-one unpaid labour is when kin living outside the household is involved. For example, each week, Natasha undertakes the food shopping for Sasha's elderly parents and delivers it to their home. Sasha, meanwhile, occasionally undertakes small home repairs for his parents.

Moreover, they both use their connections in the hospital to enable their relatives to see other doctors, avoiding a queue:

> When our relatives need medical treatment or consultation, we always help them with our connections: refer them to good doctors we know, help them to avoid queuing. In return we can always ask for help as well. For example, we often ask my father's cousin, who is retired, to do small odd-jobs. I once tried to give her 20 hryvnias for the favour, but she refused. But we always help their family and their children and grandchildren and they help us and our parents. We never pay for this help.

When one-to-one unpaid labour is conducted for non-kin (e.g., neighbours, friends), however, Sasha and Natasha tend to either receive or give token payments, gifts or in-kind labour. Neighbours, for example, have done favours for them looking after their pet cat when they were away on vacation last year. They in turn brought them a gift back from their holiday, some cigars, in return for them doing this favour. As Natasha comments, 'it would not have been right not to give them anything. You always do. That way, you do not have to give them anything back in return'.

Self-provisioning labour

Self-provisioning is unpaid work undertaken for oneself or other members of one's household. It is sometimes assumed that as the formal economy becomes more dominant, and as a commodification of society occurs, then households outsource a greater share of their domestic workload to the formal market economy, such as domestic cleaning, gardening, caring functions and so forth. This is felt to be particularly the case among more affluent households.

Sasha and Natasha show how in lived practice it is only a small proportion of the total domestic workload which is outsourced to the formal market economy. The vast majority of everyday domestic tasks are conducted by them on a self-provisioning basis. Nevertheless, they do employ a domestic cleaner two days per week who does the weekly housework, laundry and ironing. Natasha and Sasha view this as a way of liberating themselves from the routine housework so that they can free some time to conduct a wider array of more creative and rewarding self-servicing. Sasha, for example, had engaged in a do-it-yourself project to build himself a fishpond and water fountain in the garden.

This employment of a domestic cleaner, incidentally on an off-the-books basis, has also enabled Sasha and Natasha to be able to spend more time on their dacha when they get the opportunity, where they grow a range of vegetables for self-consumption. For them, this is a leisure activity which enables them to get out in the fresh air and to till the land so as to produce some organically grown fresh produce for themselves. They see this as a form of relaxation.

It is also interesting that despite the widespread perception that self-provisioning is non-exchanged labour, this is not the case in practice. Sasha and Natasha have a lot of arguments about whether they are equally pulling their weight when it comes to doing the domestic chores. As Natasha puts it:

> Sasha sees it as my responsibility. For example, he saw the employment of a cleaner as taking some work off my shoulders because I tended to take responsibility for the everyday housework whilst he did the odd-jobs when they needed doing. The problem is that he uses the domestic cleaner as an excuse to never lift a finger to help out. I still end up having to do everything besides what she does. He just doesn't seem to understand that he needs to help me out.

As Sasha puts it, however:

> I do the odd-jobs and she in turn does the housework. I also work longer hours than her so she has to take more responsibility for the housework. That is only fair isn't it.

Given this commonly expressed desire for equivalent reciprocity between partners in couple households, with one partner taking responsibility for doing one task and their partner responsibility for another, or one doing the housework because the other earned a wage, it appears that self-provisioning does indeed involve exchange and reciprocity and is in fact commonly embedded in work relations and motives similar to one-to-one unpaid labour and paid favours. Indeed, unpaid housework, an activity often viewed as wholly non-monetized and non-exchanged, can be seen as often heavily embedded in expectations of reciprocity. As Natasha and Sasha show, it is perhaps rare in couple households that domestic tasks are today wholly unpaid with no expectation of reciprocity in the future.

Conclusions

The starting point of this chapter is that it is commonly assumed that post-Soviet spaces are undergoing a transition towards a formal market economy and that the market is steadily becoming hegemonic. To dispel this myth, this chapter has examined the lives of Sasha and Natasha. If this transition towards the formal market economy was going to be seen anywhere, it would have found expression in this couple. Both have formal jobs as doctors in the Ukrainian health service and as a dual-career family, are deeply embedded in the formal market system, earning income which they then use to purchase the goods and services they need. As shown, however, once one explores the plethora of livelihood practices this couple pursue in order to both get-by and get-ahead, one starts to recognize that the transition to the formal market economy is much shallower than at first thought and that they engage in multifarious economic practices in their daily lives, of which work in the formal market economy is just one amongst many.

To show this, this chapter has transcended the conventional dichotomous depiction that simply divides work into formal economic activity that is separate from informal economic activity. Here, instead, and to capture the multifarious economic practices in post-Soviet spaces, a 'total social organization of labour' (TSOL) approach has been adopted. Depicting a seamless array of labour practices, first along a spectrum from relatively formal to more informal labour practices, and second, and cross cutting this, along a further spectrum from wholly non-monetized, through gift exchange and in-kind labour, to wholly monetized labour practices, eight forms of labour practice can be identified which exist along a borderless continua of labour practices, overlap and merge into one another as one moves along both the formal/informal spectrum and the paid/unpaid spectrum, thus showing how these multiple practices are not discrete but seamlessly entwined and conjoined.

Examining the livelihood practices of Sasha and Natasha through this conceptual lens has revealed the plurality of labour practices that they employ to secure their livelihood. The outcome is a textured mapping of the diverse economic practices that a family uses to secure a livelihood in contemporary Ukraine. It also reveals the relative shallowness of the penetration of the formal market economy. In this transition economy, which is supposedly undergoing a 'transition' to a formal market economy, this case study of Natasha and Sasha reveals the limited extent to which they are engaged in the formal commercial economy and the shallowness of its permeation into their livelihood practices and daily lives. Instead, what is revealed is the persistence of multifarious economic practices in contemporary Ukraine and quite how distant capitalism is from becoming hegemonic in contemporary Ukraine. Recognizing this plethora of economic practices is important when it comes to thinking about the transition process and the trajectory of economic development in post-Soviet spaces. What it demonstrates is that market hegemony is far from an inevitable irrefutable and irreversible process. Instead, it opens up the future to alternatives beyond market hegemony and enables one to consider the feasibility of alternative futures for economic development which recognize and value the persistence of multifarious work practices.

If this chapter therefore encourages greater recognition of the persistence of the diverse economic practices in contemporary post-Soviet economies, then it will have achieved one of its intentions. If it then encourages the future to be opened up to the feasibility of alternative trajectories for economic development beyond market hegemony, then it will have also fulfilled its other objective.

References

Chowdhury, S.A. (2007) *Everyday Economic Practices: the 'Hidden Transcripts', of Egyptian Voices*. London: Routledge.

Derrida, J. (1967) *Of Grammatology*. Baltimore: Johns Hopkins University Press.

Escobar, A. (2001) 'Culture Sits in Places: Reflections on Globalism and Subaltern Strategies of Localization', *Political Geography*, 20(1): 139–74.
Gibson-Graham, J.K. (1996) *The End of Capitalism (As We Knew It)?: A Feminist Critique of Political Economy*. Oxford: Blackwell.
—— (2006) *A Post-Capitalist Politics*. Minneapolis: University of Minnesota Press.
—— (2008) 'Diverse Economies: Performative Practices for "Other Worlds"', *Progress in Human Geography*, 32(5): 613–32.
Gibson-Graham, J.K. and Ruccio, D., (2001) 'After "Development": Re-imagining Economy and Class', in *Class and its Others* eds J. K. Gibson-Graham, S. Resnick, D. Ruccio. Durham, NC: Duke University Press.
Giddens, A. (1998) *The Third Way: the Renewal of Social Democracy*. Cambridge: Polity.
Glucksmann, M. (1995) 'Why Work? Gender and the Total Social Organization of Labor', *Gender, Work and Organization*, 2(2): 63–75.
—— (2000) *Cottons and Casuals: the Gendered Organisation of Labour in Time and Space*. Durham: Sociology Press.
—— (2005) 'Shifting Boundaries and Interconnections: Extending the "Total Social Organization of Labor"', *Sociological Review*, 53(2): 19–36.
—— (2009) 'Formations, Connections and Divisions of Labour', *Sociology*, 43(5): 878–95.
Gough, I. (2000) *Global Capital, Human Needs and Social Policies*. Basingstoke: Palgrave.
Latouche, S. (1993) *In the Wake of Affluent Society: an Exploration of Post-development*, London: Zed.
Ledeneva, A.V. (1998) *Russia's Economy of Favours: Blat, Networking and Informal Exchange*. Cambridge: Cambridge University Press.
—— (2006) *How Russia Really Works: the Informal Practices that Shaped Post-Soviet Politics and Business*. London: Cornell University Press.
Lekhan, V., Rudiy, V. and Nolte, E. (2004) *Health Care Systems in Transition: Ukraine*, Copenhagen, WHO Regional Office for Europe on behalf of the European, Observatory on Health Systems and Policies.
Lekhan, V., Rudiy, V. and Richardson, E. (2010) 'Ukraine: Health System Review', *Health Systems in Transition*, 12(8): 441–62.
Leyshon, A. (2005) 'Introduction: Diverse Economies', *Antipode,* 37: 856–62.
Polanyi, K. (1944) *The Great Transformation*, Boston: Beacon Press.
Polese, A. (2008) '"If I receive it, it is a gift; if I demand it, then it is a bribe" on the local meaning of economic transactions in post-soviet Ukraine', *Anthropology in Action*, 15(3): 47–60.
Smith, A. and Stenning, A. (2006) 'Beyond Household Economies: Articulations and Spaces of Economic Practice in Postsocialism', *Progress in Human Geography,* 30(1): 1–14.
Taylor, R. F. (2004) 'Extending Conceptual Boundaries: Work, Voluntary Work and Employment', *Work, Employment & Society*, 18(1): 29–49.
Thompson, G., Frances, J., Lavacic, R. and Mitchell, J. (1991) (eds.) *Markets, Hierarchies and Networks*, London: Sage.
Williams, C. C. (2002) 'A Critical Evaluation of the Commodification Thesis', *Sociological Review*, 50: 525–42.
—— (2003) 'Evaluating the Penetration of the Commodity Economy', *Futures*, 35: 857–68.
—— (2004) 'The Myth of Marketization: an Evaluation of the Persistence of Non-market Activities in Advanced Economies', *International Sociology*, 19(4): 437–49.
—— (2005) *A Commodified World? Mapping the Limits of Capitalism*, London: Zed.

—— (2006) *The Hidden Enterprise Culture: Entrepreneurship in the Underground Economy*, Cheltenham: Edward Elgar.

—— (2009) 'Formal and Informal Employment in Europe: Beyond Dualistic Representations', *European Urban and Regional Studies*, 16(2): 147–59.

—— (2010) 'Geographical Variations in Informal Work in Contemporary England', in (eds) E. Marcelli, C. C. Williams and P. Joassart, *Informal Work in Developed Nations*, London: Routledge, pp. 97–113.

Williams, C. C. and Round, J. (2007) 'Beyond Negative Depictions of Informal Employment: Some Lessons from Moscow', *Urban Studies*, 44(12): 321–38.

2 The story of Šarūnas
An *Invisible Citizen* of Lithuania[1]

Ida Harboe Knudsen

Šarūnas

Šarūnas[2] is a tall man with bushy eyebrows. Although only in his mid-thirties he is already progressively balding. He keeps an unshaved look, which visually adds a certain roughness to his otherwise gentle demeanour. Šarūnas comes from the northern part of Lithuania. He is a bachelor, has never married and has no children. Being a man of few words, Šarūnas approaches social interaction with a certain caution. During our acquaintance I make a few attempts to get him to go with me to the city for dinner or a beer. Once in a brave moment I suggest we go clubbing. It is all in vain. He declines subtly under the excuse that he does not have the proper wardrobe for such excursions. Yet I sense that this is more than a question about his clothes; Šarūnas does not seem comfortable with the mere idea of being out in the city or in restaurants or bars. The vibrant city life is not his scene, he feels too estranged.

Šarūnas knows that I am eager to interview him, but it is a while before he agrees. Only after a period of us having daily informal conversations does Šarūnas finally decide that we can meet for the interview. We settle for an evening after work. When asked whether I can use my dictaphone, Šarūnas objects. It 'steals your soul,' he says jokingly.[3] His irony refers back to both stereotypical ideas about anthropologists and their interaction with 'superstitious' natives, and in the same line of thinking it is a reference to how some Indian tribes once believed that getting photographed took away your soul. Irony aside, Šarūnas and I both know that the actual reason for his refusal is the illegal nature of his work and his unsettled position in relation to the Lithuanian state. Šarūnas works, as the Lithuanians phrase it, 'in the shadow' (*šešėlyje*), which means that he works without any formal employment and without paying tax. He is engaged in the construction business and conducts all kinds of repair work on houses. Šarūnas has expanded his working area to embrace two countries: Lithuania and Sweden. He works in Sweden during the summer period and moves back to Lithuania during the winter. Šarūnas pays no tax, neither in Lithuania, nor in Sweden. On top of this he has no health insurance to cover him in either of the places. He is heavily indebted to the Lithuanian state as he has received a number of fines for drunk driving and driving without a licence. As he does not plan to pay the money back he is in a precarious situation: he persistently avoids legal work (the income would be registered and state authorities would enforce payment of the debt), he cannot open a bank account (it would be registered and the state authorities would claim the money in the account) and he cannot own property, nor inherit it from his parents (this would be taken as compensation for his debt).

Šarūnas has had a drink or two before we start the interview. Now he sits in an armchair with yet another glass of white wine, which he turns round and round in his hands while we are talking. Occasionally he takes a sip. After a while the sips turn into a couple of refills. I have jotted down a number of topics and questions that I would like to talk about. Unlike many other informants I have met during my career as an anthropologist, Šarūnas does not start a long and unstoppable monologue about the general state of affairs in Lithuania according to his beliefs and personal situation that is largely unrelated to my inquiries. Šarūnas differs. He carefully listens to my questions, then considers each of them at length, before giving me an answer of few words. Šarūnas does not express any satisfaction with his situation, nor does he feel in a position to change it: 'I am out of the system,' he says in his low deep voice. So he is, and it seems close to impossible for him to get back 'in'.

I met Šarūnas for the first time in the fall of 2011. Autumn is the time of the year when he normally returns to Lithuania after having finished his working season in Sweden. This autumn he had come to stay in the city of Kaunas for a couple of months while carrying out 'shadow work': he had been hired to work on a house in Kaunas where he had to change the main part of the floors, repair the worn-down walls and paint them in refreshing colours. This lasted more than a month. For this work he earned 50 litas a day (€14.50). This was a normal salary for him in Lithuania. Depending on the nature of the work, the agreement he had with people employing him earned him from 30 to 100 litas a day (€8.70–29.00). What intrigued me about Šarūnas' situation was that in general he maintained a life largely separate from official society: he opted to live outside the radar of the state, without any property registered in his name, with no formal employment, no public health insurance and without voting at elections and referendums. And he was but one of many Lithuanians living in this way. Indeed, looking at the situation in economic terms gives us an indication of the situation. Close to one-third of Lithuania's GDP is based on the shadow economy: unregistered work, smuggling illegal goods and tax fraud.

The *Invisible Citizens* of Lithuania

Šarūnas belongs to a group of Lithuanians that I refer to as *Invisible Citizens*. By *Invisible Citizens* I mean people who opt to avoid formal and institutional relations with the state due to a general scepticism, mainly towards politicians, the police and public bureaucrats who are perceived as showing little if any attention to the problems and concerns of the lower middle class and 'ordinary people.' The *Invisible* do not register their employment and therefore pay no tax. This is more than a little moonlight work on the side; it is a way of living. In the case of

Lithuania this means that they are deprived of any kind of state support – most importantly public health insurance and economic and social support in case of unemployment – just as they will not receive an adequate pension when they reach retirement age. Yet, this is preferred above having relations with a system they do not trust. Additionally, a vast number of the *Invisible* do not exercise their democratic rights as they refrain from voting at elections. This decision is most commonly based on the argument that there is no one to vote for, that the political candidates all are corrupt, and/or that their single vote does not make a difference. While in Slovakia and Poland we have witnessed demonstrations and riots as a direct protest against neoliberal reforms resulting from EU membership (see Stenning *et al.* 2011), the *Invisible* Lithuanians express their dissatisfaction through everyday practices, not through open confrontations. Their uncanny situation is by some actively expressed as contempt for present-day Lithuania, while others, like Šarūnas, find themselves in a state of marginalized bewilderment. Although 'shadow work' and increased marginalization have been noticeable problems since Lithuania regained independence in 1990, the *Invisible* and their implicit criticism of the post-socialist state have to a great extent been ignored by the Lithuanian authorities. Indeed, only after the financial crisis struck in 2008 did the *Invisible* become an explicit point on the political agenda due to the state's need for cash, something which partly could be helped by restoring tax payments among the country's many shadow workers.

The concept of *Invisible Citizens* has hitherto been used more widely as a reference to a nonvoluntary state of being to describe people who make a claim for recognition and visibility, or people who belong to a minority. The term has been used to describe homosexuals (Vitureau 2010), stateless people in Europe (Kostapoulou 2001) or American Arabs in the USA before 9/11 (Jamal and Naber 2007). My approach differs, as I discuss a group of citizens that does not belong to a minority and is not distinguished by ethnicity, shared political goals or sexual orientation. Indeed, the *Invisible Citizens* make no claim for recognition and they have no organizational activities to promote certain rights or political points of view. However, despite the fact that their actions are expressed and exercised in a seemingly nonpolitical manner, they have serious political connotations and implications for Lithuania.

Unregistered work is most frequent in areas of seasonal and mobile employment. Thus, construction workers, plumbers, agricultural workers and other craft and tradesmen dominate the field. One additional occupation that is typical of the *Invisible* is the informal repair of cars. As these work areas are strongly gendered, the *Invisible* are characterized by an overrepresentation of males. I met far fewer women who worked illegally. Those who did often combined legal employment during the day with informal work as nannies or home teachers in the evening (see Chapter 4 in this volume). One additional occupation where women constituted the majority was the renting out of houses and rooms at holiday resorts, for example near the sea or at lakes. Furthermore, I observed that some (though not all) of my informants had minor criminal records. Criminal records were found both among young men in their twenties through to men in their late forties. Their offences were most commonly public disorder, repeated drink-driving and/or theft for which they had received fines. A few had been in prison. Debt was the most pressing problem for them. Either they did not see themselves in a position to ever pay their debt back, or, just as commonly, they refused to pay anything to the state in line with their general contempt for present-day Lithuania.

In this article I will shed light on the situation of Lithuania's *Invisible* through a detailed ethnographic description of a single informant, Šarūnas, whose story encompasses many characteristic features of working in 'the shadow'. While informal economic practices were closely interlinked with the planned economy during the Soviet regime and were often a prerequisite for its existence (Firlit and Chlopecki 1992; Ledeneva 1998; Verdery 1996; Wedel 1992), I suggest that the practices of getting around official procedures and avoiding state authorities as exercised by the *Invisible* should not be seen as a particular socialist legacy. Rather than 'restorations' of socialist patterns, these practices should be seen as direct *responses* to the new neoliberal environment rather than a heritage of a certain culture or a specific 'Soviet mentality' (Burawoy and Verdery 1999). As has been emphasized by Stenning *et al.*, such responses to neoliberalism are expressed through daily practices as people strive to make new market reforms tolerable and acceptable in their everyday life (2011). Following this line of thinking I will argue, with reference to David Kideckel's analysis of the situation of Romanian miners after the Soviet breakdown, that actions of invisibility are best linked to new forms of subalternization of labour that have emerged in post-socialist societies (Kideckel 2002). Thereby, I set out to analyse the outcomes of what Kideckel has described as the establishment of a *neocapitalist* system, which in his interpretation is understood as the wide range of negative consequences the introduction of neoliberalism has had in the previously socialist states. It is, in his own, words 'a social system that re-works basic capitalist principles in new, even more inegalitarian ways than the Western system from which it derives (2002: 115). In this chapter I will emphasize that subalternization and estrangement from society have not solely resulted in exclusion and marginalization, but have also led the vulnerable groups to adopt some of the central features of the liberalist-capitalist ideology to which they have been exposed since the Soviet breakdown. In their marginalized position they pursue a life with minimal state interference and maximum individual freedom.

Finding the *Invisible*

This chapter is based on one longer period of fieldwork and one shorter one. The first lasted one year, from the autumn 2006 to autumn 2007, and was conducted in two villages in the western part of Lithuania. The following period of fieldwork lasted half a year in 2011, before being continued for part of summer 2012. This research was conducted in Kaunas, a larger industrial city in the centre of Lithuania with more than 300,000 inhabitants.

It was during my 2006 fieldwork among small-scale farmers that I was first alerted to the complex situation of the *Invisible* in Lithuania. This was not through the farmers, but through their sons. Due to the meagre prospects of small-scale farming, most of the young men had found unofficial employment in the larger cities. The majority solely worked 'in the shadows', whereas others combined legal work in the daytime with illegal work in the evenings and weekends. Through talks, informal interviews and visits to illegal work sites, I gradually familiarized myself with their situation. I returned to Lithuania in the summer of 2011 in order to focus solely on the issue of shadow work. The goal of my research was to get a closer and more comprehensive view of the shadow workers of Lithuania, their lives, working strategies and not least their relations to the state institutions. As most workers are employed in the cities, I chose an urban site for the second piece of fieldwork, the city of Kaunas. My connections now expanded. Informants were no longer solely circular migrants from rural Lithuania, but also urban Lithuanians. Furthermore, the age range of my informants expanded to include both younger and older men. In addition, I carried out interviews about illegal work with people from public institutions: the Lithuanian Tax Inspectorate (Valstybinė Mokesčių Inspekcija), the Lithuanian Workers' Union (Lietuvos Profesinių Sąjungų Konfederacija), the Lithuanian Labour Inspection (Lietuvos Respublikos Valstybinė Darbo Inspekcija) and the Lithuanian Unemployment Agency (Lietuvos Darbo Birža).

Between the EU and the financial crisis

In the years leading up to EU membership in 2004, Lithuania, like other accession countries, underwent processes of rapid political, economic and legal change. The initial intervention of the EU in the early 1990s coincided with the undoing of Soviet features in society, the combination of which resulted in a disruptive political, legal and socioeconomic climate (Harboe Knudsen 2012). For many citizens living standards decreased, many lost their jobs, while reforms for privatization were introduced overnight, giving way to economic shock therapy and escalating inflation (Smith *et al.* 2002). As initial expectations of the country's newly gained independence failed to materialize for the *new poor*, we witnessed a growing scepticism and increasing lack of trust in the shifting governments and state institutions (Klumbytė 2008; Schröder 2008; for comparison see Torsello 2003). Indeed, as post-socialist scholars have documented, for many the break-up of the Soviet Union was not accompanied by success and greater wealth (Anderson and Pine 1995; Bridger and Pine 1998; Hann 1994, 2002, 2003; Humphrey 1995, [1998] 2001, Kideckel 2002, 2008; Verdery 2003). On the contrary, the increasing gap between rich and poor led to a spiral of downward mobility for the previously privileged workers who were more or less left to their own devices to cope (Kideckel 2002, 2008; Schröder 2010). In this regard we witnessed what Stenning *et al.* have coined as a 'domestication' of neoliberalism as people coped with the new system by filtering it through their own daily practices (2011). In the case of Lithuania, this was done by turning down interaction with the official version of the economic system and engaging in the widespread 'shadow economy'.

Society's widening gaps were reinforced when EU membership arrived in 2004: while strong political forces led a geopolitical remaking of the state, proclaiming Lithuania anew as a modern, self-conscious and liberal country, many promises were yet again unfulfilled for the poorer parts of the population, who were left dissatisfied by a perceived lack of political attention to social and economic deficits and problems of crime.

In the late 1990s the Lithuanian economy finally stabilized and grew steadily; after the Russian Crisis of 1998,[4] it had positive GDP growth for nine years in a row. Then in 2009 the financial crisis struck. After having been one of the fastest growing economies in the EU, and known as the 'Baltic Tiger', the Lithuanian economy was considerably weakened during the crisis, which again triggered an increase in the unemployment rate: from 4.3 per cent in 2007 to 17.8 per cent in 2010 ('Lithuanian Unemployment Rate' 2012). This unemployment rate should further be seen in the light of the high emigration rate from the country. From 1990 to 2008 approximately half a million Lithuanians emigrated (Kniežaitė 2010), while, according to national statistics, a further 158,990 people left the country between 2009 and 2011 (Statistics Lithuania 2012). This latter number solely testifies to the registered emigration from the country.

Only when the otherwise growing Lithuanian economy was affected by the financial crisis of the late 2000s did the issue of the *Invisible* arise in the political agenda. Economic experts and advisory boards suggested that large sums could be extracted from the country's shadow sector. Indeed, in 2010 Lithuania's shadow economy was estimated to account for between 27 and 33 percent of the country's GDP (Swedbank 2012). All in all the annual loss of tax revenue to the shadow sector amounted to 8.2 billion litas (approximately €2.4bn) (ibid.). In 2011 the Lithuanian government called for action: the State Labour Inspectorate, the State Tax Inspectorate and the police were instructed to intensify their control of a wide range of companies, and an anonymous hotline was established where concerned citizens could call in and give notice if they knew where illegal work was taking place. National campaigns were launched, both 'scare campaigns', which highlighted the criminal aspect of the act of shadow working and the consequences for workers when caught, and campaigns that strove to appeal to the shadow workers' feelings of solidarity and civic obedience, just as law-abiding citizens were encouraged to report about illegal work if they knew about such cases.[5]

Marginalization and neoliberalism

During the Soviet regime the country's shadow sector was closely intertwined with the official planned economy, and was often a prerequisite for its functions. Thus, administering property for personal gain, making use of networks, or taking goods or products from one's working place were fundamental aspects of, and interrelated with, the Soviet economy, and were necessary supplements to the daily economies of households (Firlit and Chlopecki 1992; Ledeneva 1998; Verdery 1996; Wedel 1992). This system, as during the Soviet regime, continued to function after independence, albeit in slightly different forms. In the post-Soviet era we therefore also witness how state resources have been manipulated for the sake of personal gain, just as slipping 'in and out' between formality and informality have been characteristic features both before and after the Soviet break-up (Bridger and Pine 1998; Ledeneva 2006; Mandel and Humphrey 2002; Verdery 2002). It would, however, be wrong to assume that the emergence of the *Invisible* and their current position in the country's shadow economy is a Soviet legacy. In the case of the *Invisible*, maintaining a daily living is not a question of manipulating public (state) resources or circling in and out of the official system, but rather a matter of disengaging from society as such. In line with Burawoy and Verdery I suggest that such tendencies are the result of *post*-socialist conditions and should be seen as responses to developments that people have been exposed to through the introduction of neoliberalism into society (1999).

In a critical volume David Harvey outlines neoliberalism as a theory of economic and political practices where the wellbeing of citizens is best advanced by liberating individual and entrepreneurial skills *within* an institutional framework in which the state fulfils necessary functions, including the securing of education, military defence and healthcare, and the establishment of proper legal structures to secure ownership rights (Harvey 2005). One of the problems with the neoliberal model in Lithuania has thus been that the state institutions have not kept up their side of the deal: ownership rights have only been secured for people with the right connections. Legal rights and the law can be negotiated, and healthcare is only free in theory, as in practice people have still had to pay bribes to doctors in order to secure decent healthcare, just as other state institutions have fallen short of providing basic necessities. Kideckel coins such increased inequalities as *neocapitalism*, a concept which in his use embraces all of the negative consequences of neoliberalism. In Kideckel's analysis this neocapitalist system has triggered a hierarchical (dis)placement, where workers have ended up at the bottom of society with limited knowledge of and access to labour market. This has been further exacerbated by there being limited information about privatization processes, resulting in feelings of exclusion, falling standards of living, manipulation of working conditions by unscrupulous employers, and a general devaluation of industrial work and loss of symbolic capital (Kideckel 2002). Thus, workers have been exposed to the 'forced diet' of neoliberalism, which has left them with the consequences of neocapitalism (Kideckel 2002, 2008). Dealing with the outcomes of such drastic restructuring it thus becomes pertinent to detach the concept of neoliberalism from its theoretical framework, to see how it works in practice as its ideas become implemented in people's everyday lives (Stenning *et al.* 2011).

In the case of Lithuania, the economic reforms have been closely intertwined with attempts to reform people and personhood. The goals were thus to establish a new society governed by capitalist principles far removed from the country's contaminated socialist past and, importantly, to establish a new *citizen*: like the phoenix rising from the ashes, so Lithuanians were expected to rise from the grey Soviet past as colourful Europeans. These have frequently been referred to as *New Lithuanians*: modern, successful, self-controlled and linear beings who can easily navigate Europe and succeed in and gain from the 'Westernization' of society

(De Munck 2008; Vonderau 2007, 2010). These new Lithuanians became central to the project of redefining Lithuanian identity and showing a new outer face of the country. Indeed, with a slight rewriting of George Orwell, it seemed like all Lithuanians were European, but some Lithuanians were more European than others, since European identity was assumed to be more easily embodied by some than by others.[6] Corresponding with Orwell's idea, these 'more Europeans' appeared to be better-educated people with international experience who led better lives than the majority. This politically motivated discourse has been influential in Lithuanian society in recent years, and has triggered social exclusions of the less educated, the troubled youth, the old, the not-so-internationally minded, and others who in various ways do not conform to the image of the prosperous 'new Lithuanian' (see Harboe Knudsen 2012; Klumbytė 2008; Vonderau 2007, 2010).

Through my example of Lithuania I link the negative reproduction of workers in previously socialist countries, as sketched out by Kideckel, with the emergence of the *Invisible* in the very same period. Thus, in an attempt to see the workings of neoliberalism in practice, my argument is that the introduction of this capitalist mode of thinking has ironically triggered a development where the marginalized groups have adopted fundamental neoliberalist ideas to such an extent that their lack of solidarity and their individualistic pursuits have become quite problematic for the state. Indeed, the precarious conditions after 1990 have created a situation where Lithuanian workers have become self-reliant citizens who favour the idea of minimal, if any, state interference, and largely manage their lives without consulting state institutions. As state institutions now once again advocate solidarity with society in the light of the financial crisis, people remember well that the very same state institutions were the primary driving force in destroying such feelings of solidarity in the first place. Thus, I argue, the very marginalization of the worker has resulted in the emergence of an invisible neoliberal citizen, who turns away from any state interference.

Portrait of an *Invisible*

Šarūnas, whom I introduced in the beginning of the chapter, is one of Lithuania's *Invisible Citizens*. He belongs to the generation that was brought up under the Soviet regime, and which at the peak of its youth experienced dramatic social change with Lithuania's self-proclaimed independence in 1990 and the dissolution of the Soviet Union in 1991. For a young man, as Šarūnas was at the time, opportunities appeared plentiful. Accompanying Lithuanian independence was an atmosphere of general enthusiasm, hope and high spirits. However, in the same period society was in a chaotic state as factories closed down one after another and getting or even keeping formal state employment became difficult. As the state could not employ citizens and provide the same guarantees as it could formerly, opportunities outside the state seemed to be the most promising. Some Lithuanians indeed managed to establish businesses and make fortunes at the time (see Vonderau 2007, 2010), while others, like Šarūnas, instead found that the prosperous future turned out to be difficult to access. With his lack of education, lack of knowledge about the restructuring processes, and lack of knowledge of European languages, combined with his living far away from the vibrant cities, Šarūnas did not possess the opportunities or resources to access 'new Lithuanian-ness'. While it was never exactly planned for Šarūnas, in time he found himself living more and more on the boundaries of the state as the first envisioned hopes of independence failed to materialize.

Brought up during the Soviet regime Šarunas is a fluent Russian speaker, yet he later had to struggle with learning English, which he accomplished to some extent through the 'learning by doing' method. Šarūnas finished the ninth grade around the time of Lithuanian independence. He received no further education, which meant that he started looking for employment in the chaotic period of the early 1990s. Throughout his late teens and early twenties Šarūnas had various different short-term jobs and occupations. His first job was a legal employment at a TV factory where he worked for about a year. Unsatisfied with the job he reasoned that he could do better on his own, as opposed to earning a minimal salary and being tied to a factory that had little concern for the workers' conditions. In the spirit of the time he developed the idea of opening a German-language school. With Lithuania 'moving west' and with interaction with the rest of Europe becoming increasingly important, he reasoned that German would be a valuable language in the near future. He managed to get the paperwork done and then employed a local schoolteacher to come to his school in the evening and teach his clients German. The school ran for about one year without making any real profit. At this point Šarūnas was offered a job on a ferryboat and decided to leave the language school behind, since it had not turned out to be the prosperous business once imagined. The job on the ferryboat was legal employment; he worked as a waiter in the boat's restaurant. However, the salary mainly consisted of tips, which was hardly enough to get by, especially since he, due to his shy nature, was not able to charm the guests and encourage them to leave tips in the same way as the other more courageous and talkative waiters on the boat. Unsatisfied with the working conditions and the little money he made, he decided to leave the job on the ferryboat before his contract ended. A friend had suggested to him that he take up construction work in Sweden, and it was not difficult to convince him.

Šarūnas liked the idea of working in Sweden; he could make considerably more money than in Lithuania yet work fewer hours. That it was 'shadow work' went without saying. Work was arranged through people and took place with no formal contracting. In the beginning he entered into the construction business through his friend's network, but after a while Šarūnas managed to get his own place and arrange his own deals. He has now established himself in the northern part of Sweden where every summer he rents a room in a little hotel run by a local businessman. The businessman is also the main person who arranges work for him. Whenever people in the area need cheap construction work done, Šarūnas is called. He states that he prefers to work alone. He explains that, when you work together with other people, tensions are likely to arise and disagreements appear, and you always have to check whether the work is carried out properly. Šarūnas speaks from experience, as he for a while worked together with his cousin – a cooperation which ended badly due to disagreements about work and pay. Ever since his first trip to Sweden Šarūnas has faithfully returned every year, except for two years when he was prohibited from entering the country as he had been caught by the police for overstaying his three-month visa.[7] In this period he relied on his father's income and various illegal short-term jobs. When he was once again permitted entry into Sweden he took up his previous pattern of seasonal migration.

Šarūnas leaves for Sweden in the spring, works throughout the summer and returns to Lithuania in the autumn. He manages to get by with his limited English and his few Swedish phrases. During the winters Šarūnas and his father work on building a house in Lithuania. Yet, a constant lack of money slows the project down considerably. In the winter he lives from the money he made in Sweden during the summer. Sometimes he supplements it with an additional shadow occupation of bringing firewood to people in the local area. Still, it is hardly ever enough to get him through to the spring, which makes him dependent on his father's income in the last months before he can again return to Sweden. Although Šarūnas swears by the higher Swedish salary and prefers that above working the entire year in Lithuania, it is still hardly enough to make ends meet for him. An additional problem he grapples with is that he throughout his life has collected a considerable amount of debt to the state, mainly for drink-driving, and he does not see himself in a position to pay it back.

The debt has forced him into a further vicious circle of invisibility; he does not register any income, as this would lead to a forced payback of the debt, something he deliberately seeks to avoid, since he cannot live on less money than he already does. He cannot open a bank account, as any reported money in his name would lead to the same result. The car, which he drives in Sweden, is registered in his father's name, and due to drink-driving incidents he has also lost his licence. Both in Lithuania and in Sweden he thus runs the risk of getting caught driving without a licence. As he has no job, he also has no health insurance, neither in Lithuania, nor in Sweden. If he ever needs to go to a doctor or to go to hospital, it will cost him dearly. Two years ago he made an attempt to register with the Lithuanian Employment Agency (Darbo Birža), as registration automatically leads to health insurance. However, he encountered an obstacle: he is still registered as having his own language school and thus, his own company. While the language school only exists on paper, the logic is that if he has a company, he has a job. 'Now it does not matter', he says in answer to my question of why he does not choose to shut the company down, since it has been out of business for many years. He tells me that he owns a few hectares of land and forest in northern Lithuania, which he has registered in the names of his father and his aunt respectively, as any property written in his name would be claimed by the state as compensation for his debt. The forest is used for firewood in the winter, and the land is rented out to a local farmer who pays him 500 litas a year. This is sufficient for him to buy a one-way ticket to Sweden in the fall.

His general outlook appears to be one of lost hope, with little expectation of things changing for the better, while his idea of achieving a better life is mainly connected with strengthening his position in Sweden. When asked about his opinions on and feelings towards the recent campaigns against illegal work in Lithuania, he just shrugs his shoulders in the manner of 'they gotta do what they gotta do'. He does not relate the campaigns to any required changes in himself. 'My situation is not good', he says, looking down at the floor, as he has done most of the time we have been talking. Šarūnas himself has not had an accident or needed medical care while being in Sweden, but states that if an accident did happen he would be in a bad situation. He mentions a couple of friends who likewise work in Sweden and who came to need medical care. One of them cut himself with a knife in the leg, another cut two fingers off:

> In such cases you have to pay for treatment. You just lose the entire salary, all the money you made in that season . . . I suppose Lithuanians think that they will be lucky, nothing bad will happen to them. So, they go and work without insurance.[8]

Šarūnas does not consider giving up his frequent trips to Sweden in exchange for formal employment with insurance. The situation in Lithuania is far too unstable, according to him, plus, the minimum salary as paid to uneducated workers is not enough to get him by. Only by sustaining his life on the margins, relying on his own ability to find illegal occupations, refraining from any relations with the state, by hoping that he will not need any medical care and by relying on personal networks, especially on his father, does Šarūnas see an option of making it through.

The problems of the *Invisible*

While Šarūnas initially had high hopes for himself in independent Lithuania, he soon found the general conditions to be far more difficult than initially imagined, leading him into a spiral of different work experiments before finally settling for shadow employment as the best and most promising solution. One could argue that Šarūnas' situation is the product of a number of unwise decisions and is thus the sole responsibility of a single man, but the problem arises that there are many people like Šarūnas in present-day Lithuania; the thousands and thousands of *Invisible* bear witness to a problem for the state in terms of lack of participation and lack of tax payment, but also a problem produced by the unsettled economic and social circumstances after independence, combined with growing social exclusion.

Šarūnas is one of a number of people that find themselves in a very weak position in present-day Lithuanian society. With no proper education, he is exposed to lower-paid jobs and often low-prestige jobs with few opportunities to benefit from the so-called 'new' society. With the general tendencies being, as pointed out by Kideckel, that attention to workers' rights and conditions remain a low priority in present-day neocapitalist societies (2002, 2008), few initiatives are taken to better the general situation for people who are unable to access higher or even tolerable living standards. The risk follows that employment in the formal sector in Lithuania may not even lead to a better position for the *Invisible*, as the current situation of increasing unemployment is exploited by employers, who do not secure their workers' general rights. As was emphasized by an employee in the Lithuanian Workers' Union, union members are often the last to get employed and the first to get fired, a fact which further discourages workers from joining a union at all.[9]

While the intense engagement in Lithuania's 'shadow sector' is likely to be linked with Soviet styles of engagement in the informal sector, I have shown that the *Invisible* have only emerged with the introduction of neoliberalism. On the one hand they are a marginalized group of citizens, yet on the other they are a group that actively responds to the shortcomings of neoliberalism in Lithuanian society by rejecting the state altogether and pursuing their lives with no need for the state to interfere. People living on the margins thus strive to continue their lives as unnoticed as possible by formal authorities, while state authorities have done their best to suppress the problem. Indeed, the issue of the many illegal workers was only addressed at the point when it became an economic issue for the country, while the serious social issues and lack of consideration for the working man which triggered this development remain unmentioned. Rather, through the intensified campaigns against illegal work, where blame for the country's weak position is projected towards the workers, we find a pattern which Kideckel refers to as 'blaming the victim':

> Thus, the victims of economic downturn, are held to blame for that same downturn, even as those who cast the blame – media, new entrepreneurs, parliamentarians, some state functionaries – reap the lion's share of benefits in the new political economy. (2002: 114)

Engaged in shadow work, often on the margin of poverty and petty crime, the *Invisible* neither adequately reflect nor respond to the ideas embedded in 'new Lithuanianism'. Rather, at the same time they challenge this very idea by taking liberalist thought to its extreme. The *Invisible* undermine the proclaimed progress in the realm of law and order as local normative law increasingly challenges the hegemony of the state, and by extension, the proclaimed success in EU-izing Lithuania. In a period where we ideally should witness greater legal compatibility within the EU, the Lithuanian example shows a paradoxical situation between political attempts to establish the nation as a well-functioning, modern and determined EU state on the one hand, and on the other increased reliance on normative law on the margins of society.

Epilogue

In the spring of 2012 Šarūnas returned to Sweden as usual in order to work in the construction business over the summer and make some much needed money for his next stay in Lithuania and the construction of his and his father's house. However, this year something changed, as he later explained. Although he returned to the same town as always, it proved to be difficult to find occupation in the way he hitherto had done. According to Šarūnas, the man who hosted him seemed less willing to make appointments with people from the surrounding areas, just as the Swedes' general attitude appeared to have changed to become more hostile. Things escalated when one day he drove to a nearby town to fill up his car with gas and do his shopping. While in the grocery store, Šarūnas saw through the shop window how a local man was walking around his car and checking the number plates. Only a few minutes after, just as Šarūnas left the shop, the police had arrived and were waiting for him outside by the car. They asked several questions about his occupation and his whereabouts in Sweden, indicating that he was probably or potentially there to steal. Although Šarūnas got out of the situation with no further consequences, the situation had been highly uncomfortable and added to the already changed atmosphere he had sensed in Sweden this particular summer.

Unable to find work and feeling subject to suspicion, Šarūnas decided to return to Lithuania early the same summer, having made close to no money at all. His father was not happy about his early return, especially as he did not bring any money. Deprived of his opportunity to work in Sweden and unable to access the Lithuanian Darbo Birža, he had few options ahead of him, thus increasing his dependence on his father. Finding legal work, closing his language school and entering Darbo Birža were not options in his estimation of the future. Rather, in the present he believes his prospects are to work on the house, possibly finding work 'in the shadow' during the summer, and possibly returning to Sweden the following year in hope of a better season. Another option, he considers, is to find himself another 'base' in Sweden and build up connections in a new place.

Šarūnas continues his strategies of invisibility, finding his way around official procedures and avoiding institutional interference, as do thousands of other Lithuanians, whose continued invisibility only testifies to the increasing gap between the 'official' and 'unofficial' Lithuania.

Notes

1 The research for this article has been funded by the Danish Independent Research Council for Culture and Communication (Det Frie Forskningsråd, Kultur og Kommunikation). I would like to express my gratitude for their support.
2 Pseudonym.
3 From my fieldnotes, November 2011, my translation from Lithuanian.
4 The Russian financial crisis unfolded in 1998 as a result of the difficulties Russia had in changing to a market economy, political mismanagement and abortive reform efforts throughout the 1990s. Prior to the crisis, the country's GDP had decreased by 40 percent between 1989 and 1996 (UNCTAD and UNECE secretariats 1998). The crisis hit the previously socialist countries hard, as they still exported much of their production to Russia.
5 See the homepage of the Lithuanian Labor Control: http://www.vdi.lt/index.php?-1371079622 (accessed 9 July 2012).
6 The original quote from Orwell's *Animal Farm* is 'All animals are equal, but some animals are more equal than others'.

7 This was before Lithuania entered the EU, when visas still were required.
8 Interview November 2011. My translation from Lithuanian.
9 Interview at the Workers' Union in Vilnius, October 2011.

References

Anderson, D. G. and Pine, F. (eds) (1995) *Surviving the Transition: Development Concerns in the Post-socialist World*, Cambridge: University of Cambridge, Department of Anthropology.

Bridger, S. and Pine, F. (1998) 'Introduction: Transition to Post-socialism and Cultures of Survival', in *Surviving Post-Socialism Local: Strategies and Regional Responses in Eastern Europe and the Former Soviet Union*, Bridger, S. and Pine, F. (eds), London: Routledge, pp. 1–15.

Burawoy, M. and Verdery, K. (eds) (1999) *Uncertain Transitions. Ethnographies of Change in the Postsocialist World,* Lanham MD: Rowman & Littlefield.

De Munck, V. C. (2007). 'First, Second and Finally Third Order Understandings of Lithuanian National Identity: An Anthropological Approach', *Sociologija. Mintis ir Veiksmas* 1(19): 51–73.

—— (2008) 'Millenarian Dreams: The Objects and Subjects of Money in New Lithuania', in *Changing Economies and Changing Identities in Postsocialist Eastern Europe*, Schröder, I. and Vonderau, A. (eds), Berlin: Lit Verlag, pp. 171–91.

Firlit, E. and Chlopecki, J. (1992) 'When Theft is not Theft', in *The Unplanned Society: Poland after Communism*, Wedel, J. (ed.), New York: Columbia University Press, pp. 95–109.

Hann, C. M. (1994) 'After Communism: Reflections of East European Anthropology and the "Transition"', *Social Anthropology* 2(3): 229–49.

—— (2002) 'Farewell to the Socialist "Other"', in *Postsocialism: Ideals, Ideologies and Practices in Eurasia*, Hann, C. M. (ed.), London: Routledge, pp. 1–11.

Hann, C. M. and the Property Relations Group (2003) 'Introduction: Decollectivization and the Moral Economy', in *The Postsocialist Agrarian Question: Property Relations and the Rural Condition*, Chris M. Hann and the Property Relations Group (eds), Münster: Lit Verlag, pp. 1–47.

Harboe Knudsen, I. (2010) 'The Insiders and the Outsiders: Standardization and "Failed" Person-Making in a Lithuanian Market Place', *Journal of Legal Pluralism and Unofficial Law* 62: 71–94.

Harboe Knudsen, I. (2012) New Lithuania in Old Hands: Effects and Outcomes of EUropeanization in Rural Lithuania, London: Anthem Press.

Harvey, D. (2005) *A Brief History of Neoliberalism*, Oxford: Oxford University Press.

Humphrey, C. (1995) 'Introduction', in *Surviving the Transition: DevelopmentConcerns in the Post-socialist World*, ed. Anderson, D. G. and Pine, F., *Cambridge Anthropology* (special issue) 18(2): 1–12.

Humphrey, C. [1998] (2001) *Marx Went Away – But Karl Stayed Behind.* Ann Arbor: University of Michigan Press. (Updated edition of *Karl Marx Collective: Economy, Society and Religion in a Siberian Collective Farm*, pub. 1983).

Jamal, A. and Naber, N. (eds) (2007) Race and Arab Americans Before and After 9/11. From Invisible Citizens to Visible Subjects, Syracuse: Syracuse University Press.

Kideckel, D. A. (2002) 'The Unmaking of an East Central European Working Class', in *Postsocialism: Ideals, Ideologies and Practices in Eurasia*, Hann C. M. (ed.), London: Routledge, pp. 115–33.

—— (2008) *Getting By in Postsocialist Romania: Labor, the Body, and Working-Class Culture*, Bloomington: Indiana University Press.
Klumbytė, N. (2008) 'Post-Soviet Publics and Nostalgia for Soviet Times', in *Changing Economies and Changing Identities in Postsocialist Eastern Europe*, Schröder, I. W. and Vonderau, A. (eds), Münster: Lit Verlag, pp. 27–47.
Kniežaitė, M. (2010) 'Grėsmingi lietuvių emigracijos mastai' ['Emigration from Lithuania']. Online. Available: <http://geografija.lt/2010/01/gresmingi-lietuviu-emigracijos-mastai/> (accessed 10 July 2012).
Kostakopolou, T. (2001) 'Invisible Citizens? Long-Term Resident Third Country Nationals in the EU and their Struggle for Independence', in *Citizenship and Governance in the European Union*, Bellamy, R. and Warleigh, A. (eds), New York: Continuum, pp. 180–206.
Ledeneva, A. (1998) *Russia's Economy of Favors: Blat, Networking and Informal Exchange*, Cambridge: Cambridge University Press.
'Lithuanian Unemployment Rate' (2012). Online. Available: <http://www.indexmundi.com/lithuania/unemployment_rate.html> (accessed 10 July 2012).
Mandel, R. and Humphrey, C. (2002) 'The Market in Everyday Life: Ethnographies of Post-Socialism', in *Markets and Moralities: Ethnographies of Postsocialism*, Mandel, R. and Humphrey, C. (eds), Oxford and New York: Berg, pp. 1–16.
Schröder, I. (2008) 'The Classes of '89: Anthropological Approaches to Capitalism and Class in Eastern Europe', in *Changing Economies and Changing Identities in Postsocialist Eastern Europe*, Schröder, I. W. and Vonderau, A. (eds), Münster: Lit Verlag, pp. 3–27.
Smith, D. J., Pabriks, A., Purs, A. and Lane, T. (2002) *The Baltic States, Estonia, Latvia and Lithuania*, London: Routledge.
Statistics Lithuania (2012) 'International migration by administrative territory, statisticalindicator and year'. Online. Available: <http://db1.stat.gov.lt/statbank/selectvarval/saveselections.asp?MainTable=M3020102&PLanguage=1&TableStyle=&Buttons=&PXSId=6282&IQY=&TC=&ST=ST&rvar0=&rvar1=&rvar2=&rvar3=&rvar4=&rvar5=&rvar6=&rvar7=&rvar8=&rvar9=&rvar10=&rvar11=&rvar12=&rvar13=&rvar14> (accessed 10 July 2012).
Stenning, A., Smith, A., Rochovská, A., and Świątek, D. (2011) *Domesticating Neo-Liberalism: Spaces of Economic Practice and Social Reproduction in Post-Socialist Cities.* West Sussex: John Wiley & Sons.
Swedbank (2010) 'Swedbank Analysis of the Lithuanian Economy'. Online. Available:<http://www.scribd.com/doc/48801903/Swedbank-Analysis-Lithuania-December-2011> (accessed 9 July 2012).
Torsello, D. (2003) *Trust, Property and Social Change in a Southern Slovakian Village*, Münster: Lit Verlag.
UNCTAD and UNECE secretariats (1998) 'The Russian Crisis of 1998'. Online. Available: <http://www.twnside.org.sg/title/1998-cn.htm> (accessed 10 July 2012).
Verdery, K. (1996) *What Was Socialism and What Comes Next?*, Princeton: Princeton University Press.
—— (2002) 'Seeing Like a Mayor, or How Local Officials Obstructed Romanian Property Restitution', *Ethnography* 3(1): 5–33.
—— (2003) *The Vanishing Hectare. Property and Value in Postsocialist Transylvania*, Ithaca, NY and London: Cornell University Press.
Vitureau, M. (2010) 'Homosexuals, The Invisible Citizens of Lithuania', available online: www.balticworlds.com (accessed 28 August 2012).

Vonderau, A. (2007) 'Yet Another Europe? Constructing and Representing Identities in Lithuania Two Years after EU Accession', in *Representations on the Margins of Europe, Politics and Identities in the Baltic and South Caucasian States*, Darieva, T. and Kaschuba, W. (eds), Frankfurt and New York: Campus Verlag, pp. 220–42.

—— (2010) 'Models of Success in the Free Market: Transformations of the Individual Self-Representation of the Lithuanian Economic Elite', in *Changing Economies and Changing Identities in Postsocialist Eastern Europe*, Schröder, I. and Vonderau, A. (eds), Münster: Lit Verlag, pp. 111–29.

Wedel, J. R. (ed.) (1992) *The Unplanned Society: Poland during and after Communism*, New York: Columbia University Press.

3 Moonlighting strangers met on the way

The nexus of informality and blue-collar sociality in Russia

Jeremy Morris

At the beginning of a second period of ethnographic fieldwork I am sitting in the cab of Sasha's flatbed truck at night in a garage block on the outskirts of Izluchino – a small industrial town in provincial Russia. Sasha is outside talking to a long-distance lorry driver he used to work with at the cement works. A small amount of money changes hands and Sasha passes me a canister. The Driver siphons off 20 litres of diesel fuel from his cab which I put in our truck.

'See you at Auntie Klara's on the 5th?', says the Driver to Sasha. 'Maybe not', he answers, 'I've got a *kalym* [moonlighting] job on that off-day.' The Driver indicates his cab with a twist of his head: 'Fancy a drink? Are you "on", or "off" tomorrow?' Sasha replies: 'I'd stay for one, but the wife is waiting. We're both "on" tomorrow; why don't you come by the garage on Saturday and we'll put a few away there.' The last phrase is accompanied by a sharp movement of the head, indicating his property in the next row of brick garages – an important male refuge from the domestic space. The Driver locks up his cab and walks off to the nearest block of flats 50 yards away. Sasha and I get back in his truck and drive to his own block, five minutes away.

In this brief exchange, replete with tacit mutual understanding, the nexus of blue-collar sociality, formal work status, and informal economic activity is neatly encapsulated. Let us follow the trickle of the illicit diesel and unpack the entwining of the social and economic from Sasha's encounter above. First, stealing and selling on fuel and other work-property must be understood as much for sport than profit. Petty theft is hardly an important source of income, nor is it especially widespread, despite the practice of 'filching' from work as an institution under socialism and after (Verdery 1996). Nonetheless the activity sets various important markers: it reinforces solidarity between 'workers' – in the sense of putting into relief the literal contrast, in the eyes of Sasha and the Driver, between people who 'do work', and the bosses, white-collars, managers. In the face of derisory benefits from formal employment contracts it is an entitlement 'perk' – owed to the employee, in his eyes. Finally, it is part of a 'making-ends meet' philosophy of self-provisioning, understood in its widest sense, on the part of the working poor. Such activity may encompass mushroom picking and an economy of jars (Kideckel 2004), DIY at home, or even filching diesel on the part of blue-collar workers. The fuel allowance 'perk' is facilitated by a robust and mutually-trusting network of 'sometime' colleagues. In the past, the Driver and Sasha worked together. Now they do not, but through social and kin networks they maintain a sort of arms-length friendly contact in the compressed social geography of the town. The social fact of simultaneous closeness and distance is good for reducing the risk of the Driver getting caught – there is nothing in particular to link Sasha to the enterprise from which the diesel originates, but at the same time, Sasha is not some stranger on the side of the Kiev–Moscow highway.

So in this encounter Sasha has reinforced his solidarity with a 'sometime confrere' as Burawoy calls the particular class-allegiance of blue-collar workers under socialism (1992: 123). What else has he gained and why? Russian annual inflation, especially in goods people actually need – food, fuel – has remained at about 10 per cent for a decade. Petrol and diesel are the life-blood for blue-collar workers' strategies of household reproduction. Whether you work in a factory or do own-account work, you need wheels. Disregarding the 'sporting' element of such a transaction with the Driver, Sasha has now got a full tank for perhaps $15 instead of $30. This will increase his margins somewhat in the *kalym* job he has to go to on his off-shift day tomorrow. *Kalym* refers to any moonlighting job using skills, connections or even materials related to formal work.[1] For Sasha this happens to be using his flatbed to deliver building material, from which he derives a small cash income from an informal enterprise which 'employs' him (i.e. unregistered and undocumented as a legal entity), of which more below. He calls it *kalym* because this informal work environment is dominated and perpetuated by ex-workers from his formal job.

At the same time, Sasha works as a normative worker in a German-owned lime kiln as a forklift driver. This work is in 12-hour shifts, every other day, with every third shift overnight, hence the question about 'on' and 'off' days. For Sasha, working as a delivery driver is manageable because of the 'gaps' in his shift work, although often he can barely keep his eyes open. The informal work nearly doubles his take-home pay from $350 (equivalent) at the kiln to $700 per month. Finally, our scene of informal exchange ends with an obligatory reference to the geography of not only masculine sociality among blue-collar workers: the garage block space where mechanical tinkering and drinking vodka receive equal attention from men gathering there whenever they can, whatever the weather. The 'garage', actually a substantial brick structure with electricity, a cellar, sofa, table and chairs and a hi-fi, is also a space between work and leisure where many informal economic and not-so economic activities can take place. From traders storing stock, to welders fixing cars, or just workers hanging out after the shift discussing the latest *kalym* opportunities – the garage and other places like it are key spaces where the intersection of blue-collar formality and informality is made visible.

Introduction

This chapter is organized into three parts. In the first I briefly discuss the social and economic context of in-work precarity that is crucial to understanding blue-collar informality and the perspective I take: informality on a continuum of economic activities and not detached from formal work (Harding and Jenkins 1989). I also emphasize the symbolic importance of social networks which facilitate informality, but which are as much about conserving or expanding social capital and whose actual economic significance may be marginal. Then I turn to a description of the field – a small Russian town where manufacturing and industry remain the life-blood of the local economy. This compressed social space is rich in terms of social networks' impact on opportunities in informality and its imbrications with formal work. In the final section I present an extended portrait of a composite blue-collar worker, whose household reproduction strategy straddles formal and informal employment, own-account work, odd jobs, reciprocal labour exchange and self-provisioning. Sasha's experience provides a means for discussing the pertinence of informality in the post-socialist blue-collar context. Informal economic transactions are embedded within a totalizing continuum of activities that to very different degrees contribute to household income. Such activities – collecting mushrooms for consumption, doing neighbours' gardening for cash-in-hand, own-account delivery driving, DIY at home, fixing extended kin-relations' bathrooms up, even factory shift-work, are all best understood when the economic prism is tempered by class-based (Dunn calls it 'horizontal') sociality (2004). Identity, social capital and 'fitting in', feeling at home – are often better conceptualizations of decisions about work and practices that at first glance would appear to be the purview of economics.

Social and economic contexts of informality in Russia: precarity and portfolio incomes

Discussions of informality globally link it to precarity – whether the insecurity is rooted in wages, lack of social protection or irregularity of work (Routh 2011: 208). Precarity itself is uniformly viewed by social scientists as symptomatic of structural changes in capitalism associated with globalization. Since Russia began a process of integration into the global economy in the 1990s, it has gradually become an increasingly attractive destination for inward investment in extractive and manufacturing from multinational companies seeking cheaper and cheaper production costs. The significant way this has affected labour in the field-site region of this research is explored in the following section. Regardless of the peculiarities of Kaluga Region's labour market, it is possible to generalize that since 1998 there has been a continuous expansion in formal work opportunities in both low-skill and high-skill construction and manufacturing jobs for much of European Russia.[2] For informants this means that in contrast to even the 1990s, work in production is plentiful but precarious.

The fact of permanent vacancies in many enterprises in both specialized and manual unskilled jobs with uncomfortable or dangerous working conditions means workers tend to 'try out' different enterprises in search of better conditions or benefits, while take-home pay remains uniformly low. High 'churn' in personnel is an acknowledged problem in all sectors of the economy. In short there are locally particular attitudes on the part of blue-collar labour towards formal work of this sort. Workers uniformly see unskilled and even skilled manufacturing work as 'sweating' labour. Low levels of reward, uniformity of poor conditions and benefits (the recent state-mandated social protection within labour law is minimal) as well as explicit comparison with socialist-era social and enterprise benefits, all contribute to a view of *formal* employment as precarious (Morris 2012). Informality is widely viewed as a 'normal' parallel activity to formal work, that informants can rapidly switch their time and other resources towards in the case of interruption or lack of waged labour income. Engagement in informality almost rivals self-provisioning in terms of its value as a ritualized practice that symbolizes the potential for the individual to protect himself or withdraw at least partially from formal marketized relations (waged labour) and the state's purview.[3]

If we add to this apparent 'hedging strategy' by workers the enduring social and cultural tendency in Russia to blur notions of public and private labour and property, this makes for a problematizing of separating informal and formal. It is key therefore to look at informants' economic and work worlds interpretively. If Sasha sees his 'factory' work as no more qualitatively important than cash-in-hand delivery driving, then we must be careful not to privilege normative worker status, especially in the context of Russia's formal economic policy convergence within the global economy, which results in the labelling of informal economic activity as something the state seeks to reduce (Guariglia and Kim 2006: 4).[4] A 'continuum' view (Harding and Jenkins 1989) is therefore useful in bringing to the fore links between employment, work, and the myriad micro-strategies that are used in relation to status and resources gained from the formal economy, but which involve non-formal transactions (like the diesel sale above). This necessarily entails looking at livelihood and the wider social context of the working poor (ibid.). However this is not unproblematic as scholars can end up looking at everything as the purview of the economic when this is clearly not the case; should the theft and sale of diesel really be treated as a primarily 'economic' transaction when the sense of material action that it embodies may owe as much to the social practice within which it is embedded (Gudeman 2001: 4)? When blue-collar workers get together in a garage to fix someone's truck rear axle and then they are rewarded with payment in kind that is mostly symbolic, is this best understood as an economic transaction? This chapter emphasizes that informality is often more meaningfully examined within the context of understanding how sociality sustains networks which partly provide alternative economic and productive practices. These may be marginal economically speaking but symbolically and socially they may be crucial to participants and communities.

Following suggestions by Routh (2011), this approach may avoid some of the problems associated with a 'structuralist' view of informality, which underplays the importance of the diversity of activity that is economically marginal, like subsistence agriculture, but which may be as ubiquitous for informants as formal work. Similarly an analysis of informality as social gestalt avoids a perspective where informality remains 'unconnected to the formal economy (or 'sector'), as well as subcontracted entrepreneurships linked to the formal economy' (ibid: 217). Thus, while the present research is rooted in Hart's original anthropological account of informality as a picture of self-sufficient economic transactions not dependent on organized capital and where informants are perpetually seeking 'angles' in everyday life to eke out income from their disadvantaged structural positioning within the wider economy (1973), the social fact of continual interdependence of the formal and informal is acknowledged. This is particularly important in the post-socialist case where informality is historically argued to evolve from 'parasitic' relations to the socialist formal economy (Verdery 1996: 27). While this was literally true in an important way in the socialist era, the present research draws attention to the social links between normative work and informality in context of post-socialist labour's strategies for household reproduction.

Approaching blue-collar informality – Russia's industrial towns

Ethnographic research materials for this chapter were gathered in the Kaluga region of European Russia over three extended periods, totalling six months of ethnographic fieldwork, between November 2009 and December 2010. Around 50 workers and their families engaged in a variety of economic practices over and above formal waged work comprise the core of informants. Most families include a 'breadwinner' who had varying degrees of engagement with formal shop-floor manual work. Examples of such formal labour roles encompass manufacture (including packaging and processing), assembly, repair and maintenance, extractive industry, and construction. What qualifies as 'informality' is explored in detail in the main ethnographic section of this paper; it can range from one-off opportunities to earn cash-in-hand, typically in construction, unregistered 'self-employment' with a 'hard' skill, e.g. welding, to *in extremis*, informants selling self-provisioned food (mushrooms, apples) on the highway.

The field site encompasses a district (*raion*) containing two small towns (populations 15,000 and 20,000) about 30km from the region (*oblast*) capital. During the Soviet period both towns were dominated by single employers. The smaller town, which I call Izluchino, the focus of the present research, was a 'company town' – built from scratch in the postwar period around local extractive industries and manufacturing. The 'company' was a single, extensive, industrial enterprise responsible for building the housing and other social infrastructure throughout the town and industrial zones. The enterprise provided the vast majority of the relatively well-paid blue-collar work in the town as well as work-benefits such as canteens, transport and leisure facilities to the chiefly male workers and their dependants.

Because the company town was a geographically isolated and bureaucratically discrete unit of production operating within an economy typified by shortages, it created for itself a very significant web of support and maintenance micro-operations (e.g. vehicle repair shops) designed to support core activities. This has been called a 'do-it-yourself approach' (Winiecki 1989: 367) with many jobs in peripheral activities. Many of these activities live on in inheritor businesses, now disaggregated from the main firm and fending for themselves. The existence of this relatively diverse industrial hinterland, alongside the compressed public and social geography of the town, is crucial to understanding the existence of ready-made social network resources for informants seeking alternatives to formal labour, even if they do not wish to permanently exit it.

Locating informality in an ex-'company' town

In this extended ethnographic section, discussion is structured according to a 'continuum' of formality–informality of labour, starting 'closest' to formality – informal employment with an unregistered 'enterprise', but in practice replicating much of the reality of normative blue-collar labour. Next, and perhaps most typically in terms of informality, I examine the context of 'see-saw' labour: where a diverse range of informal activities balance sometimes erratic engagement with the formal sector – Sasha from the initial discussion is the 'case study' here. Finally, the example of unregistered 'own-account' work is discussed, bringing the discussion full-circle to a practice that is close to the formal occupational categorization of the traditional tradesman.

Each section focuses on a particular informant, whose ethnographic portrait incorporates some composite elements from other collected material – interviews, observations, etc. I organize material around three anchoring quotations from informants which summarize their understandings of the social and economic positioning of their labour. The interpretation of each 'case' is shown to rest substantively on the social, historical and symbolic meanings of informality, as much as the economic. In each case, regardless of its spatial, economic or other distance from formal work, important links relating to the social network of informants can be exposed. In the first and third cases this is relatively straightforward, but even in the 'see-saw' narrative, informants can be shown to 'understand' formal–informal work as blurred. Informal activities are often strongly embedded in the formal economy.

Informal employment: 'better in every way'?

Victor: 'We work for ourselves. That means if we need to get money we go to work. If we don't want money right now then today we won't work.' (November 2010)

This was how a key informant, a 26-year-old trained electrician who had left a job in the employ of the local authority a year before, described the advantages of his informal employment as we walked to the garage meeting point from where he was picked up by car every morning. After collecting more workers, the 'Brigadier' took us all by car to the next settlement where the assembly workshop for the aluminium and uPvC window business was situated.[5] The workers in this brigade were a tight-knit social group; they had mostly followed the Brigadier, sooner or later, out of work in the cement plant, the linoleum rolling mill, or elsewhere and into the underground of the lucrative business of assembling windows on the cheap for a legal front company which then sold them retail to the general public. Victor was the youngest and the most recent recruit. His was the hardest job: sweeping up the aluminium shavings which were razor sharp, hauling by hand the 30kg glazing units from store to bench and then to despatch, and using a rubber hammer to finish the framing in the yard outside regardless of the weather. Together we spent many an hour in the November cold of the yard talking about his work history and the glazing enterprise.

Victor had wanted to stay with the local authority as an electrician. He liked the flexibility and variety of the work. He liked the people; he valued the sense both of social inclusion and his contribution to local lives that the work gave. The pay was low even by Izluchino's standards and Victor shared a room at his parents' flat with two siblings. Matters came to a head when he was unable to qualify for a subsidy of household municipal and utility payments. Eventually, despite the security of his electrical work, through his contacts he came to the uPvC site. Some of the others were suspicious. They had come from the back-breaking work of the cement plant, where you could taste the dust between shifts and workers were regularly maimed by the poorly-maintained elevated roadway trucks bringing aggregates down from the pits; why had Victor given up a job with the local authority which gave him precious autonomy, despite the poor pay? In his place, they argued, they would have made something of it: used the municipal transport and equipment at his disposal to start a lucrative private business.[6] Sure, barriers had been put in his way: the immediate supervisor of the site where Victor was based had very carefully monitored his workers precisely because of the expensive electrical equipment they had access to.

Investigating further it became clear that there were quite mundane reasons for Victor coming to the uPvC rather than striking out on his own. These are to do with both sociality and life experience. Many of the workers here were still in their twenties. While they had plenty of contacts – concentric circles of '*priyateli*'[7] radiating out – from ex-school mates to sometime-labouring-peers to neighbours and in-laws – many were not ready or, still living at home, did not have the impetus of family household provision to push them in to more independent and riskier own-account informality (explored below) let alone formal entrepreneurship with its financial and legal barriers to entry.

However, many informants, regardless of life experience, provided other significant reasons for their continued informality. 'I want to stay in the same brigade; we all know each other. It is easier that way instead of having to get to know a new lot of people and all that commotion.' In this quote, Victor's reasoning based on affect, sociality, and peer-regard intersects. Engaging even in the low-risk informality of the uPvC shop entailed a high level of mutual trust. Not surprisingly, trust and peer-regard are partly affective categories. Small-scale entrepreneurial activities in informality like the window shop are by necessity predicated on social networks for their human capital. Victor wants to stay with people he knows and trusts, and who acknowledge him as a worthy labouring subject. Informal employment and work based on networks of mutuality can be seen to provide an in-kind social benefit over and above any economic advantage to participants. Ironically, because the shop is 'underground' it relies on an integrated network of participants – from the delivery driver, to the shop-floor workers, to the front staff and financial backers. In the economic jargon, trust helps keep 'transaction costs' low.

The uPvC shop was a convenient stepping stone into the turbulent river of informality. One from which informants could quickly retreat to the safety of the dry bank of the cement works, the linoleum, etc., if they got their feet too wet. At the time of writing, Victor had spent a year at the uPvC before moving on to 'the Cement'; despite the better money, the camaraderie and the autonomy, he felt he needed the structuring framework of a shift-work job. Some peers thought him mad to go 'back' to formal work. In the end it was probably more down to personality than anything else. At the uPvC things were 'too easy', the money came too quickly and was spent just as fast. Victor's father, a hard-working engineer, put a word in at 'the Cement'. Others however had struck out further into the flow of informality – the Brigadier finally taking a share in the uPvC business and Sasha, discussed below, maintaining a more or less constant arms-length contact as delivery driver.

See-sawing between the formal and informal: just watch you don't fall off!

Sasha: 'A citizen knows many things and so won't lose out.' (September 2009)

Sasha, whom we met at the beginning of this chapter, had just returned from his village plot where he owned about half an acre of land and a tiny hut built from clinker foundation blocks 'obtained' from a building site where he had worked as a day labourer over the summer of 2009. The original house had burned to the ground in suspicious circumstances. The family received a small insurance payment nonetheless. But rather than spend it on a new summer house, Sasha had put it towards his flatbed truck. Extended family and others had put up the ramshackle replacement hut over a few days in the late summer. Sasha had used his new truck to bring building materials to the plot as well as using it for all kinds of cash jobs. This time he had been visiting a contact at the local private dairy farm some 15km out of town. A farm hand had broken his leg and Sasha had spent the best part of two weeks delivering manure throughout the district. A 'perk' of the cash-in-hand job was that he had been able to get his plot manured for free. His mother-in-law was looking forward to a bumper crop of fruit and vegetables the following year, if the smallholder neighbours didn't filch the black gold over the winter. Sasha and I were now sitting in his garage having a beer with his wife's colleague's husband Boris, a night-watchman at the paper-processing plant in the next town. Boris was a keen gardener and something of a wit:

> So you've been shit-shifting again? When are you going to get a proper job, and while we're at it, when are you going to drop a pile of the black stuff in front of our flats so the wives and old people can get going with their front gardens? You never know, you might even get on the 'Board of Honour' for it.

Boris was referring to the very prominent hoarding in front of the main municipal building which, like everywhere else in the region, continued the Soviet tradition of publicly highlighting the 'outstanding' workers, both in public and private sectors. The front 'gardens' of the blocks of flats were public property but their beautification was an important informal community activity. Sasha, being rather a gruff character, was stung. The informal work at the farm was a source of embarrassment *and* pride. On the one hand he felt good about how it linked him back to the land his grandfather had worked. He loved being at the family plot, although since his children had been born he had little time for it except for a few weekends in the summer. 'Only arse-lickers and grasses get on that board,' he retorted to Boris, following up with the aphoristic: 'a normal citizen knows many things and so won't lose out', unknowingly paraphrasing Archilochus' famous saying: 'The fox knows many tricks . . . '. Knowing 'many tricks' summed up Sasha's approach to balancing formal and informal work in such a way as never to be too dependent on a single source of income, a single group of network contacts. Others however viewed this as a serious character flaw, interpreting his 'seesawing' between work and employment as a mark of his disagreeable nature, and pride – even his best friend, making reference to his employment record, called him a 'rolling stone'. Similarly, his retort about the Board of Honour could partly be interpreted as sour grapes, more than pride in independence. But, to be fair, there were many like Sasha who valued some kind of autonomy from permanent reliance on waged labour (Morris 2012) and who often uncomplainingly lived through extended periods of near destitution.

'And if you want manure you can shift it yourself. If you come along to do the shovelling tomorrow, I can let you have half a truck's worth, how about it?' Sasha ended. Boris seemed unimpressed by this proposition; as far as he was concerned there were far better informal work opportunities that didn't involve physical work: gypsy cab driving in the autumn and spring months. Otherwise he got by with a tiny wage from his formal night shift at the gate of the paper factory. His wife earned a modest salary as a teacher. In the early summer he would usually travel to Moscow to work on construction sites for as long as a particular building project lasted – also informally.

For informants like Boris and Sasha who take a variety of occasional or seasonal odd jobs only some of which are related to formal work status and experience, access to a wide circle of acquaintances is crucial to household survival. Their approach is superficially similar to the 'portfolio' employment found among city white-collar workers by Williams and Round (2007).[8] However, as we have seen, the 'best' jobs in construction are time-limited and outside the region – meaning long-term engagement with this facet of informal work is problematic. Equally the local formal sector is viewed by all with mixed feelings. Yes, you can work at 'the Cement' for a year or so, but the wages are so very little, the conditions so bad, and the new foreign owners will brook no slacking, 'the bastards never let up'.

I have known Sasha for over ten years. In that time he has always supported his household with income derived from diverse sources. First there is the formal economy. When he was in his twenties he worked full-time at the cement works which still employs about a thousand men including Victor, discussed above. This was where he built up a network of 'confreres'. Like Sasha, most of them have moved on – to permanent own-account skilled work full-time using skills picked up in industry (our final informant portrait below), or to trading and odd jobs in the informal economy. A few have left friends and family to go to Moscow on the construction sites, but this is even more arduous than staying in the cement works and most prefer to make ends meet in a portfolio of 'work'; only some of which is in the formal economy.

Sasha is typical of informants in that he maintains 'contact' with normative employment – about a quarter of the time he works in large-scale industry, one year it will be the linoleum-rolling plant owned by the Italians, the next it will be metal fabrication, the year after, a processed-food production line. He will do a 'stint' here and there, likening all formal jobs to 'doing time', before falling out with one of the supervisors and putting his papers in.[9] Then he will dig out the illuminated 'checkers' roof sign for his car from the garage and, like Boris, spend the next two seasons 'taxiing' as a gypsy cab driver. Not lucrative and, more significantly, positively dangerous – last year two drivers were murdered by ex-prisoners from the large incarceration 'zone' nearby. His wife will finally persuade him to ask around his confreres for something else. Here the labouring lives of moonlighting strangers Sasha and Victor intersect at the workshop turning out 'euro-standard' double-glazing units in the industrial zone. After mooching on his family plot in the summer and earning beer money: cutting some muscovite's lawn, delivering vegetables to distant relatives, painting fences, Sasha, mindful that his teenage son requires a new coat for winter, takes his wife's words to heart and sets off to October Street, where in an unheated concrete tomb – formerly a store for railway carriage parts – half a dozen men are working at lathes cutting aluminium frames for glazing units. Sasha's point of entry to the workshop was provided by Boris, who had in turn had a word with his 'neighbour' from two landings up in his block of flats. The neighbour's son was part of the Brigadier's team of lathe operators at the uPvC shop. A complex but socially compressed web of contacts works to maintain informal labour opportunities that in this town can encompass any willing worker.

This is also where we retrace the flow of diesel fuel filched at the beginning of this chapter. Sasha was a serendipitous find for the uPvC shop: on the very day I had begun my fieldwork at the shop they had lost their delivery driver and his private flatbed truck. Sasha was a shoe-in, aided by his 'visiting card' as the Brigadier called Sasha's tenuous network connection to himself. Again it is worth highlighting the role of mutuality, both in terms of trust – a vital currency in a country where any sniff of officialdom still provokes fear and suspicion in equal measure – and also a kind of primitive solidarity among people who often think of informal work as qualitatively different from the precarity of sweated wage-labour. Sasha and Victor's work in the shop does not appear any different to a casual observer from the manual labour they perform elsewhere. However, to them, informality is associated with (sometime conflicting) affective and social values; much like the 'reasons' for the filching and sale of the diesel fuel, informal work and practices arise out of these values, as much as material want.

In the first two informant examples we saw how informality may have been facilitated by a social network related more or less closely to formal-work contacts and affiliations, but usually involving work and practices quite different from those the worker was used to in formal employment. In both Victor's and Sasha's cases this was at the root of the ambiguous interpretation of such work, both by themselves and by their kin and peers: such informality provided relief from precarity (better pay than the cement works), it provided some sense of solidarity and self-reliance, and possibly most importantly of all, it was associated with labour autonomy and being able to pick and choose the 'when' (and some of the 'how') of work, if not the 'what'. On the other hand there was also an undercurrent of feeling about the temporary and 'second-best' nature of such work in a context where all workers had access to social memory of a previous period of permanent and normative industrial work (whether through personal experience in those over 40, or through fathers, in-laws, etc.). Hence the exhibition and simultaneous suppression of feelings that might be called 'shame', by Sasha and Victor, which complicate the affective picture of the informal–formal dilemma.

Moving up and moving on? Informal own-account work

'I am my own keeper but that doesn't mean I'm like one of those "entrepreneurs."'[10] (October 2010)

The final informant, Grigory, at first glance seems to represent a shift towards the more normative (and semi-formalized) end of the informality–formality continuum of work: informal own-account work or 'self-employment' related to a previous job or training. For example, another such informant – Kiril – was able to transfer machine repair training, fixing conveyor belts at a poultry-processing plant, to moonlighting in a different context but doing a qualitatively similar role, say, as a bought in '*slesar*' (general mechanic) on a local construction site where day-rates are paid cash-in-hand. Kiril, like Victor the ex-electrician, had vocational training, but the formal sector provided inadequate remuneration, despite shortages of technical staff. Unlike Victor, Kiril and Grigory were able to build up a network of contacts and jobs directly related to their training but largely informally in parallel to their 'day' jobs at the poultry plant and pipe fabricators, respectively. However, looking more closely at the choices Grigory has made and his interpretation of own-account informal work sets his understanding of labour at odds with an entrepreneurial self-employment that might be readily incorporated into the formal economy.

Grigory came to Izluchino in the early 1990s – even in the darkest days of Russian industry there was a shortage of workers at the cement works. He worked in a pit as a blaster's mate for a while – very dangerous work indeed, surrounded by huge moving machinery. For six years after that he worked as a skilled welder and fitter in a small plastic and steel pipe-making company. While he had no complaints about the work there, in fact the business is both officially and unofficially lauded locally for its enlightened management, he would always complain about incommensurate wages to the skills and efforts for which he and his brigade were praised. Gradually Grigory built up a small weekend *kalym* business installing electric water heaters domestically in the town. Soon he found that he could earn as much on a Saturday as he did in the whole working-week.

When I met him he still worked at the pipe company but was mulling over the offers he had from Moscow for better paid formal work and the idea of leaving employment completely for the *kalym* work. Later the quantity of *kalym* work became such that simultaneous engagement with both formal and informal spheres was becoming untenable. Almost every weekend Grigory was working very long hours, sometimes commuting to the neighbouring region (3–4 hours drive each way) to install full domestic heating systems. When I met him again he had lost weight, looked haggard and complained about not being able to spend time with his eldest son, who had recently returned from military service. Similar to the case of Victor and Sasha, Grigory was at the centre of his own wide-ranging web of contacts that continually provided him with informal work, with payment, often substantial, by result. I travelled with him one Saturday in his battered car to meet his 'mini-brigade', hand-picked from the best workers at the pipe-plant. The job, at a small town some 70km away, was to install the plumbing from scratch in a large country residence (a *dacha* of approximately 300m^2). This took four weekends working ten hours a day for a four-man team (not counting my own incompetent participation). As foreman, Grigory earned $2000 for this job – four times what he might hope to earn in a month in industry with bonuses.

Back at his tiny one-room flat, squeezed between children and pets, we reflected on what *kalym* meant in comparison to the 'day job'. Grigory had always valued the formal status he gained from being a valued worker at the pipe company – he regularly got the best bonuses as well as informal extra payments and other perks. He had recently needed a medical operation, and the company director had paid for this without any argument. At work he had '*avtoritet*': 'authority' status-qua-worker (see Morris 2013 for an extended discussion). However, it was increasingly clear that he could translate this into work outside employment primarily by involving others in his social network in bigger and bigger informal jobs. Indeed, his employment-grounded status conferred by formal work facilitated the extension of this network 'vertically' to include important entrepreneurial contacts beyond Grigory's blue-collar circle. Thus he became one of the faces on the Board of Honour for a while outside the town hall. Ironically it was not long after that Grigory decided to quit his job. A few months later he returned from Moscow where he had been working in construction as a plumber informally. He now had even more contacts further afield.

His job in Moscow had changed him and his attitudes to informal work somewhat. While he was not going to return to the pipe company, he did not want to work again with strangers 'slumming it' in temporary accommodation in Moscow. Nor did he have any intention of officially registering as an 'individual entrepreneur', effectively becoming legally self-employed. Why not? I asked him. It is not a question of red tape – since 2011 it has become even easier to register as self-employed in Russia and taxation has been simplified; on the other hand there are no bureaucratic or tax incentives pertaining to this status either and a minimum social protection payment must be made which might be onerous to a trader with a small turnover. The answer lies more in a 'moral economy' view of labour, payment and politics more generally. Once the decision had been made to leave waged work, Grigory felt that he now owned his labour completely – why should the corrupt state with its blurring of politics and business get any of his income? Paying into the social fund? But they had closed the local hospital and when he had needed his operation he had to pay either way: 'over or under the table'. What about legal status? 'What difference would that make,' Grigory scratches his head, grinning. Despite the extension of his social network upwards and outwards, jobs and clients can still be largely 'vouchsafed' through existing contacts; trust-based versus contract-based 'transaction costs' are hardly differentiated. 'If someone doesn't want to pay, they won't pay.' Additionally, informal plumbers like Grigory are not in the same disadvantaged position of more visible 'tradesmen' I encountered – like mini-bus drivers or shop owners, where avoidance of registration is not an option.

Conclusions

While more developed as a viable form of household reproduction, it can be seen that Grigory's arguments for informality, like those of the other informants, coalesce around a fuzzily articulated but persistent sense of dignity and autonomy in labour. Finally, Grigory's case 'for' informality coincides in terms of mutuality with that of other informants too. His own-account work allows him continuing professional access to significant peers: his mini-brigade, without legal ties which 'aren't necessary . . . it wouldn't somehow be right to sign a contract with them'. Informal economic activity is closely correlated with 'informal' sociality and solidarity within blue-collar groups. Grigory talked about his relationship with workers with whom he continued to labour, after employment, and with others: 'mutual aid is still important. It is pleasant that people check up on you, even if they stayed at the factory.'[11] For Grigory, *kalym* somehow does not fit with the term 'entrepreneur'. To call himself that would mean giving up something that makes him both a 'worker' and an *avtoritet*, and this would go against the grain of blue-collar sociality.

This chapter has viewed blue-collar informal economic activities along a continuum of labour that everywhere has points of contact with formal employment and formally employed workers. Interpretively, different forms of informality are not particularly sharply delineated from each other. Formal work is seen as deficient in numerous ways by workers who value autonomy, monetary and sociality benefits of informality, though not necessarily in that order. Weak–strong ties facilitate informality, but are not necessarily 'friendly'. However, their class-based nature is a binding, perhaps bonding substance (compare Yabukovich 2005) of a blue-collar network which provides a remarkably resilient and effective means to access informal sources of income, especially related to manual and skilled trades tied to worker status. Hence moonlighters, once strangers who met on the way to informality, gradually come to develop social capital in-common. Their viability as labouring entities outside formal work means depending on a complex weave of friends, kin, acquaintances, former bosses and colleagues. Informality and sociality therefore are no strangers either, but intimate bedfellows; without accounting for the peculiar persistence of post-Fordist social networks of labour, in turn the resilience of informality both 'because of' and 'in spite of' neoliberal reform, cannot begin to be apprehended as a social phenomenon. Neoliberalism creates labour insecurity at all levels, but especially among vulnerable blue-collar workers. This pushes some more enterprising workers into informality. The same casualization and loss of permanent work that neoliberalism propagates would seem to seek to 'structurally' incorporate informality within itself (Castells and Portes 1989). However, rather than accepting their status as reserve labour, this chapter shows that entrepreneurial blue-collars with social capital resist incorporation in this manner. Their 'domestication' (Stenning *et al.* 2011) of self-employment or informal employment is predicated on long-standing moral narratives on the importance of sociality, autonomy of labour and householding and suspicion of the state.

A final point to reinforce from this ethnography of manual work is that informality occurs in a continuum, where a gradual transition within and outside formal work is possible: from informal odd jobs with a vague understanding of reciprocity (barter, favours, payment in kind), to extra cash-in-hand bonuses at formal workplaces and lucrative own-account employment whose actual work may not be different, but which qualitatively differs from formal, and normative employment. Even in an urban setting, the non-cash, socialized economies of favours remain important. The continuum prism adopted here may help collapse the dualistic conceptualization of economic practices, where formal and informal are kept at arm's length. In the Russian post-socialist context this imbrication of the formal and informal has been an unremarkable observation when examining white-collar and professional activities; the present chapter shows that it is equally relevant to looking at the working poor in a marginal urban space.

Notes

1 The word still carries derogatory meaning left over from the Soviet period due to its association with misuse of state property and informality per se, although, significantly, my informants' neutral moral attitude to differentiating this work from formal work indicates a change in nuance.
2 For example there were 29 FDI automotive projects alone in 2010, representing a 100 per cent increase on the previous year. See 'Growing opportunities Russia FDI report', Ernst and Young 2011.
3 This insight parallels Nancy Ries' analysis of the 'ontology' of potato growing in Russia: it is as much a ritual practice as a practical/calculative one (2009).
4 Guariglia and Kim take a marginal utility approach and restrict their econometric analysis to purely economic motivations for participation in the informal economy. Unsurprisingly they find a high degree of correlation between moonlighting and desire for a change in job.

5 There is plenty of disused space in the district for such underground outfits – all you have to do is pay for the electricity and 'come to a mutual understanding' with the factory site management. In the compressed social geography of the town where it is difficult to avoid bumping into even the most distant acquaintance, no one is going to 'grass' to the tax authorities.
6 Without going into too much detail, Victor's specific role in the municipality was particularly ripe for exploitation in informality.
7 '*Priyatel*' – a close and friendly acquaintance. The word is used to locate a person socially between friend and mere acquaintance.
8 Williams and Round (2007) use portfolio to refer to a variety of formal jobs worked at simultaneously in Russia and Ukraine. I argue here that for blue-collar workers, often portfolio working cuts across the formal–informal divide.
9 That both large- and small-scale enterprises will still take Sasha on at all, considering the gaps in formal employment in his 'work book', is witness to the continuing shortages of manual labour in European Russia.
10 For 'entrepreneur', Grigory uses the recent bureaucratic term 'individual entrepreneur' ('*individual'nyi predprinimatel*'') which refers to the formal tax and regulations regime for the self-employed.
11 'Mutual support' translates '*vzaimovyruchka*', which has more of a concrete meaning than the more standard '*vzaimopomoshch*'', meaning 'mutual aid'.

References

Burawoy, M., with János Lukács (1992) *The Radiant Past: Ideology and Reality in Hungary's Road to Capitalism*, Chicago: University of Chicago Press.

Castells, M. and Portes, A. (1989) 'World Underneath: The Origins, Dynamics, and Effects of the Informal Economy', in Portes, A., Castells, M. and Benton, L. A. (eds), *The Informal Economy – Studies in Advanced and Less Developed Countries*, Baltimore and London: Johns Hopkins University Press, pp. 11–37.

Dunn, E. C. (2004) *Privatising Poland: Baby Food, Big Business, and the Remaking of Labor*, New York: Cornell University Press.

Ernst and Young (2011) 'Growing opportunities Russia FDI report', Online. Available: <http://www.ey.com/Publication/vwLUAssets/Growing_opportunities_Russia_FDI_report_2011/$FILE/Russia_attractiveness_survey_2011.pdf> (accessed 31 March 2013).

Guariglia, A. and Kim, B. (2006) 'The Dynamics of Moonlighting in Russia: What is Happening in the Russian Informal Economy? *Economics of Transition* 14(1): 1–45.

Gudeman, S. (2001) *The Anthropology of Economy: Community, Market and Culture*, Malden MA; Oxford, UK: Blackwell.

Harding, P. and Jenkins, R. (1989) *The Myth of the Hidden Economy: Towards a New Understanding of Informal Economic Activity*, Milton Keynes: Open University Press.

Hart, K. (1973) 'Informal Income Opportunities and Urban Employment in Ghana', *Journal of Modern African Studies*, 11(1): 61–89.

Kideckel, D. A. (2004) 'Miners and Wives in Romania's Jiu Valley: Perspectives on Postsocialist Class, Gender, and Social Change', *Identities* 11: 39–63.

Morris, J. (2012) 'Unruly Entrepreneurs: Russian Worker Responses to Insecure Formal Employment', *Global Labour Journal* 3(2): 217–36. Online. Available: <http://digitalcommons.mcmaster.ca/globallabour/vol3/iss2/2> (31 March 2013).

—— (2013) 'Beyond Coping? Alternatives to Consumption within a Social Network of Russian Workers', *Ethnography* 14(1): 85–103.

Ries, N. (2009) 'Potato Ontology: Surviving Postsocialism in Russia', *Cultural Anthropology* 24(2): 181–212.

Routh, S. (2011) 'Building Informal Workers Agenda: Imagining "Informal Employment" in Conceptual Resolution of "Informality"', *Global Labour Journal* 2(3): 208–27. Online. Available: <http://digitalcommons.mcmaster.ca/globallabour/vol2/iss3/3> (accessed 31 March 2013).

Stenning, A., Smith, A., Rochovska, A., Swiatek, D. (2010) *Domesticating Neo-Liberalism: Spaces of Economic Practice and Social Reproduction in Post-Socialist Cities*, Wiley-Blackwell.

Verdery, K. (1996) *What Was Socialism, and What Comes Next?*, Princeton, NJ; Chichester, West Sussex: Princeton University Press.

Williams, C. C. and Round, J. (2007) 'Beyond Negative Depictions of Informal Employment: Some Lessons from Moscow', *Urban Studies*, 44(12): 321–38.

Winiecki, J. (1989) 'CPEs' Structural Change and World Market Performance: a Permanently Developing Country (PDC) Status?', *Soviet Studies* 41(3): 365–81.

Yakubovich, V. (2005) 'Weak Ties, Information, and Influence: How Workers Find Jobs in a Local Russian Labor Market', *American Sociological Review* 70: 408–21.

4 Nannies and informality in Romanian local childcare markets

Borbála Kovács

Introduction

I had been recruiting families to talk to about the care arrangements of their youngest children through public kindergartens[1] in spring 2010. I was setting up a meeting when a mother asked whether I would be able to talk to another carer in the family. The mother, Erika, told me I would be talking to the girls' granny. I went to the specified address early in the morning, but no grandmother was there, only Erika's father. He said that Piroska néni[2] and Erika should both arrive soon. I surmised Piroska néni was the paternal grandmother. I was puzzled: why not meet at her place then?

Piroska néni kept returning to her experience caring for Erika's older daughter, some eight to nine years ago. As she started reminiscing, she became very friendly and adopted a confiding tone.

> We lived in the same block of flats, you see. They lived on the ground floor and I lived . . . live on the seventh . . . I didn't know them before, but I came to really like the little girl, as my son is not home and he lives abroad . . .

Piroska néni kept talking about her single son living in Germany and her sadness over not having grandchildren of her own as it dawned on me that I was talking to no grandmother, but to someone who in my understanding was a *nanny*: an elderly woman paid for her time and energy to look after the children of a working couple that had no other informal help to rely on.[3] Erika, the mother, had passed her off as the girls' grandmother, yet she was no grandmother. Or was she?

In close to two hours I had learned quite a lot about Erika's daughters': their daily routines while growing up, how pretty and smart they were, what kinds of personalities they had, how much they loved each other and Piroska néni, what sports they did and what medals they had recently won, etc. Piroska néni was the long-term nanny of these girls, but she spoke about them and their mother as if they were her family:

> It's six or eight hours and it's only me there, caring for the little one. Instead . . . if there was anything during the afternoons, too, she would just call me and I'd go, so . . . or she'd come up. This is how we were . . . mother and daughter . . . type of relationship. And this is the same to this very day.

68 *Borbála Kovács*

Although money was changing hands, the relationships between Erika, her girls and Piroska néni bore semblance to those within an extended family. Piroska néni had been offering 'bespoke' childcare services on and off for close to ten years, but her involvement caring *for* the girls transformed over time into a relationship defined by caring *about* them. Piroska néni had opened her home to the two girls and offered her best in terms of attention, affection and knowledge. She invested energy and method into the girls' development and supported and shaped their turning into 'endlessly smart' girls with her best intentions and undivided focus. As some kind of vindication by fate for her forced early retirement in 1990, the emigration of her son and his bachelor lifestyle, Piroska néni transformed the chance to work as a nanny into the opportunity of becoming a grandmother, a much desired and highly prized identity. For Piroska néni, Erika and her young family – very close, very dependent and very sweet – became the perfect surrogate daughter and granddaughters.

Erika's mother-in-law had died and her mother was still working full-time when her first baby was born. So close, so eager to help, so loving with her daughter, Piroska néni came to embody for Erika the most suitable substitute carer during her first daughter's early years. Her availability, helpfulness and flexibility recommended her as a trusted carer for Erika's second daughter, as well, when Erika's own mother was dying. But Piroska néni was more than the long-term paid carer of the girls. As a result of the organic growth of the relationship between nanny and children, Piroska néni became Piroska *mama*:[4] their (surrogate) grandmother.

The encounter with Piroska néni revealed that the affection and intimacy of paid carer–child relationships can, in time, efface the self-interested pragmatism and primarily exchange that contractual relationships are often characterised by at their onset. The flexibility of the exchanges that took place between this mother and nanny and the mutual dependence and trust that developed reinforced a relationship that was increasingly less economic, pecuniary and needs-driven. Instead, the cash-for-care relationship changed into a familial one, Piroska néni's caring and Erika's financial assistance forming the core of a repertoire of practices through which these women were 'doing family' (albeit a surrogate one) (Silva and Smart 1999: 8–9). The informal economic exchange of cash for childcare between these two women may be seen as a textbook illustration of what Pfau-Effinger (2009: 91–3) called solidarity-based undeclared work.

Informal childcare services for payment are not necessarily provided within social networks, however. Zita, the main informant of this chapter, had been working informally for a high-income family with two young children as a cleaner, nanny and housekeeper in addition to her full-time job as a cleaner at a bank in downtown Tîrgu Mureş. With this informal job, she tripled her meagre bank salary. In the context of the bank's closure in March 2012 and her employing family's successful business, Zita made the atypical transition from being a full-time informal domestic worker for this family to being an employee in their family business in April, retaining her domestic responsibilities. Younger and with a family of her own, Zita's affections for the two children she cared for were more reserved than in Piroska néni's case. Furthermore, she regarded their mother, Dorina, as her employer. In contrast to Piroska néni, Zita expected to be financially rewarded for her 'invaluable' caring work, especially when it involved extras, and was reluctant to make herself available at any time. In spite of a trusting rapport, Zita worked hard to maintain a *contractual* relationship with Dorina. She expected her salary to be paid on time, to be financially rewarded for extras and she expected to be talked to as if to a 'worker' rather than as to family. Equally, she invested a lot of energy into being professional in her work for Dorina: she made a point of being on time, developed the cleaning standards and routine and, most importantly to her, intervened in the children's upbringing by openly insisting on her own methods and expectations. And although Zita's main source of income was employment by this family, she reiterated her intentions of quitting after incidents that felt to her to be violations of a contractual relationship.

The childcare work of these two women may be read as real-life illustrations of the ways in which personalised childcare services in children's homes for under-threes have been provided and purchased in Romania over the last ten years at least. Piroska néni's story of surrogate grandmotherhood is illustrative of the experiences of women of her generation who were rendered economically redundant through successive waves of forced early retirement (Hrzenjak 2012). Zita's experience of constantly combining formal and informal employment offers an insight into what might be considered Romanian urban working-class families' survival strategies in transitioning post-socialist economies (Stănculescu 2002). Childcare and domestic services emerge as an important currency of escape from poverty within informality for women of all ages in contemporary Romania. In addition, these women are indispensable to the formation of an emerging urban middle class formed by high-income couples of enterprising men and professional women. Working in demanding and high responsibility jobs, living in spacious, purpose-built family homes and engaged in what Lareau (2011) called the concerted cultivation of their children, i.e. a constant preoccupation with stimulating children's growth and development through a multitude of activities and social encounters, women in such couples are faced with an overwhelming triple burden of job, domestic work and childrearing in the absence of any help from their entrepreneur husbands. This type of affluence creates the need (and generates the resources) for a nurturing person who, in the intimacy of the family home, can act as these women's extension in some or all things domestic.

In the context of increasing income differentials and the particularities of caring as both work and relationship, looking after (privileged) young children was experienced as both labour and pleasure by those performing this kind of 'labour of love' (Graham 1983). Both Piroska néni and Zita appreciated and took pride in the affection and attachment of the children they were caring for. Both regarded their caring and involvement in childrearing as invaluable due to the dedication and love they had for the children. But their relationships with those whom they were helping and the grounds on which they were offering their help differed significantly.

This chapter is structured in four parts. The first section details the primary data that informs the analysis in the last two sections. The focus of the second is a review of the different types of informality characteristic of the Romanian context especially and the different explanatory factors that have been seen to drive Romania's informal economy. This section also discusses informal childcare services as a particular form of undeclared work and its estimated extensiveness. The third part aims to provide an analysis of what may be called supply-side factors in explaining undeclared childcare and domestic services more generally. Zita's narrative especially serves to bring into focus the meanings and tensions of informality and the role that undeclared work, informally provided childcare especially, has for those who deliver such services.

There seems to be a certain degree of consensus in the literature focusing on post-socialist countries' informality that undeclared work is in particular driven by the supply side (Djankov *et al*. 2003; Parlevliet and Xenogiani 2008; Pfau-Effinger 2009). Analyses of informality dwell especially on undeclared work as a survival strategy (Wallace 2002; Pfau-Effinger 2009: 84–9) in depressed economies with low levels of investment, low to negative job growth and large supplies of cheap labour as a result of abrupt and radical economic restructuring (for Romania, see Rose 1994; Mungiu-Pippidi *et al*. 2000; Neef and Stănculescu 2002). However, the quintessentially self-driven and mostly self-sufficient form of informal economic activity, subsistence agriculture, has been on the decline in Romania. At the same time, the number of those working informally in sectors other than agriculture doubled between 1995 and 2005 (Parlevliet and Xenogiani 2008). It would appear, therefore, that both supply *and demand* for informal employment have been on the rise in Romania (as elsewhere, in fact). Drawing on the experiences of the two nannies featured in this chapter, the fourth section discusses what might be seen as demand-side factors underpinning local informal childcare service markets. The fifth section concludes the chapter.

Data and methodology

This chapter draws primarily on in-depth interview data. I met Piroska néni in March 2010 in Tîrgu Mureş, a city of 140,000 in central Romania. She and the mother she was still occasionally helping with childcare, Erika, were among the earliest participants in a larger study the fourth section of this chapter also draws on (see below). Zita was recommended to me by a bank employee, a mutual acquaintance. I talked with her at length twice during March 2012, in Tîrgu Mureş, and once later, in July. Given that close to half of the city's inhabitants are Hungarian (or speak Hungarian as their first language), it was a coincidence that both nannies were Hungarian. While Piroska néni's narrative may be paired with that of Erika's, I never met Zita's employer, Dorina. The fourth section of the chapter focusing on the demand side of informal home-based childcare services draws on 68 in-depth interviews with mothers, fathers and grandmothers in 37 families whose children were aged between one and five at the time of the interviews, in spring and summer 2010. Of these families 21 lived in Tîrgu Mureş and the other 16 in two villages at some distance from the city. Discussions focused on children's care arrangements and transitions in care arrangements during their first five years of life, these families' access to different state family provisions (in cash and in-kind, in the form of services), as well as reliance on informal – paid and unpaid – childcare.

In the light of the narratives of the 68 familial carers, Piroska néni emerged as a typical nanny of the loving kind. Zita's experience of informality as a nanny was less typical due to her age (she was 30 when she started caring for Dorina's older son) and labour market status (she was in formal employment), but especially because she was offered, after seven years of working informally for Dorina, an indefinite work contract. At the same time, however, Zita's undeclared work (including working as a nanny) in combination with formal employment illustrates a different role that informal home-based childcare can play in the lives of carers: the main avenue of securing a regular second income almost continuously since leaving school. Informally provided 'bespoke' childcare formed an essential component of Zita's working life, best understood as a succession of jigsaws of formal and informal employment during the working day, the working week, the working year. This type of market activity makes Zita typical not as a nanny, but as a semi-skilled, middle-aged worker in a middle-income transitioning economy and a thriving local childcare market.

Informality in Romania: survival and 'envelope' incomes

Among the member states of the European Union, Romania has been described as the country with the highest incidence of undeclared work since the early 2000s (Renooy *et al.* 2004). The size of the shadow economy in Romania was estimated to represent 30–40 per cent of GDP during the early 2000s (Parlevliet and Xenogiani 2008), although official statistics estimate that only 16–21 per cent of GDP originates in undeclared work (Renooy *et al.* 2004: 142; European Commission 2007a). More recent studies have suggested that undeclared work in Romania has remained constant (European Commission 2007a), although the impact of the economic crisis has likely resulted in an increase in informal economic transactions.

Romania also stands out as an economy with a large share of the working population engaged in undeclared work as an alternative or complement to formal labour market participation. Stănculescu (2006) estimated that in 1998 65 per cent of the population regularly combined formal employment with undeclared work in some way, many self-employed in subsistence agriculture: 2.8 million individuals in 2005. In other words, undeclared work in the Romanian context has more frequently amounted to unregistered self-employment in subsistence agriculture than informal *waged* work for an employer. However, informal employment tripled between 1995 and 2005 (Parlevliet and Xenogiani 2008; Stănculescu 2006).

Perhaps the most relevant particularity of undeclared work in Romania is the polarisation of the involved workforce in terms of the conditions under which informality is undertaken. Romania's shadow economy is what has been called two-tiered (Fields 1990; see also Parlevliet and Xenogiani 2008: 25–6). On the one hand, a large proportion of individuals work exclusively informally as a survival strategy in response to the economic shocks of the 1990s in particular (Djankov *et al.* 2003; Mungiu-Pippidi *et al.* 2000; Neef and Stănculescu 2002; Rose 1994). Undeclared work as escape from poverty has been explained as the direct outcome of mass layoffs in urban industrial enterprises especially in the 1990s against the backdrop of land restitution that took off in 1991 (Djankov *et al.* 2003; Renooy *et al.* 2004). Self-employment in subsistence agriculture, 'subsistence enterprises' (Djankov *et al.* 2003: 65) and informal labour market participation in depressed local economies with very limited formal job opportunities (see Mungiu-Pippidi *et al.* 2000) are the most common examples of this type of informality. But while these types of survival strategies were most common during the 1990s (Ciupagea 2002) and in decline by the early 2000s, (Mungiu-Pippidi *et al.* 2000) the propagation of undeclared work as poverty escape survives in spite of overall economic growth due to regional asymmetries in the development of provincial local economies and the negative effects of employment history fragmentation on employability among economic migrants (see Stănculescu *et al.* 2011: 114). On the other hand, another tier of the informal economy comprises professionals and companies of all sizes offering a broad range of services in sellers' markets that carry out some of their activities partly informally to reduce their tax burdens and social security contributions (Djankov *et al.* 2003: 63–5; Renooy *et al.* 2004). A key symptom of this type of informality is the so-called 'envelope wage', i.e. the systematic under-reporting of earned income of formally employed workers (European Commission 2007b). This type of informality has been explained by the direct and indirect costs associated with paying taxes and social security contributions for *de facto* gross incomes, as well as generalised distrust of the state (Djankov *et al.* 2003; Parlevliet and Xenogiani 2008; Renooy *et al.* 2004).

Household services, cleaning and childcare included, have been described as involuntary informal employment (Parlevliet and Xenogiani 2008) or precarious labour of migrant women in the context of a global care chain, especially in the advanced economies of the global North (see for instance Ehrenreich and Hochschild 2003; Hrzenjak 2011; Lister *et al.* 2007). The degree of precariousness of such work has been seen to vary with the conditions under which it is performed and by whom. In Western Europe and the US, such work has been documented to be often carried out by illegal migrants in live-in situations that undermine their control over working hours, personal privacy, greatly limit their possibilities of exiting employment situations and erode their wages as a result of the room and board included in their employment agreement (see Lister *et al.* 2007). The informality of the cash-for-care exchange may originate, then, especially in workers' inability to undertake such work within the existing provisions (and protection) of the law.

But neither Piroska néni's, nor Zita's experience working as nannies (and as a domestic worker in Zita's case) is accurately explained by any of these determinants of undeclared work. Their informal employment may only be considered a poverty escape strategy in the broader sense since the circumstances that led them to undertake childcare for pay were not the lack of income. Both of them are natives of the city where they work. The informality of their caring work should be understood as a defining feature of this type of service throughout Europe. In Romania, 7 per cent of respondents – a low figure in comparative terms – who had undertaken some informal activity said they provided domestic services, almost half with some regularity (European Commission 2007b). In the light of the experience of these two nannies and that of over 30 informant families with young children, a more convincing explanation seems to point to the complex interactions between the demand side and the supply side in *local* mixed economies of childcare (Daly and Lewis 2000). In other words, informality seems to arise from the ways in which the local demand and supply of *all types* of childcare services play out, shaped by structural factors such as the quality and accessibility of public childcare services, aggregate employment and unemployment levels, local income inequalities, as well as the particularities of the regulatory framework pertaining to childcare services generally. Arguably, the greater the number of high-income middle-class families with wide-ranging expectation is and the less regulation pertaining to 'bespoke' home-based childcare services, the greater the local informal nanny market.

Furthermore, the informal character of home-based informal childcare services must also be seen in the light of the symbolic particularities of this type of labour. The kind of childcare that nannies are meant to provide, a labour of love in the private home of the child and his/her family, seems to be incompatible with the connotations of formal work relations. Caring, although labour, too, is invariably desired to also be a strong affective relationship between child and his/her carer. Childcare has long been seen to command a particular *moral* rationality (Finch and Mason 1993; Kremer 2007; Waerness 1984), one that stresses 'the right thing to do' for the child especially rather than a self-interested rationality more characteristic of economic exchanges (Duncan *et al.* 2003; Duncan and Edwards 1999; Folbre 2008; Vincent and Ball 2001). Moreover, the location of childcare performed by nannies – in a familial setting, 'informally' – has long been understood, in post-socialist societies, too, as the opposite of the state and the labour market, the location of economic transactions (Goven 1993; Magyari-Vincze 2006). Therefore the possibilities of formalising an economic exchange that is strongly wished by parents to be affective and familial rather than economic and formal should be seen as greatly undermined by the very nature of services rendered, in this case childcare. Zita's narrative reveals the tensions of her care work for pay in a private household, but her experience also shows that it is informality that generates the opportunities through which she is able to navigate these tensions.

The supply side

At the time of our conversations, both Piroska néni and Zita had been working for their respective families for over seven years. Theirs were long-term, exclusive relationships of economic and affective dependence: neither Zita, nor Piroska néni combined the care work they did for Dorina and Erika, respectively, with other informal activities. In Zita's case the main reason was her workload: she worked six-to-seven hours a day for Dorina during standard working hours and another two hours after 4pm in what was, officially, her full-time formal cleaning job at the bank. During her time as a cleaner for the bank, Zita had successfully negotiated the expansion of her work contract from initially four hours a day to a full workload, while at the same time reducing the number of hours actually spent cleaning, allowing for time to undertake other (undeclared) work.

The shortening of the number of hours Zita spent in her formal job occurred against the backdrop of the deterioration of her employment relations. Zita was not the employee of the bank, but that of a contracted cleaning company. For more than eight years Zita had earned the same 400 RON a month (~ €95) that she started out with working part time. When her employer sub-contracted the refurbishment of the entire building later on, Zita was left to do the subsequent general cleaning completely by herself. Around the same time, her employer had also ceased to carry out the quarterly general cleaning that Zita had been used to, leaving her to work in an environment in which 'dirt dominated' despite her meticulous daily routine. Her cleaning company also failed to regularly cover her transportation costs amounting to 100 RON/month (~ €24), i.e. a quarter of her post-tax salary. As a result, in months when her transport money was not paid in spite of her formal request, she took home 300 RON (~ €70) from her formal job. In response, Zita negotiated an unofficial reduction in her actual working hours with her immediate superior, the director of the bank. As long as she got her routine cleaning done, she could come and go as she pleased. Zita made sure she worked no more than two hours a day for her meagre salary on this full-time contract.

Interestingly, however, the precariousness of Zita's formal employment provided her with opportunities rather than hardship given the high demand for informal cleaning services among the overwhelmingly female middle-class workforce of the bank. Her cleaning job provided her with social security and health insurance coverage and, equally importantly, functioned as a springboard for much more lucrative and less demanding cleaning jobs. It was mostly bank employees or managers of other banks who were familiar with her cleaning services and who offered her extra cleaning jobs. Zita described employees at the bank and other 'directors' 'begging' her to take on regular cleaning responsibilities in their homes, suggesting that she (and her labour) had always been in high demand. Although her job at the bank offered her no financial security, it served as a shop display and a business card for *her* – rather than her company's – cleaning services.

Zita's employment at Dorina's ensued after Dorina's sister, also working at the bank, had 'begged' her for weeks to at least go and assess the cleaning work that Dorina required after the construction of their family home. Zita went, assessed the work and agreed to clean twice a week, during standard working hours. Although her formal job took precedence over this and other cleaning jobs, Zita's main source of income was the totality of her unregistered activity. Before agreeing to also take on care responsibilities for Dorina's son a few months later, Zita's working week was a jigsaw of formal and informal cleaning jobs for private individuals and companies. In addition to her job at the bank, her week was organised thus: 'Mondays I'd head to the enterprise, Tuesdays to Dorina's, Wednesdays to the enterprise, Thursdays to Dorina's and Friday's to Ani's, from the bank.' The enterprise she was referring to was a local company that constructed and sold windows and doors made of PVC and whose 'junior director' had recruited her to do cleaning work without a contract. Ani was the manager of the bank and Zita had been cleaning for her almost since she had started work at the bank.

Just as in Piroska néni's case, whose employment as a nanny was facilitated by the affinity between her and Erika's daughter, Zita's transition from being a cleaner to a nanny in Dorina's home occurred as a result of Dorina's son's attachment to Zita. In both cases it was the mothers, engaged in running their husbands' businesses, who proposed the informal arrangement and the financial one accompanying it. In Zita's case, the additional workload that childcare constituted – childcare and cleaning five days a week rather than just cleaning on two – led to the refusal of any other kind of extra jobs apart from her formal employment. At the time of our talks, Zita's schedule consisted of six to seven hours of cleaning and childcare at Dorina's house for a total of 800 RON/month (~ €190), a quarter of which was for public transport, and around two hours of cleaning at the bank for 300 or 400 RON/month (~ €70 or 95), depending on whether transport was covered or not.

As already suggested, this kind of patchwork employment had characterised Zita's entire working life. After graduation from secondary school in the early 1990s, her first job was informal: she looked after a pre-school-aged boy for around a year, just before giving birth to her own son. Her transition back into the formal labour market was facilitated by the mother of the children her own mother was caring for at the time, during a period of generalised economic decline (Ciupagea 2002). After five years spent working as an unskilled worker in a small clothes factory, Zita spent a few years in and out of formal jobs. While working in a small factory making envelopes and boxes, she and some of her colleagues were offered the opportunity to do the same type of work at home, informally, for significantly more pay. In addition, she also helped her parents care for an elderly couple for pay around this time. This type of patchwork employment, constituted by formal employment and undeclared work doing the same or a variety of different kinds of activities, was characteristic of Zita's extended family, as well. Her husband worked as a welder combining a full-time formal job with additional short-term contracts on construction sites, informally. Zita's brother-in-law, working as a technician for the national gas works, had always 'earned very well'. This was particularly the case during the 2000s, when private households started purchasing central heating, informally employing technicians from the national gas works to get the paperwork signed and put the central heating system in place. Zita's father, in a fashion characteristic of socialist times (Renooy *et al.* 2004; Verdery 1996), 'had done a lot' of moonlighting after hours as a plumber. Zita's mother, who was sent into early retirement on health grounds before turning 45, had made a post-retirement career of looking after children of 'directors'. In a post-socialist local economy in which wages remained compressed and living-wage-paying jobs scarce, informality was, among the more enterprising, the main fall-back strategy to avoid spells of poverty (Mungiu-Pippidi *et al.* 2000;

Stănculescu 2002). 'Work-loving' and 'fair' people like Zita received constant undeclared job offers, keeping her (and her family) in the grey economy.[5]

Zita took ownership over her labour in part as a response to the similar message that seemed to originate with her informal employers. The undeclared character of the extra cleaning jobs Zita was 'begged' to accept sat comfortably with what seemed to be everyone's tacit acceptance that the work was Zita's, not her employing company's, therefore one hired her, not her employing company, for the job. Furthermore, Zita took pride in the fact that she was such a sought-after cleaner and carer, but this pride originated in more than her self-appreciation of the quality of her work. She often provided details of her informal employers, remarking they were 'directors' of some kind or owned a 'SRL', i.e. a private limited company. Resonating with recent socialist-time points of reference when the hardworking everyman was an employee[6] and being a director placed someone at the pinnacle of local social hierarchies, Zita's reference to her employers' managerial posts or entrepreneurial leanings was her working-class shorthand for designating the local elite. Even if these 'directors' lived in a socialist-era concrete flat just like herself, even if those who 'had an SRL' were, in fact, shopkeepers who stored their goods in their wardrobes at home, Zita sought to emphasise that they were respectable, different from your typical labouring employee. But, somewhat confusingly, they were working people all the same – like herself or her husband. Being sought out by such respectable people, regularly working in their homes unsupervised and regularly chatting with them was, to her, the opportunity to rub shoulders with them. And being accepted, valued and socialising with these 'directors' and SRL owners reinforced a sense of equality reminiscent of what Anderson (1999: 316–21) called relational *democratic* equality: the possibility to stand as an equal in front of others.

Zita negotiated the confusing incoherence of class signifiers that she constantly encountered through a narrative of what might be called differentiated equality. Ani, Dorina and her parents' neighbour, the 'junior director' of the PVC carpentry company, were all 'directors' or 'had an SRL': they were different from her, only a cleaner, especially in terms of the things they could afford. But Zita often asserted that they were different *only* in that respect. As people they were 'no better' than she was. Zita expressed her sense of equality through various actions whose aim was to challenge and question what she interpreted to be her employers' enactment of superiority: she made a habit of gifting them with cake she baked; she openly criticised them for what seemed to her to be unjustified arrogance; she refused her services if she felt she was not being appreciated even if her work was deemed impeccable; and she used sarcasm to express dissatisfaction and anger if she felt wronged. Zita navigated the contradictions and tensions of the class inferiority she was constantly encountering in dealing with 'rich' people (like 'directors' and SRL owners) through cultivating a self-image of the indispensable domestic employee. Unlike Piroska *néni*, who wanted to be family to Erika and her daughters and greatly enjoyed being Piroska *mama*, Zita resisted becoming family to Dorina and her children despite the apparent pressure they exerted to make her feel 'one of them'. It was important for Zita to remain the trusted employee rather than become 'one of them' because she feared that otherwise extras – e.g. childcare at weekends – would go unpaid. And, ultimately, Zita was working for Dorina to be able to afford her own son's designer clothes, motorcycle and holidays abroad, not acquire a second family.

The reasons for Zita's entering undeclared employment relations after finishing school has been described in the literature as a widespread response to risks of poverty among hardworking working-class urbanites in a post-socialist economy where living-wage-paying jobs were hard to come by. Personal initiative in the face of poverty, materialised as undeclared cleaning and care work, was 'rewarded' in Zita's case by a constant demand for her services. In spite of the tensions of class hierarchy that her undeclared work for wealthier individuals exposed her to, Zita stuck to her 'career' of domestic work and childcare for people higher up the income ladder and class hierarchy. While part of her reasons to accept and stick to her informal employment in domestic services were purely material in character, her narrative suggests that the material benefits derived from work in the grey economy had symbolic meanings at least as important as escaping poverty. One such symbolic benefit was the possibility to exercise equality with these 'rich' 'directors' and SRL owners. With a precarious formal cleaning job, Zita would have remained 'just' a poorly paid cleaner. By working informally as a trusted, indispensable domestic worker, Zita exercised power in her employment relationships and the assertion of power in relationships with wealthy people (e.g. when putting them down for their arrogance or refusing to work for them any longer) gave her a sense of (differentiated) equality and self-respect.

Given her extended family circumstances, Zita could have afforded not to work extras, but undeclared work and the additional income generated from informal employment carried additional symbolic meanings for her. Zita's husband, a trained welder, had always earned a mediocre income that he, too, complemented with work 'done black' (*la negru* in Romanian, *feketén* in Hungarian), i.e. informally. The couple had one son and lived with Zita's mother-in-law, who had her own income in the form of a pension. Zita had been freed from childcare responsibilities during weekdays while her son was young by her own mother. In short, Zita lived in an extended family situation in which all adults had their own incomes and care responsibilities were divided in such a way as to facilitate employment among the younger generation. However, in the context of the rivalry between her own family and that of her sister-in-law, whose husband – working for the national gas works – was making an easy substantial additional income from moonlighting jobs, Zita and her husband were driven to earn as much as they could. This rivalry was maintained by her mother-in-law's differentiated treatment of her own two children and Zita suffered as a result of her mother-in-law's reminders of her and her husband's alleged inferiority. Therefore making as much money as possible was another type of reiteration of her equality, this time as part of an extended family. By earning extra, Zita was asserting her equality by keeping pace with her sister-in-law's consumption habits and therefore being on the same class footing with her.

Economic need and financial security, as well as the myriad ways in which Zita asserted her sense of equal worth with those higher up the income ladder especially – whether her employers or members of the extended family – do not alone explain the reasons for Zita's longstanding informal employment relationship with Dorina. The *undeclared* character of her work for Dorina seems to be rooted in the path-dependency of exchanges that have a caring component, in particular care *for* and *about* employers. Although Zita had been offered formal employment by Dorina at least once before our talks, she had refused the formalisation of her caring job because she was keen on retaining her circle of friends at the bank. Zita described her well-educated, professional 'colleagues' at the bank as her family, people she had started her cleaning job with and people who were members of a team she was also part of. Caring *about* her colleagues compelled her to stay in her precarious formal job, as switching to a formal work contract with Dorina's family business would have meant ending a set of relationships at the bank which were important to her. A similar attachment made Zita decide to keep working for Dorina after a particularly hurtful episode when she was the target of anti-Hungarian racist remarks in Dorina's home. Zita explained her decision not to quit as a result of her desire to avoid hurting the children because she 'knew how much they would lose' if she decided to leave. What seems irrational altruism in Zita's case may be read as an expression of a moral rationality of caring (Duncan and Edwards 1999), which makes the welfare of those cared for the most important consideration. Similarly, Zita accepted Dorina's offer to become her employee with a work contract for 1,000 RON/month (~ €240) plus extras[7] starting April 2012 despite her expectation of at least 1,500 RON/month in cash plus extras (~ €360). In spite of her distress as a result of what she saw as a much lower income than she had expected, Zita accepted the formalisation of her long-term informal caring and cleaning responsibilities due to her caring *about* the children and Dorina.

In the context of massive job shortages in the 1990s, undeclared work in household services emerged for Zita as an accessible option for income generation through the contacts of her mother. In what seemed a depressed local economy in which most jobs were manual, requiring little-to-no skill, poorly paid and in addition few and far between, the idea of job growth and a career quickly deserted her. If in need of extra income, the informal market of low-to-no-skill household services was easily available. Driven by family rivalries and increasingly costly consumption habits, extra income was always welcome, keeping Zita with one foot in the grey economy even in times when she had a full-time formal job. Her domestic work led to the development of close relationships with her employers, with the possibility of formalisation sometimes seen as threatening her friendships with the people she came to care about. All these put together seemed to prevent Zita from attempting to carry out the work she was doing undeclared within the boundaries of a formal work contract.

The demand side

Interviews with 68 mothers, fathers and grandmothers of young children revealed one commonality as regards nannies: it was always parents who had to find them.

From parents' vantage point, paid informal childcare was more often hard to come by than not, with supply often insufficient. It was a symptom of this unmatched demand that some of the parents 'dared' to ask their neighbours whether they might look after their children, 'hoping' for a positive answer. It was another symptom of demand exceeding supply that some dual-earner couples who had no grandparental help to rely on encountered only refusals in their search for a nanny. Similarly, this same mismatch between high demand and low supply explained why higher-earning parents refrained from the use of what they saw as very beneficial and cheap formal childcare services and hired instead a nanny full-time: 'everyone knew' that no nanny came to care for children only when they were sick.

In dual-earner households with no familial childcare resources during standard working hours, the hiring of a nanny most often served to bridge the care gap between the time when the paid parental leave came to an end – usually around the time when children turned two – and when they started kindergarten, in most cases the September closest to their third birthdays. As cheap as a full-time nanny sometimes came, prices ranged from 50 RON/month (~ €12) for six hours a day in one of the villages to 500 RON/month (~ €120) for eight hours a day, it was still regarded as a luxury partly because these childcare costs were often compared to the cost of public childcare services in crèches and kindergartens, ranging from 60 to 120 RON/month (~ €15–30). Still, in the case of parents who could afford this 'luxury', nannies were sought exclusively informally.

Part of the reason for hiring someone to act as nanny without any kind of contract was the evident reduction in the costs of her services. No contract meant, as much literature has suggested, no taxes and social contributions paid. It also meant saving on the burdensome legwork and paperwork that the registration of a contract would have meant for the employing parents. But, as in Zita's case, another key reason for keeping the cash-for-care exchange informal was because this is how it was usually done and everyone felt comfortable with such transactions being made informally. Parents, similarly to nannies such as Zita, would have needed a good reason to *register* the cash-for-care arrangement they were entering since paid childcare services – and any other kinds of personal services in fact – had always been purchased informally since time immemorial. Although much of the literature has attempted to explain why private individuals and members of private households purchasing goods and services informally do *not register* their transactions, the real question seemed to be, why should they?

The norm of informality in respect to home-based paid care services may be traced back to socialist times (Renooy *et al.* 2004). Personalized services represented the least developed component of socialist welfare states, particularly in the poorer nations of Eastern Europe such as Romania. Although state propaganda continually reiterated the Romanian socialist state's success in catering to households' and families' every need, in truth the Romanian economy was fraught with massive shortages in the supply of both consumer goods (Verdery 1996), as well as services of all kinds (Einhorn 1993). Those who could afford to purchase personal and household services during the socialist decades did so informally, often from people who had no reason to decline extras outside their jobs moonlighting

(Renooy et al. 2004) or by 'scavenging' for goods and services of one's workplace (Verdery 1996: 50–3). Such transactions were always person-to-person and, as a result, services rendered could be easily personalised, tailored to actual needs. It might be argued that post-socialist societies have inherited a notion of personal services, home-based childcare included, being for purchase primarily informally.

The lag in the development of a regulatory framework and user-friendly procedures for the purchase and sale of person-to-person services has likely reinforced the widespread informality in this sector of the economy during the 1990s. In Romania, home-based childcare services – and other domestic services in fact – have been granted what could be considered only marginal attention in the development of a regulatory framework after 1989. There is no regulatory body that might set standards of training and good practice in relation to 'bespoke' home-based childcare services. Nor have nationally applicable guidelines and procedures been developed for becoming home-based paid carers. Due to the lack of any kind of regulatory framework pertaining to this type of household service, the local supply and demand in the localities where interviews were conducted were fragmented, unstable and informal in character. Lack of regulation created market failures such as the mismatch between demand and supply, as well as informational asymmetries. Those who required 'bespoke' childcare services in their homes often risked not finding appropriate helpers because they did not have access to a proper market of potential 'suppliers', i.e. nannies. Due to lack of formalisation, there was also no streamlined system for the professionalisation of women who might have wished to work as nannies, nor was there any incentive to do so in the absence of any punitive mechanism. Around half of the parents who had relied on paid help for childcare had had negative experiences and had to change their nannies. In other households, parents minimized the time they planned to rely on paid help by maximising their paid parental leave and making the transition into formal childcare (kindergarten) as soon as possible. Although Romanians now have at their disposal a multitude of ways to formalise person-to-person cash-for-care transactions, informality in the purchase of childcare services has remained a widespread norm and practice.

Furthermore, the care ideal (Kremer 2007) that a majority of formally employed parents I talked to seemed to adhere to – especially in relation to children under age three – was what Kremer (2007) called the 'surrogate mother' care ideal. In the context of the imperative for paid work, the most appropriate care alternative for children under kindergarten age appeared to be informal childcare by those whose caring came closest to that of the mother: grandmothers and people *like* a grandmother. In contrast to 'cold' professional carers in public institutional settings, these maternal replacements were seen to supply the best kind of childcare in mothers' absence. At the heart of caring offered by grandmothers and ideal nannies were love, attention and selfless giving, which were seen to transform the labour of caring for a young child into pleasure. The relationship between toddler and paid help was thought to emerge organically, as in the case of grandmother and grandchild, and was seen either to be there or not. Piroska néni was an exemplar of this ideal nanny image. As the quality of purchased childcare services was seen to emanate from the chemistry between child and nanny, and not the generosity (or lack of generosity) of the cash-for-care exchange, many parents saw no motive to insist on the formalisation of the exchange. What could a contract add to a care relationship that was excellent anyway? Nothing: and what improvements could a contract make to a poor care relationship?

Inherited norms and practices in respect to the purchase of household services, reinforced by an informality supported by the absence of any kind of regulatory framework that could contribute to the formalisation of local paid childcare service markets, led to an overwhelmingly informal demand for home-based childcare services over recent decades. With formalisation driving up the price of childcare services, offering no added value to a relationship widely seen to emerge organically between carer and child and securing no additional safeguards towards children's emotional and physical safety, parents wishing to hire a nanny saw no reason to do so with the hassle of a contract. In addition, it was uncommon to hire your nanny with a contract: why would they risk losing their *tanti* over a 'triviality' such as a contract?

Conclusions

The narratives of the two nannies, Piroska néni and Zita, and those of the close to 70 familial carers I talked to revealed what seemed an intuitive incompatibility between childcare – a labour of love, located in the home and anchored in relationships between private individuals – on the one hand, and formal work contracts – the realm of entrepreneurship, the tax office and more generally the distrusted state – on the other (see also Vincent and Ball 2001). But the informal character of the cash-for-care exchanges between nannies and their families had a less straightforward origin than this symbolic incompatibility. Zita's narrative especially revealed that little-to-no skill household services – such as cleaning and childcare – represented a reliable source of income when no formal jobs were available or when formal jobs allowed for time to be spent doing other jobs. Her experience of constantly combining formal full-time employment with more lucrative and time-consuming undeclared work was suggestive of the embeddedness of informal economic transactions alongside typical income-generating activities among Romanian working-class urbanites. Regardless of her motives explored in section three above, childcare and cleaning undertaken without contract represented to Zita the most rewarding type of employment in both financial and emotional terms. With her labour in great demand, Zita felt she had control over who she worked for, how much and for what money. Although she could have done the same with formal contracts, the main reason for operating in the grey economy seemed to be habit and a sense of normalcy: childcare and cleaning had always been purchased informally.

As a result of the decades-long inheritance of informality in local markets of personal and household services, reinforced by the lag in the development of a user-friendly framework for the easy formalisation of person-to-person transactions and a complete lack of formalisation of home-based childcare services, parents of young children needing such services had to operate in informal local markets of 'bespoke' childcare services. With formal contracts seen to add nothing except extra costs to a relationship built on the organic emergence of affection, mutual attachment and trust between child and nanny, transactions that have at their heart caring about and for a small child were perceived to have no reason to be *formalised*.

Indeed, in the light of Zita's, Piroska néni's and interviewed parents' experiences, the question why informality in cash-for-care transactions 20 years after the fall of communism still persists seems normative in character. This chapter reveals that the true question Zita and any couple seeking the services of a good nanny ask is not 'What reasons do we have to do this informally?', but rather 'What reasons do we have to do this *formally*?'.

Notes

1 Kindergartens – *grădinițe* in Romanian – are pre-school education institutions whose staff are trained educators and employees of the Romanian Ministry of Education. Kindergarten attendance is not compulsory and it is free at the point of access (with the exception of meals). In the 2007/2008 academic year, over 80 per cent of the relevant age group of children in Romania (between ages three and six) were enrolled in kindergarten.
2 Piroska is a first name. *Néni*, or *tanti* in Romanian, is a Hungarian term used alongside the names of elderly women not members of the extended family, for instance neighbours, to denote familiarity. The fact that many parents referred generically to nannies as *nénik* or *tanti* (using the plural) suggests local perceptions about the age of potential nannies (members of the generation of parents' own parents), as well as their relationships to the parents (neighbours, neighbourhood acquaintances).
3 The term 'informal' is used in a dual sense throughout the chapter. More commonly, informal is used as a synonym for undeclared, unregistered, forms of work that take place in the grey economy. When used alongside childcare, most frequently 'paid informal childcare', informal means childcare performed within the private sphere of the family and the home, i.e. outside formal institutional contexts of childcare.
4 In Hungarian, *mama*, the equivalent of *buni* in Romanian, is the generic name attributed to grandmothers.
5 Wallace (2002: 277) reports on research in the UK suggesting that in the aftermath of the first decade of de-industrialisation in the 1980s, households that were more likely to participate in the informal economy were not those without any kinds of labour market attachments, but those that were also active in the formal labour market. Differences were not between households with formal and informal economic activities, but 'work-rich' and 'work-poor' households.
6 Employee in Romanian is *angajat*. Zita referred to people in employment as 'angajalt', the tweaked Romanian term instead of the proper Hungarian one, *alkalmazott*.
7 With extras for transportation (that she was going to receive in cash outside her contract) and meal tickets, Zita earned the equivalent of 1,400 RON/month (~ €330 and a little under the national average post-tax salary in Romania in April 2012, see the data of the Ministry of Labour, Social Solidarity and Family at http://www.mmuncii.ro/j3/images/Date_lunare/s017-13.pdf. Interestingly, she did not seem to attach value to these extras amounting to 40 per cent of her net income, nor did she seem to care about the amount that was registered officially in her new work contract (the minimum wage). In other words, Zita seemed to judge jobs not in terms of formality and the benefits associated with working formally, but in terms of the amount of income generated.

References

Anderson, E. (1999) 'What is the Point of Equality?', *Ethics* 109(2): 287–337.
Ciupagea, C. (2002) 'Romania', in Neef, R. and Stănculescu, M. (eds) *The Social Impact of Informal Economies in Eastern Europe*, Aldershot: Ashgate, pp. 113–18.
Daly, M. and Lewis, J. (2000) 'The Concept of Social Care and the Analysis of Contemporary Welfare States', *British Journal of Sociology* 51(2): 281–98.
Djankov, S., Lieberman, I., Mukherjee, J. and Nenova, T. (2003) 'Going Informal: Benefits and Costs', in Belev, B. (ed.) *The Informal Economy in the EU Accession Countries*, Sofia: Center for the Study of Democracy, pp. 63–80.
Duncan, S. and Edwards, R. (1999) *Lone Mothers, Paid Work and Gendered Moral Rationalities*, Basingstoke: Palgrave Macmillan.
Duncan, S., Edwards, R., Reynolds, T. and Alldred, P. (2003) 'Motherhood, Paid Work and Partnering: Values and Theories', *Work, Employment and Society* 17(2): 309–30.
Ehrenreich, B. and Hochschild, A. R. (2003) *Global Woman: Nannies, Maids and Sex Workers in the New Economy*, London: Granta.
Einhorn, B. (1993) *Cinderella Goes to Market. Citizenship, Gender and Women's Movements in Central and Eastern Europe*, London: Verso.
European Commission (2007a) 'European Employment Observatory Review: Spring 2007'.
European Commission (2007b) 'Undeclared Work in the European Union: Report', Special Eurobarometer 284.
Fields, G. (1990) 'Labour Market Modelling and the Urban Informal Sector: Theory and Evidence', in Turnham, D., Salome, B. and Schwartz, A. (eds) *The Informal Sector Revisited*, Paris: OECD Development Centre.
Finch, J. and Mason, J. (1993) *Negotiating Family Responsibilities*, London: Tavistock / Routledge.
Folbre, N. (2008) *Valuing Children: Rethinking the Economics of the Family*, London: Harvard University Press.
Goven, J. (1993) 'Gender Politics in Hungary: Autonomy and Antifeminism', in Funk, N. and Mueller, M. (eds) *Gender Politics and Post-communism: Reflections from Eastern Europe and the former Soviet Union*, London: Routledge, pp. 224–40.
Graham, H. (1983) 'Caring: A Labour of Love', in Finch, J. and Groves, D. (eds) *A Labour of Love: Women, Work and Caring*, London: Routledge & Kegan Paul, pp. 13–30.
Hrzenjak, M. (2011) 'The Regulation of Paid Domestic Work: A Win–Win Situation or a Reproduction of Social Inequalities?', in Dahl, H. M., Keranen, M. and Kovalainen, A. (eds) *Europeanisation, Care and Gender*, Basingstoke: Palgrave Macmillan, pp. 59–74.
Hrzenjak, M. (2012) 'Hierarchisation and Segmentation of Informal Care Markets in Slovenia', *Social Politics* 19(1): 38–57.
Kremer, M. (2007) *How Welfare States Care: Culture, Gender and Parenting in Europe*, Amsterdam: Amsterdam University Press.
Lareau, A. (2011) *Unequal Childhoods: Class, Race and Family Life*, Berkeley: University of California Press.
Lister, R., Williams, F., Anttonen, A., Bussemaker, J., Gerhard, U., Heinen, J., Johansson, S., Leira, A., Siim, B., Tobio, C. and Gavanas, A. (2007) *Gendering Citizenship in Western Europe: New challenges for citizenship research in a cross-national context*, Bristol: Policy Press.
Magyari-Vincze, E. (2006) 'Romanian Gender Regimes and Women's Citizenship', in Lukic, J., Regulska, J. and Zavirsek, D. (eds) *Women and Citizenship in Central and Eastern Europe*, Aldershot: Ashgate, pp. 21–37.

Mungiu-Pippidi, A., Ioniță, S. and Mândruță, D. (2000) 'Social Costs of Economic Transformation in Central Europe: In the Shadow Economy', *SOCO Project Paper no. 80*, Vienna: IWM.
Neef, R. and Stănculescu, M. (eds.) (2002) *The Social Impact of Informal Economies in Eastern Europe*, Aldershot: Ashgate.
Parlevliet, J. and Xenogiani, T. (2008) 'Report on Informal Employment in Romania', *Working Paper no. 271*, OECD Development Centre.
Pfau-Effinger, B. (2009) 'Varieties of Undeclared Work in European Societies', *British Journal of Industrial Relations*, 47(1): 79–99.
Renooy, P., Ivarsson, S., van der Wusten-Gritsai, O. and Meijer, E. (2004) 'Undeclared Work in an Enlarged Union. An Analysis of Undeclared Work: An In-depth Study of Specific Items', European Commission.
Rose, R. (1994) 'Who Needs Social Protection in East Europe? A Constrained Empirical Analysis of Romania', in Ringen, S. and Wallace, C. (eds) *Societies in Transition: East–Central Europe Today*, vol. I, Aldershot: Avebury – CEU.
Silva, E. and Smart, C. (1999) 'The New Practices and Politics of Family Life', in Silva, E. and Smart, C., (eds) *The New Family?*, London: Sage, pp. 1–12.
Stănculescu, M. (2002) 'Romanian Households between State, Market and Informal Economies', in Neef, R. and Stănculescu, M. (eds) *The Social Impact of Informal Economies in Eastern Europe*, Aldershot: Ashgate, pp. 119–48.
Stănculescu, M. (2006) 'Informal Economy and Unregistered Work in Romania', paper presented at the *EU-ILO Project on Social Dialogue as a tool to address unregistered work in Turkey*.
Stănculescu, M., Stoiciu, V., Alexe, I. and Motoc, L. (2011) 'Impactul crizei economice asupra migrației forței de muncă românești', Bucharest: Friedrich Ebert Stiftung.
Verdery, K. (1996) *What was Socialism, and What Comes Next?*, Princeton: Princeton University Press.
Vincent, C. and Ball, S. J. (2001) 'A Market in Love? Choosing Pre-School Childcare', *British Educational Research Journal* 27(5): 633–51.
Wallace, C. (2002) 'Household Strategies: Their Conceptual Relevance and Analytical Scope in Social Research', *Sociology* 36(2): 275–92.
Waerness, K. (1984) 'The Rationality of Caring', *Economic and Industrial Democracy* 5(2): 185–211.

5 Drinking with Vova

An individual entrepreneur between illegality and informality

Abel Polese

'According to macro economic data we should all be dead.'
(Interview with school teacher, autumn 2005)

Prologue

The first time I met Vova, in April 2003, he was working as a taxi driver at night, earning €1–3 per fare, trying to recover from a long legal battle that had cost him his health, passport, property and several months of his life. However, seven years later in the summer of 2011, Vova took his wife, children and even grandchildren on an all-inclusive holiday to Turkey spending more than $3,000 for a week-long stay. How this was possible, and how he recovered from disgrace, is the main focus of this chapter.

Small, or even individual, entrepreneurs in Ukraine, a country of 48 million inhabitants, make up a large section of the national economy. The official figure is 1.3 million entrepreneurs registered officially, of which slightly more than 250,000 are in Kiev, 100,000 in Dnepropetrovsk and almost 95,000 in Donetsk (Ukrainian Statistical Committee 2011). Those figures give the number of small and medium business companies registered officially. If we move away from official accounts, *de facto* everyone is potentially a small-scale entrepreneur. On their way home, company employees pick up random passengers to boost their income; truck drivers on their off-days take a car and drive people around to secure extra cash; pensioners hide in some *podzemnyi perekhod* (subterranean underpass: an important urban site of informality in cold winter months) and sell garden-plot produce; officially unemployed people trade icons, repair computers for friends and acquaintances, work part time as 'fixers', translators without being registered and without, obviously, bringing any revenue to the state.

Unrecorded transactions occupy a large part of many economies, both in developed and developing countries (Feige 1990). In the case of post-socialist economies a dual attitude is observable: such transactions are condemned according to an official narrative but there is a tacit agreement that they may be tolerated, at least to a certain extent. This may well be the evolution of the *kompromat* practice (the collection of compromising material on individuals by authorities and employers), where everyone has something to hide and is therefore liable to manipulation by others on the basis of incriminating information. However, widespread informality may also reflect the social acceptability of practices outside the law. In this respect, it helps to refer to the matrix legal/illegal and licit/illicit (van Schendel and Abraham 2005), where what is illegal may still be licit (or socially acceptable) and what is legal might be illicit (not socially acceptable). What should be one's attitude towards a pensioner trying to sell pickled mushrooms or a sack of apples in the street? There is an official position of the state demanding the police crack down on these activites; however, policemen asked to go to *perekhody* and chase away all those 'illegal sellers' might find themselves in a very awkward situation when they consider that their grandparents might be doing the same thing somewhere else, or worse that they themselves might be selling apples in a few years, since state pensions do not secure survival in today's Ukraine (Polese 2010).

In previous studies on public workers the visible tension between the licit and the legal has systematically emerged. A doctor accepting an informal payment after visiting a patient is technically accepting a bribe. According to a generally accepted definition of corruption (the use of a public function for private gain), that person is corrupt. However, people in such situations might not automatically be classifiable as public workers (or 'hundred percent public workers', see Polese 2008) since, at least in theory, a public worker works for the state and receives sufficient compensation to live, which is not always the case in post-socialist spaces. Several studies have highlighted the social acceptability of certain practices (Humphrey 2002; Lonkila 1999; Morris 2011; Polese 2012; Williams and Round 2007; Williams *et al.* 2013). It has been suggested that the approach of international organizations should be adapted to local cases to ensure a less normative and more pragmatic approach (Morris and Polese 2014; Wanner 2005, Werner 2003).

This chapter is intended to illustrate practices on the boundary between legality and illegality in order to shed light on some of those engaging in diverse transactions. Challenging the vision of a 'culture of corruption' (Miller *et al.* 2001) and that 'no discount' should be applied to corrupt practices (Papava and Khaduri 2001), the starting question of this chapter is: what makes a practice 'corrupt' or illegal? In this respect I suggest the need to contextualize and de-normativize illegal practices, since they depend on both social and legal norms. From a juridical standpoint a law is a law, but the value and applicability of a law is ultimately decided by people in social practice. What if there is a law and the state is unable to enforce control or punish anyone because a substantial number of citizens do not follow it? There is a growing body of literature challenging the very significance of written law in a context where other rules may apply. For instance, Wanner has remarked how a new moral order may be applied to some spheres of Ukrainian life where the state's protection is felt to be lacking. How illicit or immoral is it to try to bribe a court if the same court is issuing an order on the basis of false evidence produced against you (Wanner 2005)?

The present chapter raises questions about the validity of international reports and policy analysis on Ukraine, and possibly on the rest of the former Soviet world, that see illegal practices only as a social evil to eradicate. This is the position of a number of strands of developmentalist thought which uncritically reject possible alternatives (Nederveen Pieterse 2006), positing that it is only a matter of time before transitional countries adopt a functioning neoliberal model. In contrast, it has been argued that monetary transactions do not encompass or adequately explain all economic activity – this is evident from the work of the growing school of diverse economies (Community Economies Collective 2001, Gibson-Graham 1996, 2008). In addition, economic 'effectiveness' might not mean the end of non-market oriented transactions (Williams 2005), which may also serve to partially challenge the de-personalisation of power relations in the labour market and the separation between the social and economic sphere predicted by Polanyi (1944 [1957]); see also Hann and Hart 2009). Empirical evidence has shown that 'success' may also be measured by satisfaction of spiritual obligations, activity in social life (Pardo 1996) and that even the meaning of money differs depending on the social and economic norms of a society (Parry and Bloch 1989).

When marketization is introduced into a country, as happened in post-1991 Ukraine, neoliberal ideas maintain that economic reforms will lead to more effective allocation of resources and, in the long run, remove dysfunctional elements that do not allow the economy to develop as it should. What happens if those reforms conflict not only with socially accepted norms but even involve an economic loss for one, or several, segments of a society?

When the costs of overt challenge to a regime, or simply a policy, are too high, it has been shown that people engage in a silent and unorganized resistance (Scott 1985) or swing between legality and extra-legality (de Soto 2002). The case presented here may be interpreted as nested within a practice that challenges a system that is hostile to a particular social category, in our case entrepreneurs. A set of alternative practices and unwritten rules are generated from the gap between 'how things should work' and 'how things work in practice'. Such practices are constantly changing and adapt to similarly changing social–legal conditions, but it is not possible to predict whether, and for how long they will continue. What may be said is that some of them are caused by the very rules and norms which seek to prevent or reduce them. It is by expecting too much from entrepreneurs that the state actually generates informal economic practices instead of preventing them. It is the sum of the state's unrealistic expectations and obligations that entrepreneurs have to fulfil that prompts informal economic practices to develop to a finely honed, complex degree, with companies existing purely to defraud the state and state workers who try to maximize their benefits in the absence of control.

What follows is an account put together during several years of fieldwork in Ukraine. It is the case of a single entrepreneur who survived the 1990s (the toughest period in the history of Ukrainian, and post-socialist, business) and went through several phases of social and economic disgrace and misfortune and then success. A single case study approach is not necessarily something novel, other scholars (Craciun 2009, Rivkin-Fish 2005) have used it in a short-hand, illustrative form of wider processes, and my argument would similarly be that 'by focusing the comparison on the way in which social interaction is constituted and channelled in different systems rather than on the institutional features of different societies, it is possible to ignore the question of scale in membership when constructing the dimensions for

88 *Abel Polese*

comparison' (Barth 1981: 133). This means that the following case study has been created mostly from the accounts of one informant, but that findings have been triangulated through interviews with other informants, across different spaces and longitudinally. This has then helped me to build up a picture arguably representative of the current situation of SME entrepreneurs in Ukraine. Material for this chapter was collected between 2003 and 2011, during which period I lived, taught and carried out research in Ukraine for more than four years. In 2008 I started devoting almost all of my research to informal economic practices, thanks to the financial support of the EU (Marie Curie IOF grant 219691). Living in the country gave me the chance to experience narratives of informality as well as witness firsthand situations, upon which I would then reflect with friends and colleagues from local universities and abroad. My main base has been Kiev and Odessa for some years; however, I also visited regularly a number of other cities (L'viv, Simferopol, Donetsk) and talked extensively with entrepreneurs. Material from other informants has served to better understand and clarify the case study I am presenting. Meeting entrepreneurs does not guarantee the collection of meaningful information. However, all those informants I have benefited from were people I have been meeting for years and who have helped me to gain an insight into their professional life and the micro-entrepreneurial situation of the country. Throughout I have chosen to keep the atmosphere informal and use only informal interviews. I have met my informants during, and especially after, their workday, chatted, eaten and drunk with them. As in similar anthropological scholarship my role may be questioned and my identity – who I was when interviewing them – can be subject to debate. I believe, however, that this has given me the chance to construct a picture that is sufficiently representative of the current situation of SME entrepreneurs in Ukraine.

The chapter is structured around 'Vova', a Ukrainian entrepreneur. Vova is, as in most cases in anthropology, a pseudonym I have used to anonymize my informants. It is also a name in Russia redolent of the 'everyman': 'Vova' is the main character of many jokes and anecdotes. I use it here to highlight the attitude most entrepreneurs have to acquire in the course of their life: use irony and take everything philosophically, otherwise you'll never make sense of the business environment in Ukraine. In the following sections Vova, the real 'author' of this chapter, speaks in the first person and the researcher's comments are only used to clarify and expand on the context. To avoid confusion, the sections that are direct comments by Vova have a [V] at the beginning and the researcher's, [P]. Each section results from a conversation on a different subject. I introduce Vova's vision on informality in the next one, whereas the following deal respectively with non-monetary exchanges, relationships with the authorities and tax regulation. The final part wraps-up the chapter and shows how Vova was capable of emerging from a difficult situation thanks to informal relations with other economic actors.

Learning the glossary

[V]You want to learn about the shadow economy (*tenevaia ekonomika*) and here it comes. Do you know what I need to do when I want to pay myself a bonus from the money my company has earned into my salary? In Ukraine income taxes can reach 90 per cent if you consider that they'll tax the source (the company) and the beneficiary (the employee) so that paying *po-chestnomu* (honestly) is not an option. What I do, and companies like mine do, is called *obnalichivanie* (cashing of capital) through a *firma babochka* (butterfly company). I call a fixer, in my case Konstantin (I am sure this is not his real name) and pay him an amount of money. He will keep 10 per cent and bill me for the money I gave him, so that I can claim those were necessary expenses for my company. He then gives me the 90 per cent in cash. The name *firma babochka* is due to the fact that they live very short lives, like a butterfly. In Ukraine companies have to fill a tax declaration every three months. Butterfly companies may exist between two tax declarations and declare bankruptcy or just disappear a few days before they are due their first tax declaration. Their employees and board will also disappear to reappear somewhere else, under different names and registration numbers, to continue doing the same business.

[P]Technically, there is little difference between the operation called *obnalichivanie* and what is investigated at the international level as money laundering. A main difference is that the money cleared may not be coming from illegal operations but from entrepreneurs who have earned their income relatively honestly and do not want to pay most of it in double taxation. Had Ukraine a more pragmatic attitude, and tax code, there would probably be less fiscal fraud and more legal financial operations. The lady from whom I normally buy biscuits in Kiev explained: 'I earn here 1,500–2,000 hryvnia per month (around €200 at the 2012 exchange rate), I have to pay for this stand 800 hryvnia and almost 1,000 hryvnia in taxes; if I follow the law I have to pay to stay in business.' This conversation emerged from her story of how she had gone to protest in front of the parliament with other entrepreneurs who, like her, are over 60 and in business because their state pension does not pay their bills.

It is possible to see a fundamental tension between what the Ukrainian state would like people to do and what they are capable of/necessitated in doing. The state sets the standards, too high to be respected, and then fails to apply the necessary control making most kinds of fiscal fraud inevitable, not to say desirable. Why? According to Vova there's a sort of constant *kompromat* pending on every single person in Ukraine. The authorities know that everyone has something to hide but will target only those they have an interest in. Those could be the richer ones, from whom they can get extra payments, the ones politically active that need to be silenced or quietened or for any other strategic reasons. This acknowledgement of the quasi-legality and contested nature of all state–citizen interactions, is not very far from the Soviet institution of *kompromat* that eased manipulation of political leaders and people in general. In a state with absurd rules every citizen is guilty but their guilt is 'discovered', or pulled out of the hat, only when that person becomes a burden to someone more important. In all other cases it is 'put on hold' or temporarily forgotten. Political analysts have suggested that (current president) Yanukovich had been chosen by president Kuchma as successor because his past made him easy to manipulate even when occupying the highest state position. In his work on state effectiveness Darth (2006) has maintained that a state can be effective even when based on blackmailing and constant silent threats in the parliament and administration, given that power is not shared formally but informally.

[V]Tax payments expectations are absolutely *nerealnye* ('unrealistic', alternatively: 'fantasy') in Ukraine. Some companies are registered in Panama, with which Ukraine has no double taxation agreement, but this is a trick that only richer companies can play. All the others have two options: if they are large enough and more exposed to state control such as Kyivstar (the main mobile telephone company in the country) they choose, and can afford, to follow the rules. They know that they are too profitable and should they fail to comply with something, state and tax officers would be on to them immediately. Otherwise everyone has to perform small (or less small) irregularities and in a sequence of little secrets, from the least to the most important person. They falsify an invoice for which someone will vouch for them, then this person will have to pay someone else to get 'covered' in an endless *kompromat* chain. This means that when tax inspectors come to you they can solicit money not to check your books thoroughly. Which would you prefer? Everyone has something to hide. Isn't it better to offer a present? They will have to share their extra payments with their superiors who, allegedly, know about their extra incomes and will demand a share to cover up for their irregularities. The system is not based necessarily on cash payments but also favours. For instance, policemen may be asked to provide their physical labour, either during working hours or during holiday, to build a dacha for their superiors. Bribery is thus a risky transaction for us. If you offer too little money, tax inspectors (but also policemen and all those dealing with cash payments) may decline your offer and take you to a court for attempted bribery. Obtaining a bribe has a cost for them and too little money is just not worth it. In this respect the nineties were much easier.

When I opened my first company our office was opposite a tax office. One day some people came and asked me to buy them mobile phones. I gave them the money and told them to go themselves to the shop but discovered they wanted the phones to be officially registered with my company, a thing that in the end I did. They also offered me a way out by saying that if I pointed the finger at a bigger company where they could demand more money they would leave me in peace.

[P]Fiscal legislation is perhaps the trickiest aspect of unregistered economic transactions among Ukrainian entrepreneurs as it opens a series of possibilities and raises a series of questions to which it might be impossible to respond. It has been suggested that honesty in tax matters is positively associated with incentives and negatively with control, at least in OECD countries (Bovi 2001). The better the controls and the higher the prize for diligent tax payers, the lower fiscal evasion. But in the Ukrainian case, as in many others, there is a gap between the official discourse and reality. Institutions are set up and work according to principles inspired by international organizations. Consultants from the IMF, the World Bank and other international institutions are paid thousands of dollars to instruct local tax inspectors and train them to higher standards. But are local tax inspectors and officers really interested in working effectively? Are they offered enough incentives to do so and are they liable if not? Why blame them if they see an easy gain and are pushed by their superiors to collect money and share it with people higher in their hierarchy? This is made particularly easy by the complex legislation and the high taxes that not many are able to pay. Everyone is potentially liable to be blackmailed, and the amount of money circulating between companies, butterfly companies, tax inspectors and state revenues is much higher than official figures show. I am not sure one can call it an alternative to capitalism but there is a system in place; it does not work in a way public finance experts would label as effective, but it has a logic, rules and dynamics that make it sustainable.

There is another consideration. Vova and many other people often refer to 'the system' as something put into place by civil servants or 'people from the authorities' to maximize their gain. It is of course natural that people see as conspiracy and design an arrangement that results in anarchy and a way out of it. However, it is more accurate to see this as the sum of micro actions, driven by individual interests and not contested, or only to a limited degree, by other forces.

Every stick has two ends (Russian saying)

[V]I do not know how to talk about *blat*. It is a good and bad thing at the same time. When I moved to a new flat I had to sign a contract with a gas supplier and this was extremely difficult, not to say impossible. I went to the company managing gas supplies and started swinging from one room to the other. Everywhere there was another document missing and waiting time for a simple installation would be more than six months. As an alternative I was shown that one could contact one of the companies whose contact numbers was on a board in a corridor.

I went to the board and selected the only company providing a land line phone (all the others gave a mobile number and one could not even be sure they existed). I called the number and an old Jew said that he was ready to assist me to get a contract. It turned out that he had worked in the gas company for several decades and knew everybody who counted, but also all the rules and exceptions. We met up, agreed on a sum, and I was shocked at how easy it then became to get a contract. All doors immediately opened. The fixer was a wise and reasonable man, who asked a reasonable price, found an exception to the rule (why I had to jump the queue) and knew whom to inform about the exception. Ever since, I have maintained contact with him and whenever there is an issue to be solved I know I can go to him.

[P]Giving favours in exchange for money may not technically be *blat* as it has been studied by other scholars (Humphrey 2002; Ledeneva 1998). However, one should also note the different role money has come to play in different times. Objects are what they come to be (Thomas 1991) and their meaning and significance changes depending on context (Parry and Bloch 1989). The significance of money and commodities has been changing since the end of the USSR, a culture of chocolate and cognac (Patico 2002) has given way to a widespread use of money and its perception as a commodity (Polese 2008). Money, in this case, is now used with a social function and can help establish a relationship, as other scholars have noted (Ledeneva 2006). For instance, one of my informants befriended her doctor thanks to the fact that the first two or three times she had paid extra money, a pattern that Rivkin-Fish has also observed in the Russian context (2009).

[V]The bad thing about *blat* is that it may be used foolishly. My IT specialist lives in Irpin (a small town outside Kiev) in a very big house. Once I went to his place and I was surprised by the amount of space he has at his disposal. He said he wanted to buy a car and asked for help to choose it. In the end he picked a very expensive jeep and bought it with cash. I asked him, 'how are you going to drive this car if you have no driving licence', and he replied, 'I can get one by *blat*', to which I said 'I'll be honest with you, I am very wary of people like you because driving around without having spent time learning is dangerous. I live far from here but I would be afraid to let my children go out on the street knowing that there are people like you who could drive irresponsibly.'

[P]Whilst this position is easy to understand, the other side of the story is also very telling. Vova's wife had to get a driving licence in 2009 in order to buy a car. She still had to pass the test but, once she went to take it, Vova made sure that a policemen he worked with sat next to her and 'helped her' with the answers. I am trying not to be judgemental here and will not discuss what is more serious or dangerous: getting a licence without even passing the test or passing the test with some assistance; my point here is that other people's irregularities are often perceived as more of a threat than our own. Vova could easily argue that he knows his wife, she is a responsible person and he knew that she would pass the test even without assistance but . . . one never knows. The IT specialist could easily argue the same: that he had been studying hard and simply had no time to take the test. What I am trying to highlight here is the additional amount of discretion or subjectiveness that *blat* allows. Informal practices give certain individuals, or most of them, if such practices are so widespread, an asset that other people do not have. A driving test is supposed to test if you are a danger to other citizens or not. Once you have the chance to judge by yourself this has many implications, for one thing it raises questions about the role of the state and its ability to protect citizens from themselves. The conception of a state moves away from a welfare model to a more Weberian sense or, in some cases, to a primitive society without the state. A state can be considered a state when it acts as such – it fulfils its functions (redistributes revenue, provides basic services), not when it simply calls itself a state (Polese 2007).

Social norms come to replace law when this is lacking or ineffective, regardless of the level of development. In a small community decisions are likely to be made on the basis of social and unwritten norms, but this is possible thanks to good informal control mechanisms. You know everyone and are responsible for your behaviour before everyone, a social restraint on action that does not apply in the anonymity of the city where flaws in the rule of law are not compensated by a social surveillance mechanism. This should not be seen as uniquely negative; there might be cases in which it is a blessing. In my previous research on smuggling between Ukraine and Moldova I suggested that illegal imports could be seen as an alternative to the monopoly some large entrepreneurs have imposed in order not to have competitors (Polese 2006), with the result of lowering choice and quality of goods available in certain markets. In places where bureaucracy or politicians prevent other people entering a market or have access to a good, informal practices are possibly the only alternative, as ultra-liberals maintain (Acemolu and Verdier 2000; Leff 1964), or the best we can do given the current conditions, as the rest of my conversations with Vova will show.

Squaring the circle: customs and excise

[V]Customs is the real racket of this country. There is no difference between before and after the 'Orange Revolution', no matter how Western or reform-oriented is our president. Customs was and will be one of the most corrupt places in Ukraine. There are too many interests and too much money involved; things simply cannot be done honestly there. Sometimes customs serve the interests of some parliamentary deputy, who has a company selling a good and does not want competition (especially from cheaper and better goods); in other cases it is just a matter of money, custom officers know you need what you are importing and will blackmail you or demand a share of your earnings. Ukrainian customs legislation is unintelligible to most and import duties are so high that they push you towards smuggling if you really need to import something.

When I started my business I needed some electronic parts that were not available in Ukraine. The cheapest supplier was based in Shenzhen, China and I ordered a sample piece to test it and ensure it would work as I expected. When I received the parcel I went to the customs to pay the duties. I was told that I would need three registration certificates to import such a type of good into Ukraine. My item had to be evaluated by a special commission that would decide on the amount of import duties to be paid. I was puzzled and asked if there was any way to make things faster since I only had one item and needed it urgently. They showed me a door and said '*idi i sam dogovarivaisia*' (go there and negotiate yourself [with the responsible officer]). I entered the office and explained the situation. Without changing his facial expression the civil servant wrote '$2,000' on a piece of paper. Two thousand dollars to import a single item, a sample version of a tool, into Ukraine . . . that was too much.

I sent the parcel back and started thinking of an alternative strategy. One item was already problematic. What would happen once I ordered a whole job lot when receiving them on time (and at a reasonable price) would be crucial to my company's survival? I looked further afield from Ukraine. Russia? Too similar, customs officers would make my life much worse in Moscow. Belarus? Romania? In the end I called the customs office in Chisinau, enquiring about import duties into Moldova. The answer was very simple, they said, 'We charge 10 per cent on any item, we do not care what you're doing with it or what kind of material it is as long as it is legal.' I could not believe my ears, things were so simple! I simply had to pay 10 per cent of the declared value (and it was still possible to ask the

Chinese partners to declare an amount lower than the real one). The next issue was to bring things into Ukraine.

But in Ukraine, as you know, we have *sviatoi gorod Odessa* (the holy city of Odessa), where everything is possible. I found out that I could arrange for someone to pick up the box in Chisinau and pay a minibus driver to bring it to Odessa. A local associate would go to the bus station, pick the box and bring it to the train station, where he could find a train inspector willing to take it to Kiev for a small amount of money. This, so far, is the 'easiest' solution I have found but I believe that there is no other way than accept the unwritten rules and smuggle if you want to survive as a small business entrepreneur, otherwise the cost of all transactions would be too high.

[P]According to the author's personal experience it is hard to challenge this statement. When living in Kiev and writing my PhD thesis I ordered €58-worth of books from France. A week later I got a phone call from customs asking to pay €62 in import duties. It was useless to explain that I was not getting any profit from the transaction, which might even advance scientific knowledge in and on the country. There were some rules, they said. In the end I decided not to collect the books that were then sent back so that I could get a refund. I re-ordered the same books but this time I got them delivered to a friend in Poland who 'smuggled' them across the border two weeks later.

[V]If I have to mention what is different from the nineties, perhaps we are less naive. True, in the nineties things were much easier and a registration or a permit could be obtained with a good bottle of cognac or offering foreign currency which almost guaranteed that any offer would be accepted. But the nineties were also much wilder an environment. My partner Kostia once told me 'if you know of someone carrying $50,000 or more just tell me. I'll kill him straight away and give you $10,000'. That same person once had his car stolen, a good Mercedes. The only person who might have had a spare key was his mechanic, to whom he immediately went. He pointed a gun at his leg and asked, 'where is my car', but the chap did not know; he asked again and after another negative answer Kostia fired. At this point I suggested 'maybe he really does not know for real where your car is', and his answer was 'I agree with you. I understood after firing that if he had known anything he'd have shared it with me, let's go now.'

The nineties were a period when such actions remained largely unpunished. Now also there is little punishment but at least you cannot kill someone in broad daylight and there is slightly more control. In this respect now it's better, in six years my company has never received any visits from tax inspectors, we are too small. In the nineties your size did not matter, if someone thought they could squeeze money out of you, albeit a little, they would come to you. But nowadays it is also harder to find an escape (a way out) if the law that applies to your company is more damaging than beneficial. No one will even accept a bottle in exchange for a favour. I paid a box of cognac bottles to register my first company but this is no longer possible. There is apparently more control and some partners told me that the price of *vziatki* (payments or bribes) has risen, civil servants are now afraid to take bribes and have introduced a 'risk tax'; they would say 'do you

Between illegality and informality 95

know how much I am risking by taking this money from you? This could be the last payment I receive so I will not risk for so little money, I want extra to cover the risk'.

'Victims or accomplices' (after Miller *et al.* 2000)

[V]I think a major mistake our government makes is to build *nerealnye ozhidaniia* [unrealistic expectations] with regards to tax revenue. They create an environment in which taxation is so high, and registration procedures so complex, that people simply cannot comply with them. I am sure a lower level of taxation would bring in much more income than the current system, which everyone is trying to defraud as much and any way they can. When I worked for SBS (fictive name for a major telecommunication company in Ukraine) my official salary was 600 hryvnia ($100), but I also received $700 in a white envelope every month. This is something many companies do. To have you employed they need to pay taxes but they will pay the minimal amount needed to keep someone on their books, providing tax-free (for them and for the worker) top-up payments (to produce the necessary clean cash they will use a butterfly company, issuing an invoice for things they never bought). It is almost impossible for someone to find a job in the private sector if you do not agree to such practice, even if it curtails your rights, and sometimes dignity, as a worker. When we had to get a mortgage to buy a property we had to use my wife's income, who has a public job and receives everything *po-chestnomu* (honestly). Another minus is that if they want to punish you or force you to leave they can simply decrease the amount of money in the white envelope. You cannot complain because you have no legal basis and have to either agree or leave. When working for SBS my line manager was an 'untouchable': a relative of the company's president and we had no way of challenging him. Our department's workers did not see a salary increase in years; my salary was still $800 when my contemporaries already received $1,000. Everybody knew he was one of the greediest individuals in the company and I suspect he was taking too much money for himself to allocate further funds for our salaries. I once discovered that he was marking up the price of imported items but nobody had ever bothered checking. He became incredibly wealthy due to this practice and nobody could utter a word since he was kind of protected, being related to the president. I think other people were aware of this but were too afraid of retaliation to do anything.

In some way he learned that I knew of his practices and became afraid of me. He never confronted me but one could sense the tension in our department. I never challenged him directly but he probably was aware that I had more initiative than other colleagues and looked for a way to get rid of me without making too much noise. The chance came when I went on holiday with my family for two weeks, the very next day he fired me for misconduct and ordered all my colleagues not to contact me. He knew that after two weeks the iron would be cold and it would be harder for me to raise any *skandal.* I got to know this because a colleague broke the embargo and phoned me, but calling the office would mean they would look for the employee who blew the whistle and I was not ready to betray anyone. In addition, I knew it would be very difficult to win my post back. Once back in Ukraine, I simply signed a resignation letter (in Ukraine, even if a worker is fired, he is still given the chance to resign himself so not to preclude further employment elsewhere).

[P]The statement about lower level of taxation that would bring more revenue would need to be discussed further, since few people would be happy to pay taxes at any level; it is also a matter of cost–benefits and control (see Bovi 2001). However, what is more important here is that the situation described is not simply a transaction or a practice; it is a whole system with its unwritten rules and codes. On paper everything is the way it should be, we have book keeping, tax declarations, inspections, controls, salaries and even official resignation letters. However, each of those words has a completely different meaning to those inside and outside the system. In the case of a naive foreign company getting information from official reports, they would see that from a legal point of view the Ukrainian business environment is immaculate and everything works according to the rules. They might frown when learning that most workers are on a $100 salary but that's what figures say and companies are audited and inspected by tax officers. However, it is not difficult to imagine the smile on the face of tax inspectors when they come and check a company employing people at $100 per month in Kiev, where a rental in the worst area is no less than $300.

The game companies and inspectors play is 'I know that you know that I know', and possibly a way to 'accommodate things' will be offered, when needed. To break any link in the chain of this circle is difficult, as it is equally difficult to understand what category is to be targeted first. Tax inspectors, as all public workers in Ukraine, have to survive on a meagre salary. Yet, working as tax inspector is a highly desired job and a number of positions may be bought for some thousands of dollars, especially in big cities. Companies that comply with all aspects of business law can be counted on the fingers of one hand, in all other cases a redistribution of the company income is not recorded on any books. This is a very convenient situation also for politicians, for any company could be shut down if needed; it would be sufficient to conduct a thorough check and it would not be a matter of whether there are irregularities but the extent of irregularities in a given firm. When a company becomes too important, too disruptive or dangerous for a business or sector already monopolized by other companies with connections in the government (or people in the government, given that 'conflict of interest' is an alien concept in the local parliament) it can be hindered or even shut down with relative ease.

It would be at least naive to see this situation from a conspiracy theory standpoint, as many locals opine when they trot out the formulae 'they are stealing' or 'they have set up such a system', assuming that there is a divine design by some high-placed people. This is the situation created by a sum of agencies (entrepreneurs, politicians, and ordinary people) and there is little to gain in understanding who started it. The system as it is works 'perfectly', although not necessarily democratically. It guarantees survival of its actors, redistribution of wealth and sustainability (should stakes change, demand and supply would adapt). A main feature is that it is short-term oriented, it is a carnival of short-term planning with workers, companies and tax inspectors trying to have their jam today because it is unclear what will happen tomorrow. In the end the amount of money paid in 'gifts', and the time spent on walking the tightrope between legality and illegality might be higher than the costs of staying legal in the long run (de Soto 2002), although in some cases to operate fully in legality might be impossible and few people have the time, or the capacity, to think long term as it is unclear what will happen tomorrow.

Epilogue

[P]Vova was not willing to fight to get his post back for various reasons, but possibly the main one was that while working in that company he had been able to register his own company and tap from his employer's network of clients to build up his own and start earning money on the side. Such contacts allowed him to earn enough money to pay for the holiday mentioned at the beginning of the chapter. The way all this happened is also very telling.

[V]One day I received an email; a major bank was asking if we could get some radio equipment fixed. I went to my line manager (the person who would later fire me) and proposed it. We had the knowledge and resources to get the equipment fixed cheaply and could earn a decent profit but he was uninterested; he was already earning more than he could spend just by marking up invoices. In the end I went through my contacts and learned that it was possible to buy spare parts very cheaply. I bought the radio equipment, got a friend to fix it and resold it for twice the price. The clients were happy and contacted me again in the following months, during which I built up my relationship; after a while they considered me a reliable person and a resourceful fixer, able to arrange things when needed. Thus, when after the umpteenth order I explained the situation the client was fine with such arrangements: I explained that I was doing all this on a personal basis, that my company was uninterested in all this but that I would provide the agreed service through another company (my own company that I had meanwhile registered). The manager on the other end of the phone agreed and proposed a deal: an exclusive cooperation between my own company and his bank. Whatever was needed in his department he would contact me in the first instance to provide the service. In exchange I had to mark up by 10 per cent whatever invoice we would issue and pay him out 10 per cent on every order. For me it was perfect, his *otkat* (cut) would not come from my money but from his bank's money and we rapidly increased the business turnover in the following months.

This relationship lasted two years. One evening, he called me to say that on 30 December (in Ukraine, the New Year is more important than Christmas as a holiday so this was a serious matter) he was be interrogated using a lie detector. He asked me to cover for him if I got a call from the bank. I thought it was all over, he was not going to lie at such an interrogation and they would ban my company for misconduct. The top managers of the bank were present and they would all know about me. On 4 January the manager was fired and I thought they would get to me at some point. Then a week later I got a phone call from the bank telling me that I had won the tender from the previous year and I was to come in and sign the agreement the next day.

I was puzzled; I did not know whether this was a trap, but went along anyway and was received in the vice director's room. I remember it was the penultimate floor (the floor at which an office is indicates the importance of a manager in the bank hierarchy, the penultimate floor is normally for the two vice directors) and I was welcomed by one of the vice directors with whom we signed an agreement that is still valid today.

I never got to learn what had happened nor was I able to speak with the manager after he had left the bank but I believe he was fired for other, and more serious, misconduct. He must have taken much more money from other sources so they did not bother to check up on me, because the amount of money we were dealing with was relatively insignificant.

Concluding remarks

How different is Vova's story from the story of thousands of Ukrainians? In my own experience, not much. Chronology, twists and turns of fate and other details may differ but the substance is the same. For a long time survival according to the rules of the game has not been possible for anyone in Ukraine. Or it is better to say that survival according to the *written* rules of the game is not possible and the reason is the extremely divergent dual system with regard to people's relations to rules and power that in Ukraine have been developing since Soviet times. Some years ago someone mentioned that in my home town, Napoli (Southern Italy), traffic lights do not give you orders but merely suggestions; that is, you are not obliged to follow the red and the green, but your relationship with the authority might improve if you do. Also, it was proposed that if you fastened your seat belts the police would stop you because such obliging people (in a place where no one does) might have something to hide. In Ukraine not only is it de facto impossible to comply with the dozens of written rules, often contradicting one another, it is also not expected and if you do so tax inspectors or even your peers will grow suspicious. How is it possible that this person is doing everything by the rules? He must be hiding something bigger.

In a continuation of Soviet logic, the state demands something that is not possible to achieve, or would starve people to death if achieved, and the people diligently pay only lip service to it. The gap between the official version, where everything is perfect, and what really happens is the real essence of the Ukrainian business environment and can be seen from two standpoints. One is what international organizations suggest and how things should be in order for the economy to work properly. They use nice terms such as good governance or transparency (Haller and Shore 2005) assuming that strategies that have worked elsewhere will work also in this case, which is not necessarily true (de Soto 2002). However, they neglect the importance that social norms and social capital may have even in industrialized countries. Often the models of governance proposed by international consultants are not even properly applied in their home countries in Europe or the US,[1] not to mention that the social consequences of such reforms are ignored. Who is going to trust an entrepreneur who has no secrets? Especially when everyone is under threat of *kompromat,* such a situation becomes a sort of identity, a thing that unites people. If money makes us relatives (White 1994), being on the verge of illegality generates a sense of solidarity, a collective identity, a position against the state that unites. The state, and in general higher authorities, are not seen as something protecting citizens but as something trying to rip them off, through high taxation, corrupt custom officers, low salaries. As a result, short- or long-term alliances are formed to limit damages, like in the case of the bank contact. For Vova this was a way out of his difficult situation and for the bank employee it was a stroke of luck to have found a reliable and goal-oriented person in what was usually a not-so-reliable environment. In a highly unstable environment, where current rules do not always allow contracts to be honoured since companies disappear and courts are overloaded with cases and judges can ultimately be bought, such alliances are particularly valuable and to be kept. In such an environment, human values, such as personal loyalty, count more than written laws and allow business to develop, things to be achieved and a 'normal' functioning of services.

In a functioning and effective state, entrepreneurs will behave better and in more 'civic' ways, but how long this will take is an unanswerable question. How long does this 'transition' need to last before one considers whether Ukraine is not simply aligning or converging onto 'the right path', but instead pointing towards a new direction with regards to the way governance is implemented and socio-economic life develops? If it lasts 'too long' that might not be a transition, but simply another system working whether 'properly' or not.

Note

1 I am grateful to Thomas Carothers for this remark (during the workshop The International Dimension of Political Party (System) Development, 14–15 November 2008, Amsterdam). I have found a similar argument in Sampson 2004.

References

Acemoglu, D. and Verdier, T. (2000) 'The Choice between Market Failure and Corruption', *American Economic Review* 90(1): 194–211.
Barth, Fredrik (1981) *Process and Form in Social Life*, London: Routledge & Kegan Paul.
Bovi, M. (2003) 'The Nature of the Underground Economy – Some Evidence from OECD Countries', *Journal for Institutional Innovation, Development & Transition* 7: 60–70.
Community Economies Collective. (2001) 'Imagining and Enacting Non-capitalist Futures', *Socialist Review* 28(3): 93–135.
Craciun, M. (2009) 'Trading in Fake Brands, Self Creating as an Individual', in Miller, D. (ed.) *Anthropology and the Individual*, Oxford: Berg, pp. 25–36.
Darth, K. (2006) 'The Integrity of Corrupt States: Graft as an Informal State Institution', *Politics and Society* 36(1): 35–60.

de Soto, H. (2002) *The Other Path: The Economic Answer to Terrorism*, New York:
Feige E. L. (1990) 'Defining and Estimating Underground and Informal Economies: The New Institutional Economics Approach', World Development, 18(7): 989–1002.
Gibson-Graham, J. K. (1996) *The End of Capitalism (As We Knew It): A Feminist Critique of Political Economy*, Minneapolis MN: University of Minnesota Press.
—— (2008) 'Diverse Economies: Performative Practices for "Other Worlds"', *Progress in Human Geography*, 32(5): 613–32.
Haller, D. and Shore, C. (eds) (2005) *Corruption: Anthropological Perspectives*, London: Pluto Press.
Hann, C. and Hart, K. (2009) *Market and Society: The Great Transformation Today*, Cambridge: Cambridge University Press.
Humphrey, C. (2002), *The Unmaking of Soviet Life: Everyday Economies after Socialism*, Ithaca, NY: Cornell University Press.
Ledeneva, A. (1998) *Russia's Economy of Favors: Blat, Networking and Informal Exchange*, Cambridge University Press.
—— (2006) *How Russia Really Works: The Informal Practices That Shaped Post-Soviet Politics and Business*, New York: Cornell University Press.
Leff, N. (1964) 'Economic Development through Bureaucratic Corruption', *American Behavioral Scientist* 8(8): 8–14.
Lonkila, M. (1997), 'Informal Exchange Relations in Post-Soviet Russia: A Comparative Perspective', *Sociological Research Online* 2(3). Online. Available: (accessed 31 March 2013).
Miller, W. L., Grodeland, A. B. and Koshechkina, T. Y. (2000) 'Victims or Accomplices? Extortion and bribery in Eastern Europe', in Ledeneva, A. and Kurkchiyan, M. (eds), *Economic Crime in Russia*, London: Kluwer Law International, pp. 113–28.
Morris, J. (2011) 'Socially Embedded Workers at the Nexus of Diverse Work in Russia: An Ethnography of Blue-Collar Informalization', *International Journal of Sociology and Social Policy* 31(11–12): 619–31.
Morris, J. and Polese, A. (2014) 'Informal Health and Education Sector Payments in Russian and Ukrainian Cities: Structuring Welfare from Below', *European Urban and Regional Studies*, forthcoming.
Nederveen Pieterse, J. (2006) *Development Theory*, London: Sage.
Papava, V. and Khaduri, N. (1997). 'On the Shadow Political Economy of the Post Communist Transformation, an Institutional Analysis', *Problems of Economic Transition* 40(6): 15–34.
Pardo, I. (1996) *Managing Existences in Naples: Morality, Action and Structure*, Cambridge: Cambridge University Press.
Parry, J. and Bloch, M. (eds) (1989) *Money and the Morality of Exchange*, Cambridge: Cambridge University Press.
Patico, J. (2002): 'Chocolate and Cognac: Gifts and the Recognition of Social Worlds in Post-Soviet Russia', *Ethnos* 67(3): 345–68.
Polanyi, K. (1957) *The Great Transformation*, Boston, MA: Beacon Press.
Polese, A. (2006) 'Border Crossing as a Daily Strategy of Post Soviet Survival: the Odessa-Chisinau Elektrichka', *Eastern European Anthropology Review* 24(1): 28–37.
—— (2007) 'Ukraine: the State is Public, the Private Sector is Private, the Public Sector is . . . ?', Workshop Paper on Property in Eastern Europe, New European College, Bucharest 14–15 June.
—— (2008) '"If I Receive it, it is a Gift; if I Demand it, then it is a Bribe"' on the Local Meaning of Economic Transactions in Post-soviet Ukraine', *Anthropology in Action* 15(3): 47–60.

—— (2010) 'At the Origins of Informal Economies: Some Evidence from Ukraine (1991–2009)', Working Paper, Friedrich Schiller University of Jena.

—— (2012) 'Who Has the Right to Forbid and Who to Trade? Making Sense of Illegality on the Polish-Ukrainian Border' in Bruns, B. and Miggelbrink, J. (eds), *Subverting Borders: Doing Research on Smuggling and Small-Scale Trade*, Leipzig: VS Verlag, pp. 21–38.

Prato, G. (2006) 'The Devil is not as Wicked as People Believe, Neither is the Albanian: Corruption between Moral Discourses and National Identity', in Pardo, I. and Prato, G. *Between Morality and the Law: Corruption, Anthropology and Comparative Society*, Aldershot: Ashgate.

Rivkin-Fish, M. (2005) 'Bribes, Gifts and Unofficial Payments: Rethinking Corruption in Post-Soviet Health Care', in Haller, D. and Shore, C. (eds), *Corruption: Anthropological Perspectives*, London: Pluto Press, pp. 47–65.

—— (2009) 'Tracing Landscapes of the Past in Class Subjectivity: Practices of Memory and Distinction in Marketizing Russia', *American Ethnologist* 36(1): 79–95.

Sampson, S. (2004) Too Much Civil Society? Donor-Driven Human Rights NGOs in the Balkans in Dhundale, L. and Andersen, E., Revisiting the Role of Civil Society in the Promotion of Human Rights, Copenhagen: Danish Institute for Human Rights, 197–220.

Scott, J. (1985) *Weapons of the Weak: Everyday Forms of Peasant Resistance*, New Haven and London: Yale University Press.

Thomas, N. (1991), *Entangled Objects: Exchange, Material Culture, and Colonialism in the Pacific* (Cambridge, MA: Harvard University Press).

Ukrainian Statistical Committee (2011). Online. Available: <http://www.gorstat.kiev.ua/p.php3?c=953&lang=1> (accessed 11 March 2013).

van Schendel, W. and Abraham, I. (2005) 'Introduction: The Making of Illicitness', in van Schendel, W. and Abraham, I. (eds), *Illicit Flows and Criminal Things: States, Borders, and the Other Side of Globalization*, Bloomington: Indiana University Press, pp. 1–37.

Wanner, C. (2005) 'Money, Morality and New Forms of Exchange in Postsocialist Ukraine', *Ethnos* 70(4): 515–37.

Werner, C. A. (2002) 'Gifts, Bribes and Development in Post-Soviet Kazakhstan', in Cohen, J. H. and Dannhaeuser, N. (eds) *Economic Development: an Anthropological Approach* (Walnut Creek, Lanham, New York and Oxford: Altamira Press), pp. 183–208.

White, J. B. (2004) *Money Makes us Relatives; Women's Labor in Urban Turkey*, London and New York: Routledge.

Williams, C. (2005) *A Commodified World? Mapping the Limits of Capitalism*, London: Zed.

Williams, C. and J. Round (2007) 'Re-thinking the Nature of the Informal Economy: Some Lessons from Ukraine', *International Journal of Urban and Regional Research* 31(2): 425–41.

Williams, C. J. Round and P. Rodgers (2013) *The Role of Informal Economies in the Post-Soviet World*, London and New York: Routledge.

6 When is an illicit taxi driver more than a taxi driver?

Case studies from transit and trucking in post-socialist Slovakia

David Karjanen

Introduction and overview

I begin this chapter with an anecdote from past fieldwork in Slovakia in 1999. An informant living a few blocks away and I had the following exchange over an espresso: 'David, if you want to understand the economy, you should talk to my friend, Peter.' I asked, 'Who's Peter, an economist?' 'No,' he replied. I asked again, 'Oh is he an academic or an official?' His reply: 'no, no, (shaking his head), much more important, he drives a taxi.' Eventually, Peter did become extremely useful to me as a taxi driver, but he was far more valuable as a window into the operations of informal economic exchange. His cab, for instance, ferries everything from contraband cigarettes to people needing medical care at the regional polyclinic, and all done as an unregistered business, paid for in cash. In short, Peter, along with his old beat up Škoda Favorit, is a vital node in the movement of people, goods, and services from various points within a spectrum of informal and formal economic activities. The aim of this chapter is to explore the operations of informal work and its relationship to economic restructuring, drawing on case studies in the transportation and trucking/logistics industries as a way to re-examine the persistence of informal practices in the post-socialist Slovak economy.

In this chapter I look at three case studies in two industries: transportation and shipping/logistics. The transportation industry includes informal taxi drivers, while shipping and logistics includes truckers, warehouses, and related occupations. The main distinction between the two industries is what they move. Transportation firms move people, while shipping and logistics firms move and warehouse goods, generally speaking.

The research discussed here was conducted in Slovakia from 1995–2007, and included both surveys and ethnographic studies of economic practices during the transformation from state socialism. This chapter draws specifically on case studies of specific firms within these two industries. Although there is good anecdotal evidence to suggest that these are typical for the broader Slovak economy, there are no surveys large enough to determine the extent of these practices in specific industries like trucking/logistics and transportation precisely.

The chapter is organized into the following sections. The first part of this chapter discusses the theoretical issues surrounding informal work and its relationship to the formal economy. In the next section, I look at the context of Slovakia's economy and the emergence of the informal economy in the post-socialist context. In the third section, I present case studies of informal work and forms of informal exchange, including exchanges dependent on kinship ties and those involving bribery in the context of the transportation and logistics industry. I conclude with a theoretical discussion and some observations on the future of informal sector research, particularly in the post-socialist context. My broad aim is to explore what theoretical issues informal exchange in these case studies brings out, particularly related to how we understand different distinctions of exchange, such as gifts versus purely economic transactions, or in some settings bribery versus gift exchange, and also kinship based exchange versus gift exchange.

The 'grey economy?'

Since independence in 1992, the Slovak economy has undergone different periods of economic restructuring, ranging from economic contraction, stagnation, and sporadic periods of growth. Consistent with the dissolution of the centrally managed economy, however, are long-term trends of economic dislocation and regional disparities in economic outcomes. Most importantly, the twin problems of rising unemployment and poverty have changed the economic decision-making practices of households and individuals, but also opened up new spaces for entrepreneurialism.

As state-owned enterprises were privatized or simply dissolved, rising unemployment has characterized much of the labour market since the mid-1990s, peaking at around 20 per cent, and then dropping to below 10 per cent, but rising to 13 per cent in 2010. The reliance of smaller municipalities on a single large-scale state enterprise for the bulk of employment has been particularly problematic. In several towns where this research was conducted, unemployment stood at nearly 45 per cent in the late 1990s and persisted often through to 2006. This reflects a broader uneven development of the regional economies in Slovakia (Smith 1998), wherein different regions, often tied to different industries, are moving in different directions out of the socialist economy.

Informal and illicit trade has emerged as part and parcel of the economic transition from state socialism. During the postwar period, varying degrees of unofficial economic activity occurred in Czechoslovakia. Data on the 'second economy' or 'black market' were not systematically kept, nor are available data (official statistics) typically considered accurate enough to derive stable estimates of the informal economy prior to 1992. Only scant data are available for the 1960s and 1970s, showing that a very small percentage (two per cent) of work occurred outside 'official' employment in the non-agricultural sector (Adam 1984). By the 1970s shortages of major consumer goods, and high-cost items such as cars and housing were not meeting demand, spurring increased second-economy activity to supply them (Korda 1973). Estimates vary during this period, but World Bank figures put the 'grey' or 'second economy' at 6 per cent of Gross Domestic Product (GDP) in Czechoslovakia in 1989 (Kaufman and Kalibera 1996). By 1993, estimates of the informal economy in Slovakia were 15.1 per cent, and by 2005, 18.2 per cent of GDP respectively (Kaufman and Kalibera 1996). Other estimates, however, using a similarly conservative currency demand model, put the informal economy of Slovakia at approximately 18.9 per cent of GDP in 2000 (Schneider 2002). In terms of employment, the estimates for informal sector jobs show significant growth. In 1995 informal sector employment was estimated at 17.4 per cent of total employment, increasing in 1996 to 19.2 per cent, in 1997 to 23.1 per cent, then dropping slightly in 1998 to 21.8 per cent (ILO 2003: 268). In a different set of estimates from the Slovak Statistical Office (2011) undocumented household expenditures have been estimated in billions of Slovak Koruna from 1996–2007. The overall trend in these data is a general increase, particularly for health services, rented housing, service sector tips, and bribes in health services, with an estimated 26 billion SKK paid in 1997 rising to 34 billion SKK in 2007. Unfortunately there are no data for specific industries or occupations such as trucking/logistics or transport. In sum, the trends show both informal economic activity and employment increasing in the wake of state socialism's collapse.

Why trucking/logistics and transport industries?

I have often told graduate students preparing for fieldwork that one of their best informants may turn out to be a taxi driver. Taxi drivers are often some of the first people one encounters when arriving in a new country, they often speak some English, they know their way around a city, and most importantly, from a research point of view, they know about the local and regional movement of people; everyone from businessmen and women to tourists, government officials, and prostitutes rely on taxi cabs, not to mention the use by the general public. Knowing about the movement of people from place to place, and what they may be doing there, provides a unique set of insights into the daily operations of an economy. The same holds true for truck drivers; they have an enormous wealth of knowledge about the economy from a vantage point which most researchers never access. Alvarez (2005) is a notable exception and illustrates how useful the perspective of truck driving can be to understand both regional and transnational processes.

Trucking and logistics became a large area for informal entrepreneurial activity in the post-socialist context for several reasons. First, there was dearth of private sector transportation companies after the collapse of the state-managed economy. Firms trying to get goods and services either to or from markets faced a limited range of options. New firms which were operating legally with the required licences and trained truck drivers were charging high prices. In this environment, some firms decided to move their own goods. Manufacturers provided their own trucking support, and small, often family-run businesses used their own private vehicles to move goods.

This is in part a reflection of lower rates of car ownership and registered commercial vehicles in Slovakia. Car ownership has risen by nearly 70 per cent since 1990, from 163 per 1,000 population to an estimated 287 per 1,000 population in 2010, which is still far below the rates for Western Europe and most industrialized countries (which are typically three to four times higher) (EIU 2012). Similarly, for commercial vehicles, although there has been an increase, total registrations of new (light and heavy) commercial vehicles in 2008 were 32,300, 10 per cent higher than in 2007, but still below the averages in Western Europe (EIU 2012).

A second reason that trucking and logistics was a growth area for informal work is the nature of market entry. Very little training, expertise, technical equipment, permits, or capital is needed to start a trucking or taxi company. All one needs is a reliable vehicle, mobile phone, and the ability to read a road map. Indeed, many small start-ups in Slovakia during Slovakia's economic transformation have relied on personal equipment, vehicles, and other resources to operate.

An additional reason for the growth of informal work in this industry is the location of transportation and logistics in relation to other growing sectors. Transportation workers are by definition at the intersection of numerous firms. For those workers who are ambitious, entrepreneurial, or who have an interest in earning additional income, informal work in transportation and logistics provides numerous opportunities. This is in part due to the lack of oversight on the part of state authorities, as well as the legal parameters governing the shipment of goods within the country (international shipments are, of course, subject to far greater scrutiny, costs, and regulations). Thus, as the case studies in this chapter shows, the ability of delivery drivers to foster not only relations between themselves and new clients but also between clients contributes to a growing informal network of economic activity. These networks can often expand along with the transportation and logistics businesses, sprouting parallel businesses. This I refer to not as 'marketization from below', but rather 'marketization from within', because the economic activities are not street-based 'penny capitalism' as is seen in many parts of the developing world, but rather are embedded within the very formalized institutions and practices of the economic transformation from state socialism to a market-driven economy.

Informal exchange in trucking and logistics

How does the trucking/logistics industry rely on informal economic practices? My first case study illustrates the complexity and range of informal exchange and relations within this industry. As we see with the Petrov warehousing and logistics firm, informalization is in part a response to the rapidly changing market conditions they experience.

Truck driving has changing periods of demand. The Petrov Company relies on additional drivers hired and paid in cash during the peak hauling season for produce from farmers, as well as during periods when they have unusually high volume demand. One summer, for instance, construction materials and concrete product movers were running short of carriers. The Petrov Company was called to assist a number of companies on a large construction project. As subcontractors, the Petrovs were largely able to set their own business practices as long as they delivered materials on time. To meet this additional demand, they hired two extra drivers for a short-term period, all paid in cash, and without any labour contract.

These workers were truck drivers for other firms, but 'moonlighted' and worked on weekends for the Petrov firm while the construction demand was high.

This arrangement, in turn, has generated new exchange relationships. One of the firms providing a driver has negotiated with the Petrov firm for a shared labour arrangement. Even though they are competitors, the Branov trucking company, which deals mostly with construction materials, waste, and debris hauling, negotiates with the Petrov firm for the movement of drivers between them. When one firm is short of drivers, they call the other firm and vice versa. This system of labour sharing provides limited benefits when demand is slack, but the arrangement has many benefits during peak periods both for the firm and the drivers. For drivers, this gives them the opportunity to work more hours, if they choose to do so, and for firms it provides them with an immediate, trained, trustworthy, cash-paid source of commercial vehicle driver. In essence, these firms have bypassed the labour intermediary of a temporary employment agency in order to share labour with each other, even though they are competitors.

The reason this works is that both firms occupy different market segments within trucking and logistics. Petrov deals mostly with agricultural products and consumer goods, while Branov largely transports construction materials and waste. In a way, this flexible labour-sharing agreement gives both firms an advantage over their nearest rivals within the trucking and logistics market. Of course, all of these relations are completely based on trust, social ties built over time, and are not reported to the state as labour. This saves money for both the employee and firm in taxes and human resource costs as well. In sum, this is an informal relationship, 'off the books' within the very formal practices of two legitimate firms.

It is not just labour that is shared within and between firms, however; it is also equipment, such as forklifts and trucks, and warehouse space. Once again, the movement of these economic resources within the formal sector is entirely informal, and outside of the view of any state regulation. In the case of trucks being used informally, this occurs mostly among drivers. The illustrative case in the Petrov firm is a driver named Istvan, who also has ambitions of owning his own trucking and moving firm some day. He began taking one of the smaller trucks home, typically an Iveco flatbed or cabin truck, to do odd jobs back in his hometown or in nearby towns. Along with his brother, Ivan, they have a nascent moving business, all paid for in cash. They have moved entire flats, automobile engines, artwork, and in one instance, a dozen pigeons in boxes. This moving business is too small to merit Istvan investing in his own truck, and he earns about an extra €100–200 per month doing the work, but the ability to use his employer's truck for the work makes this possible. The employer is not being entirely altruistic, however;, he nets a €35 fee each time Istvan uses the truck. If anything should happen to the vehicle, the company insurance covers the damage, a premium increase to be paid by Istvan if it occurs.

In addition to renting out transport on a cash-by-use basis to employees, some companies also rent out warehouse space, sometimes to employees, and sometimes to other firms. Again, the presence of these types of arrangements depends in part on supply and demand and an extant system of trust and reciprocity which exists between the firms and the firms or individuals renting the space. As a result, the Petrov Company has a warehouse wherein three other firms are actually doing business. The insurance companies would not permit such an arrangement unless there were higher premiums, but the Petrovs and their lessees prefer not to pay the higher premiums and instead take the shared risk if there is a fire or other loss.

In another case, the Skanda Company also relies on informal ties to ensure the smooth operations and profitability of different aspects of its operations. The Skanda logistics and transportation operations began in the garage of the family-owned firm. As their business expanded, the company decided to lease warehouse space from another company in town which had a relatively empty warehouse. By leasing part of this warehouse from the other company, the Skanda firm saved a significantly higher amount of money than it would leasing on its own, but it also built critical ties with a larger firm from which it could then develop new commercial ventures.

A mobile phone accessories company, Unitel, and the trucking company, Skanda, increased revenues simply by their proximity and shared space. One of the advantages of the proximity of the two firms was in billing shipping charges to customers. The Unitel firm charged a fee to send the good to Skanda, adding this to the total shipping fee. In reality, all this entailed was pushing a dolly with a pallet of products a few metres across the warehouse floor. As a distributor for Unitel, Skanda was able to take advantage of the proximity of its warehouse (within the same building).

The transportation industry: taxi drivers

One of the more striking conversations I had when surveying Bratislava and Dunajska-Streda area residents about their jobs was how many owned taxi companies. In one day I met nearly half a dozen men in their thirties and forties who owned their own cab company. When I asked how many employees they had, each answered 'one, me'. These sole proprietorships have emerged as part of the growth in the transportation industry, and it is at the smaller, family run or single-owner taxi company where much of the informal work and exchange occurs (see also Morris's chapter in this volume and Morris 2012).

So called 'gypsy cabs' are a world-wide phenomenon, even in New York City, where the number of informal cabs outnumbers the registered by two to one (Sassen 1988). The reasons for the development and persistence of these economic practices are multiple. First, as in the case with other industries, informal networks and cooperative or mutual aid relations in the socialist period have been expanded in the post-socialist one. For instance, having a car during socialism was often a luxury, very expensive to maintain; those who had access to a vehicle had a means to barter for other services or goods. It would, in fact, be quite surprising if such a set of exchange relationships in the post-socialist context did not continue; the difference now, however, is that such relations are increasingly commoditized. The second reason for the continued development of informal transit operations is the growth in the vehicle ownership rate and access to capital among a far larger portion of the population than during socialism. In short, the barriers to market entry have dropped substantially for operating home-based taxi companies, just as for trucking and logistics businesses. Third, this is a type of industry which is amenable to small-scale, sole proprietorships, and therefore is often outside of the purview of state regulation and oversight.

Finally, there is market demand. Registered cabs only work in larger, urban areas, and the public transit system is not adequate for residents, particularly in rural areas and small towns. While it is impossible to provide any quantification of the market demand for informal taxi rides in Slovakia, some examples of the need in smaller towns suggests that the demand is particularly great. For example, many elderly residents in small towns who require medical care depend on informal taxi companies to shuttle them to and from health clinics or hospitals.

In one such case, an elderly pensioner in a small town in the Dunajska-Streda district needed to get to the local polyclinic for continuing treatment. She had been at the polyclinic several weeks before for testing, but received a phone call stating that more tests had been ordered because the results were indicative of a potentially serious heart condition. This was not an emergency, but urgent enough for her to call for an informal taxi and pay the fare to get the tests done rather than wait for her daughter to arrive home from work and take her in her car. Renata described how 'her' taxi driver has driven her and so many of her residents in a small block of apartments, who were also largely pensioners, that they are on a first name basis, and now received a 'discount' for trips to the hospital. Renata's cab driver, Karol, has been working as a taxi driver 'off the books' for several years, and provides fares based generally on three tiers: in town, across town, and further than town. He splits these fares into equal categories, except out of town trips are by distance, but for elderly trips to the clinic or hospital the fee is reduced, as it is for families with small children. What Karol's customers get by being ferried in his four door Škoda wagon is a personalized service, at a lower cost than the registered cabs which would have to drive down from Bratislava or Dunajska-Streda. In this case, it is often difficult to discern whether or not this is a purely commercial transaction or a form moderated by considerations of mutual aid.

Theoretically the issues here are problematic: is this economic exchange or a gift economy? Or is it something combining both which forces us to rethink the social processes and relations of exchange and their relation to informality. This is, indeed, the recurrent theme of these case studies: forms of exchange which blur the boundaries of conventional rational economic models. In the case of transportation services, family members typically provide rides, which are often compensated, again blurring the lines between profit-driven and non-profit-driven enterprises and exchange.

Another theoretical question informal transit raises is, why this particular industry? The obvious answer is that during state socialism public transit sufficed to a certain extent, but with the development of the market economy informal market opportunities have made the increasingly costly and less efficient public transit system inadequate for many residents who need to travel. There are two other answers to this question, however. The first is that transit itself has become critical in the post-socialist economy precisely because mobility has become more important. Internal migration alone has shifted large numbers of Slovak residents, families have relocated, industries have restructured, labour market flexibility has been introduced, and these new conditions demand greater spatial mobility. The second reason for transit emerging as such a widespread informal area of exchange is sociality. Sharing a ride with someone, or paying someone for a ride on a regular basis, is in part a means of developing social ties across socioeconomic and spatial lines. The taxi driver, Peter, for instance, is in effect a central node in a large social network. He even helps connect business people to potential partners.

Kin-based informal exchange

How do informal social structures and relations of kinship influence informal economic activity in the post-socialist context? The role of kinship in informal economic relations is often critical, as informal exchange often relies on non-contractual but binding relationships, and kinship is the basis of many of these (Roberts 1994). The availability of trustworthy personal relations, consequently, is often vital to the economic success of informal enterprise. Enterprises rely heavily on kin or co-ethnics for their labour force and on informal social networks of clients, suppliers and bankers, rather than on contracts, in organizing their economic activities (Bailey and Waldinger, 1991; Portes and Stepick 1993). Also, for those with more limited capital, expertise, or other resources, strong kinship ties can substitute, providing greater entrepreneurial or informal work opportunities (Waldinger 1986; Waldinger and Ward 1990).

In the case of post-socialist Slovakia, kinship serves multiple purposes in relation to informal economic exchange. First and foremost, kinship is, as other scholars point out, an organizing structure of non-contractual relations which serve to undergird a more formal economic enterprise (see Chapter 10 in this volume). Of course, organized crime families are an infamous and well-discussed example of this, but the operations I discuss here are not organized criminal operations. Instead, kinship is used as a set of social bonds to foster more flexible economic exchanges, avoid state oversight, and increase profits.

The ways that informal exchange operates across kinship lines varies. The best case is the Bartos family which has a son in the trucking industry, as discussed above. In this case, the son has access to trucks and goods through distributors, and access to side-door businesses through family. Conceptually, he is a node within a socioeconomic network which is overlaid by kinship lines. His brother also works for the logistics company, and an uncle runs a firm which ships with the logistics firm. What occurs throughout the operations of these firms is a form of mutual reciprocity based on informal kin relations which supports the formal economic relations of the firms. For instance, if Ivan is making deliveries between family members, he often takes small packages or loads of goods from kin to kin, but uses the lorry from work. He earns cash in hand for this type of delivery, and also builds goodwill between the firms and himself. This type of informal delivery may be infrequent, but it provides direct cash profit for him, allows him to reinforce social ties, and paves the way for future work between the firms for himself. Another type of exchange which moves along kin lines and informal ties, but also in relation to formal economic practices, is the transfer of goods between firms based on kin relations.

Also, kinship allows for the growth of mutual trust. This is critical in informal economic exchange, particularly with regard to payments and finance. The best example of this is the relationship between the Bartos trucking company and an in-law's advertising agency. Monika, the owner of the agency, provided the Bartos Company with two calendar years' worth of advertising materials, including design, printing and contracting out for other marketing materials such as pens and calendars. Like many family-based transactions, the specific payment details were all made orally; no contract was drawn up as she agreed to do this over the phone and never sent a formal contract to sign prior to the work being done. When she did send a bill, Gyos, head of the Bartos trucking firm, said that the cost was too high. After negotiating the price, Gyos agreed to pay Monika for her work, but only for the products already provided – as some of the items, like holiday flyers and other materials were not going to be provided until later that year. He did not want to pay for things 'up front'. Monika agreed, but only if there was a good faith statement on his part that if he liked the work he would sign a more formal contract for future years' work, guaranteeing her a steady business in the future. Gyos agreed, and a payment schedule, with some flexibility, was set up for the advertising campaign. Of course this entire process could have been avoided if a bill and sales agreement was drawn up at the beginning, but the critical point here is that the negotiation process and payment schedule (and there was a need to re-negotiate after a drop off in the Bartos business about mid-year), would not have been possible without the mutual trust of the kinship relations between Gyos and Monika: they are cousins.

Finally, there is the movement and circulation of labour along kinship lines both within and across firms. The Petrov logistics company is a case and point. It handles regional- and occasionally national-level shipping and distribution for a number of companies in the Bratislava area. Many of these companies have highly fluctuating shipping needs depending on the time of year: they are seasonal firms. One company may sell camping equipment, which usually ships in the early spring and in the late summer, the rest of the year is rather light, another company ships crates of processed apple products – juice, apple sauce, cider, and so on, and these ship after the fall harvest has come in. And of course, certain holiday periods are particularly busy. As a small firm, the Petrov Company has only three people working in its warehouse, and four truck drivers handling deliveries. When high volume periods come, however, these figures double or triple, and most of the new employees are family. In the spring and fall, very busy periods, two brothers of the company director come to help. One works in construction and drives the company forklift, another works in accounting and helps manage the office work, while several cousins and nieces and even gymnasium-level students who are friends of the nieces and nephews all help out for a week or two to earn extra money. This type of labour employment arrangement may or may not be legal, depending on the circumstances (Slovak labour law requires that all employees are registered and appropriate taxes and benefits paid), but cash-in-hand work for mutual aid or payment for labour may fall outside of this depending on how one actually interprets the law). As an informal process, this response by kinship systems supports a highly flexible labour market arrangement: it allows firms to keep staffing low, increasing at times of higher demand, and paying below market rates for the short-term labour.

We might consider that Mauss's (1954) classic distinction between gifts, which aim to foster social relations, and commodities, which exchange for money. Blurring the two are informal exchanges, like *blat*, and many forms of social relations within formal exchange systems, such as kinship-based hiring, which blend the two forms of exchange together. In the post-socialist case, these conditions emerge widely, and force us to rethink both the transition 'towards' a purported 'market driven' economy in which we supposedly see informal practices and exchange vanish, as well as the fundamental distinctions more broadly in systems of exchange, whether formal or informal. What we see from emergent and transforming exchange practices in post-socialist Slovakia, like the rest of the region, is not neatly bounded within a single or dualistic moral framework. Rather, I would argue that there are multiple, often competing moral and economic forces at work at each point of exchange.

Bribery in the trucking and logistics and transportation sectors

Bribery (*uplatok*) is far more prevalent in Slovakia than in Western Europe. Overall, one in four have paid bribes in Slovakia, whereas the average in Western European countries is one in 16. In the case of businesses, data are not clear, but nearly 40 per cent of Slovaks say that businessmen are the most corrupt, followed by public officials. In any event, it is clear that informal payments are seen to be central to how the private sector operates in Slovakia.

One of the concerns I have in thinking through bribery in the Slovak case is that the general category of *uplatok* is far too homogenizing. There are both qualitative and quantitative differences in the ways that payments which may be technically illegal occur. Bribes by consumers to get goods and services are one thing, bribes by investment firms are another (as was recently found out in a political scandal ensnaring large numbers of prominent Slovak politicians). Payments in this study are restricted to payments during business transactions. In this case I am referring only to payments between and among firms, not between firms and customers. The reasons for payments which are made on a cash basis are varied in the transportation and logistics industry. Among drivers there are numerous opportunities to receive cash payments. Sometimes it is for meeting a delivery timetable or looking the other way when filling bills of lading. In some cases drivers will demand payments to 'look the other way' regarding the transit of goods which have not paid the proper taxes, are contraband, or are otherwise illicit.

There is also evidence of widespread payments to officials. While I never witnessed bribes paid, all the firms in this study report having paid some form of bribe to an official. These payments varied from very small, to up to €100. These payments were made for a variety of reasons. On the small end, there are payments simply to 'speed up' the bureaucratic process. For instance, the Petrov Company, in making modifications to its warehouse, had to obtain several permits for construction and property line verification. The company was initially told it would take several weeks to several months to get the permits, losing valuable time in expansion. For a small fee paid in cash, however, they were told that the process could be prioritized for their permits, and they could then get the paperwork approved in as little as one week. They paid the fee (approximately €30) and got the paperwork in ten days. In the case of unlicensed taxi cabs, the most frequent fee is simply for police for avoiding tickets and potential arrest for unlicensed transport businesses. Other fees are paid for vehicle licensing and registration, also to 'speed up' the process.

The payment of local bribes is also complicated by social ties. In the case of unregistered cabs and local police, I was often puzzled by how they coexisted. After all, everyone in small towns knows who runs the local, unregistered transit company, they even advertise on local bulletin boards and have business cards printed up to hand to passengers, but the police appear not to stop them from doing this, despite the need for being a registered business (including paying the proper taxes, having insurance, etc). The reason for this in some towns, is that a quid pro quo exists between those who drive unregistered taxis and law enforcement.

Some taxi drivers who are well known in a particular town make regular payments to police in order to avoid facing prosecution, while the police ignore the lack of licensing and illegal running of small-scale taxi companies, and reaping an informal payment for *not* enforcing the law. What complicates matters is that some taxi drivers have kin in law enforcement. In this case, the payments are not construed as 'bribes' or *uplatok*, but rather as *Jednorázový poplatok*, or a one-time fee. The term *poplatok*, rather than *uplatok*, indicates the differentiation of bribe versus fee. The former is associated with a corrupt act, the latter with a payment for a market-driven transaction where both parties agree to the change for ostensibly mutual benefit.

These payments raise the theoretical issues of how we view payments in relation to extant models of economic exchange. Are these bribes in the conventional sense which Western economists use, or are they simply payments to encourage or foster economic transactions and relations? As Polese (2008) argues, Western distinctions between bribe and gift fail to grasp the local and often context-dependent understandings of such payments, and thus some patterns of what appear to be corruption are actually forms of 'brift': something between a gift and a bribe.

The difficulty in discerning the motives for such practices means that it is not always possible to discern the context for each party in an exchange. For instance, some people may have closer ties than others in forms of exchange along kin lines. A police officer may have just had an unanticipated expense, is short of money, and may seek greater extraction of payments at a particular point in time.

Transit and trucking in Slovakia 113

The rumour is that during the Christmas holidays, everyone winds up spending more on informal payments because people need to purchase gifts. We might see this as ironic: that the social obligation of a gift-giving holiday encourages greater extraction of informal payments, but this is precisely the point: that these systems of exchange are intertwined, overlapping, and often mutually reinforcing.

Informality and illicit flows

The final set of qualitative data which illustrate the complex interplay of various types of informal/formal economic practices concerns illicit goods. In this case, as discussed elsewhere (Karjanen 2011), the quintessential good is contraband cigarettes. These are sold in all sorts of locations, from formal businesses to side-door businesses. It is the side-door enterprise which provides another case study in the interaction between hitherto often separated analytical spheres; formal/informal, licit/illicit, kinship/non-kin, etc.

Contraband cigarettes (where state taxes or duty have not been paid) are only one of a range of goods or services that the side-door business may sell. For instance, two of the larger side-door sellers of cigarettes I am familiar with are families who have friends or family members who are already in the trucking, logistics or transport business and simply provide a retail outlet for some of the goods. One family with a father experiencing long-term unemployment turned to selling cigarettes, knock-off Adidas shoes, and Chinese-made plastic slippers after their eldest son got a job working as a driver for a trucking firm that did business with an import/export firm which provided access to all of these goods. In exchange for transporting the goods over the border successfully (without having to pay the proper duties or state taxes), the son gets a share for his own distribution. In turn, his family then sells these goods from their home, largely to friends and family, or colleagues, but also to other small businesses. These sales were highly irregular as there is no clear way to determine what is moving through the trucking containers each week.

In this case, the circulation of the contraband produces benefits for multiple parties across what might be construed again as dichotomous economic spheres: formal/informal, licit, illicit. First the supplier shipping (smuggling) the cigarettes has avoided both taxes, and if they are imported, the excise duty on cigarettes, although these are somewhat offset by the slightly higher shipping costs which are charged by the trucking company. The driver siphons off some of the goods which then get sold out of his house through trusted family networks. As a result of this arrangement the son has provided an intermittent but nevertheless important stream of income for the family. The monthly profit from this enterprise varies greatly, but on average amounts to €135 per month. This is approximately a quarter of the mean wage for Slovakia in 2005. As a related bonus, some small businesses have purchased cigarettes directly from this family's burgeoning 'side-door' business. In effect, the retailer becomes a small-time distributor within the broader network of illicit goods. This additional source of income greatly aided the mother's cleaning business. Over the course of a year, the family invested

€1,000 in fixing her car, providing for new supplies, and paying for local advertising. As part of her cleaning business, she now sells Adidas shoes and cigarettes to her more trustworthy clients. As this final case demonstrates, the web of formal/ informal, legal/illegal and licit/illicit exchanges is complex, requiring theoretically moving beyond simplistic dichotomies.

Informal work and exchange: marginal or heterogeneous?

Research on informal work and exchange has shifted in perspective, providing a more complex picture of the range of informal practices in various economic circumstances. Early research tended towards supporting the idea that informal work was done primarily by those who are at the margins of the formal economy: the 'marginality thesis'. This approach views informal work and exchange as concentrated in marginalized groups and/or areas (e.g., Blair and Endres 1994; Button 1984; Castells and Portes 1989). Although there is some evidence to support this perspective (Kesteloot and Meert 1999; Leonard 1998; Wilson 2006), the range of informal work: its scope, types, location within the economy, and who actually does it, vary greatly. It is clear that some exploitive 'off the books' work does occur, but that this type of work also occurs among the affluent, and may in fact be supplemental to a more formal wage earned in a different occupation (Williams and Windebank 2001, 2003).

There is growing evidence that informal work includes the self-employed, who often work as sole proprietorships and entrepreneurs (Leonard 1994; Warren 1994; Williams 2004; Williams and Windebank 2001), and in some cases this type of work is done by more established 'formal sector' firms, either through subcontracting (Karjanen 2011) within or by individuals and firms themselves which in turn subsidize capitalist development (Wilson 2006). Thus, Williams and Windebank (2004) argue that our understanding of underground work has progressed a long way from the conventional depiction of highly exploitive work done by marginalized populations, and that it is more productive to view such economic activities as a spectrum of underground work organized along a range of whether for-profit or not-for profit motives predominate. They suggest that heterogeneously three broad varieties of work exist informally: income-oriented organized underground work; income-oriented self-employment and not-for-profit paid favours (2004: 14).

The scholarship of informal exchange and work in post-socialist economies, however, underscores how many forms of exchange may blur the relationship between economic interests (profit) and reproducing social relations (favours). *Blat* (Humphrey 2002, Ledeneva 1998, Polese this volume) is a type of relationship which involves both promoting personal ties and for-profit motives. Reflecting on the case studies presented in this chapter, I conclude with several theoretical areas for further research.

First, there is the issue of moving beyond the standard dualisms of economic versus social motives for exchange; something which the end of the substantivist and formalist debates in anthropology never fully satisfied. In the case of informal

Transit and trucking in Slovakia 115

work, the relationship between what are often seen as competing motives for exchange are obviated: it is clear that exchange is both economic and social. What has shaped the debate about this topic has been the question of which motive takes precedence: economically driven incentives and market rationality, or the maintenance of social ties and other forms of sociality. It is precisely the experience of state socialism, with a mixture of state, market, and social relations operating informally, as Dunn (2004) describes, as 'horizontal sociality' which may help maintain the continued significance of informalization now in the post-socialist context. This is not to say that the situation is entirely 'path dependent' (Martin and Sunley 2006), but rather is a product of an interaction between past, present, and changing socioeconomic circumstances. For instance, illicit cab driving can be seen as both a new economic practice emergent from the gaps in state- and market-economy provisions for transportation in the socialist and post-socialist contexts, but it is also a form of sociality and network formation. As Peter, my cab-driving informant and guide expresses, he has more friends in town than anyone else largely because he has driven nearly everyone somewhere at some point, or at least someone in each family. The same situation holds true, of course, for kinship-based enterprises. These are rooted in sociality. The key point here is that engaging in the debate about economic versus social motivations (a formalist versus substantivist/economist versus anthropologist) debate overlooks the crucial point of multiply simultaneous motivations and how such motivations may shift along a continuum depending on context – such as informal versus formal work, social ties, economic pressures, and so forth.

The cases presented in this chapter also suggest a second area where theoretical innovation and further research is needed: the relationship between the state and informal/formal transactions, particularly in an era of growing global economic integration and the restructuring of states. Typically, the informal sector is defined by the level of state regulation: it is outside it, whereas formal sector firms are regulated by states. There are many grey areas—such as those where informal work occurs within formal firms. There are also areas where states, or at least their proxies, such as local police or regulatory offices know of illegal practices, but ignore them (indeed, sometimes these state proxies participate in them!). What this suggests is not only that the very concept of informal/formal is difficult to define along the dimensions of state regulation or not, but furthermore that it raises the issue of how states themselves are social bodies. As such, states, as an ensemble of social practices, may act in very different, often contradictory ways – enforcing some boundaries regarding informal work, or not. In the case of trucking and transit, for instance, local police often allow the business to continue, not for economic reasons, that is, not simply because they can extract payments in the form of bribes, but for social considerations as well. Local police may turn a blind eye to illegal taxi companies which are transporting the elderly to a hospital for *moral* reasons. To quote a local officer who knows Peter, the illegal taxi proprietor, very well: 'Someone is driving someone's grandmother to the polyclinic, and the grandmother pays him. Why should that be illegal? That's what you do!' In contrast, consider the issue of contraband cigarettes, also sold widely in illicit trade and open air markets in Slovakia. There has been a strong campaign to stop these sales, and in particular the smuggling of such cigarettes. Why the distinction? In part the scale: contraband sales of cigarettes cost the state millions of Euros every year, but also there is a moral framework: one good is unhealthy, but driving someone to the clinic is a moral obligation.

Finally, in broader terms, these cases raise questions about how we understand economic processes, in particular social and economic change, comparatively. To return to the case of Peter, our well-known taxi entrepreneur, he is more than just a cab driver. He is a node in a massive social network spanning across town and even into other towns. He has intimate knowledge of people's lives; he also serves as a medium through which people can be connected. He also circulates goods and services; he drives sex workers to clients, he drives people to work when their car breaks down, he drives the sick and elderly to the clinic. All of this is good for his business, and it increasingly fosters social ties in what has been a very socially atomized society at many levels (Karjanen 2005). What this suggests, I argue, is that we move beyond the typical dualisms of gift/bribery and formal/informal, and focus empirically on practices: their structure, function, relationships. This opens new avenues for both research and theory building; as I have shown with Peter, it is possible for an informal taxi driver to actually be far more than a taxi driver.

References

Adam, J. (1984) 'Regulation of Labour Supply in Poland, Czechoslovakia and Hungary', *Soviet Studies* 36(1): 69–86.

Alvarez, R. (2005) *Mangos, Chiles, and Truckers: The Business of Transnationalism*, Minneapolis: University of Minnesota Press.

Bailey, T. and Waldinger, R. (1991) 'Primary, Secondary, and Enclave Labor Markets: a Training Systems Approach', *American Sociological Review* 56: 432–45.

Blair, J. P. and Endres, C. R. (1994) 'Hidden Economic Development Assets', *Economic Development Quarterly* 8: 286–91.

Button, K. (1984) 'Regional Variations in the Irregular Economy: a Study of Possible Trends', *Regional Studies* 18: 385–92.

Castells, M. and Portes, A. (1989) 'World Underneath: the Origins, Dynamics and Effects of the Informal Economy', in A. Portes, M. Castells and L. A. Benton (eds), *The Informal Economy: Studies in Advanced and Less Developing Countries*, Baltimore: Johns Hopkins University Press.

Dunn E. C. (2004) *Privatising Poland: Baby Food, Big Business, and the Remaking of Labor*, Ithaca, NY: Cornell University Press.

Economist Intelligence Unit (2011) 'Automotive and Truck Industry Report, Slovakia', London: EIU.

Humphrey, C. (2002) *The Unmaking of Soviet Life: Everyday Economies after Socialism*, Ithaca, NY: Cornell University Press.

International Labor Organization (ILO) (2003) *Key Indicators of the Labor Market*, Third Ed. ILO, Geneva.

Karjanen, D. (2005) 'Social Atomization and Structural Violence in the Transition from Socialism', *Anthropology of East Europe Review* 23(1): 30–7.

—— (2010) 'The Informalization of the Economy: Subcontracting and Cash-In-Hand Work in the U.S. Service and Construction Sectors', Paper presented at UCLA Institute for Research on Labor and Employment, 20 October.

—— (2011) 'Tracing Informal and Illicit Flows after Socialism: A Micro-commodity Supply Chain Analysis in the Slovak Republic', *International Journal of Sociology and Social Policy* 31(11/12): 648–63.

Kaufman, J. and Kaliberda, A. (1996) 'Integrating the Unofficial Economy into the Dynamics of Post Socialist Economies', World Bank Policy Research Working Paper No. 1691. Washington DC: World Bank.

Kesteloot, C. and Meert. H. (1999) 'Informal Spaces: the Geography of Informal Economic Activities in Brussels', *International Journal of Urban and Regional Research* 23: 232–51.

Korda, B. (1973), 'A Decade of Economic Growth in Czechoslovakia (1962–73)', *Soviet Studies* 28(4): 499–523.

Ledeneva, A. (2006) *How Russia Really Works: The Informal Practices That Shaped Post-Soviet Politics and Business*, New York: Cornell University Press

Leonard, M. (1998) *Invisible Work, Invisible Workers: The Informal Economy in Europe and the US*, London: Macmillan.

Martin, R. and Sunley, P. (2006) 'Path Dependence and Regional Economic Evolution', *Journal of Economic Geography* 6(4): 395–437.

Mauss, M. (1954) [1924] *The Gift: Forms and Function of Exchange in Archaic Societies*, London: Cohen and West Ltd.

Morris, J. (2012) 'Unruly Entrepreneurs: Russian Worker Responses to Insecure Formal Employment', *Global Labour Journal* 3(2): 217–36. Online. Available: <http://digital commons.mcmaster.ca/globallabour/vol3/iss2/2> (accessed 31 March 2013).

Polese, A. (2008) '"If I Receive it, it is a Gift; if I Demand it, then it is a Bribe": On the Local Meaning of Economic Transactions in Post-Soviet Ukraine', *Anthropology in Action* 15(3): 47–60.

Portes, A. and Stepick, A. (1993) *City on the Edge: The Transformation of Miami*, Berkeley: University of California Press.

Roberts, B. (1994) 'Informal Economy and Family Strategies', *International Journal of Urban and Regional Research* 18(1): 6–23.

Sassen, S. (1988) 'The Informal Economy', in Mollenkopf, J. and Castells, M. (eds), *Dual City: The Restructuring of New York*, New York: Russell Sage Foundation, pp. 79–102.

Schneider, F. (2002) 'Size and Measurement of the Informal Economy in 110 Countries Around the World', paper presented at Workshop of Australian National Tax Centre, ANU, Canberra, Australia, 17 July 2002.

Slovak Statistical Office, (2011) 'Study of Unofficial Payments in the Slovak Republic', SSO, Bratislava.

Smith, A. (1998) *Reconstructing the Regional Economy: Industrial Transformation and Regional Development in Slovakia*, Cheltenham: Edward Elgar.

Waldinger, R. (1986) 'Changing Ladders and Musical Chairs: Ethnicity and Opportunity in Postindustrial New York', *Politics and Society* 15: 369–401.

Waldinger, R. and Ward, R. (1990) *Ethnic Entrepreneurs: Immigrant Business in Industrial Societies*, Newbury Park: Sage.

Warren, M. (1994) 'Exploitation or Co-operation? The Political Basis of Regional Variation in the Italian Informal Economy', *Politics and Society* 22: 89–115.

Williams, C. C. and Windebank, J. (2001) 'Re-conceptualizing Paid Informal Work: Some Lessons from English Cities', *Environment and Planning A* 33: 121–40.

—— (2003) *Poverty and the Third Way*, London: Routledge.
—— (2004) 'The Heterogeneity of the Underground Economy', *International Journal of Economic Development* 6(2): 1–23.
Wilson, T. D. (2006) *Subsidizing Capitalism: Brickmakers on the U.S.–Mexican Border*, Albany: SUNY Press.
World Bank and USAID (2011) 'Corruption in Slovakia, Results of Diagnostic Surveys', Washington DC: World Bank.

Part 2

At home abroad? Transnational Informality and the invisible flows of people and goods

7 From shuttle trader to businesswomen

The informal bazaar economy in Kyrgyzstan

Anna Cieślewska

At the time I was introduced to her, Olga, a 52-year-old Russian woman who was trading at the Dordoy bazaar, the biggest in Central Asia, asked: 'Are you a foreigner? Really? Ah-ha, you are from Poland! I was in Poland once at the beginning of the 90s. You used to have big bazaar in Warsaw.' Olga developed her story while sitting in her realm – a small metal shipping container packed with clothes where she works throughout the year, no matter what the weather or other circumstances. 'Who is guilty of all those calamities?' – she waved indicating the bazaar environment – 'Gorbachev of course!' Her friend who was sitting with us nodded assent.

In Soviet times, Olga worked an industrial plant in Bishkek. During privatization this place closed and the majority of equipment was taken to Russia, including the enterprise's documentation.[1] She was dismissed without any notice period and she had to find a new source of income very quickly. Her situation was not an exception at the beginning of 1990s. As a result of liberalization and privatization in Kyrgyzstan as well as the whole former Soviet Bloc, the number of state enterprises was reduced; consequently, employment and wages declined. From 1991 to 1996, the share of the public sector in employment decreased from 74 per cent to 27.5 per cent. Many professionals – teachers, doctors, engineers, etc. – lost their jobs (UNDP 1999).

Olga is only one of numerous examples of people who have been living from trading in Kyrgyzstan in the aftermath the dissolution of the USSR. During that period the rapid shift from a central to a market economy triggered unemployment on an unprecedented scale which further resulted in an increase of informal forms of generating income, with bazaar selling as one of the most popular occupations.

Some have argued that the artificially maintained inefficient labour market of the USSR had to be reorganized, making room for unrestricted and unlimited private initiatives which should have absorbed the labour force previously employed in the public sector, and that the expansion of informal employment is only a transition phase which will be self-regulated in time. There are also other claims that the informal economy encourages entrepreneurial skills, provides jobs for the poor, and reinforces the transition towards markets, since the income it generates can help the economy to recover (Kandiyoti 2006).

Conversely, however, despite over 20 years of various reforms and market alteration, in Kyrgyzstan the labour market has not stabilized, but instead, a part of the workforce was absorbed by Kazakh and Russian markets, making up about 27 per cent of Kyrgyz GDP in 2011 (Slay and Bravi 2011). For those who remained in the country, the bazaar remains a last resort.

This chapter aims to examine the phenomenon of the bazaar economy in connection with the social, economic and political changes of the last 20 years in Kyrgyzstan. I examine the emergence of the bazaar trade during the transitional period from a centrally planned economy to a market economy, showing the consequences of the rapid deregulation of the labour market after the system's transformation. I focus mainly on the creation of bazaars in Kyrgyzstan in the aftermath of perestroika and on the activity of suitcase traders, commonly called *chelnoki*. This is illustrated by the narratives of people involved in trade on the Dordoy and in the *chelnok* business.

The chapter is based on field research conducted in Kyrgyzstan in 2006 and supplemented by more recent material collected over a total of seven months in 2011–12 during my work for OSCE, and for the NGO, Eastern-European Democratic Centre. During research I interviewed 24 traders at Dordoy market in Bishkek, and a number of employees of Kyrgyz and international NGOs, and managers of the Dordoy. I used a participatory approach as well as in-depth interviews as the main methods of research. In most cases, I was introduced by friends to my interlocutors or I selected people randomly at the market place asking them to devote their time to talk with me. Some stories were reported in a very informal way during meetings with friends for dinners, so they were only written down later, other interviews were given in the bazaar where I spent many days, sometimes sitting with people, observing bazaar life, in conversation with customers and so on. In the case of interviews with officials and NGO workers, most of the meetings took place in the offices of the interlocutors.[2]

Within the framework of this study I argue that, despite the 20 years that have passed since the USSR collapsed, the labour market has not stabilized in Kyrgyzstan, and bazaar trading is still one of the biggest sources of income for many citizens. Even the situation of those traders who achieved relative success is still uncertain due to the unstable economic and political situation in the country.

From rigid rules of central economy to free market

During the period of the USSR, statistics indicated almost no income from other activities than official ones. Joblessness was virtually a criminal offence, and for this reason each person of working age, unless he or she had a valid excuse, had to be employed. This artificial system of securing jobs for everybody resulted in low rates of capital concentration. Hence, salaries were low. Consequently, people boosted their income in other ways, a fact which contributed to the spread of different kinds of informal economic activities. In reality, the state tolerated limited forms of independent entrepreneurship, such as selling surplus agricultural production from Sovkhoz and Kolkhoz (collective farms) or providing some types of services – such as in private workshops. Nevertheless, this parallel economy was subject to various taxes and penalties, even if the situation changed over time and differed among various Soviet-type economies (Granick 1987; Wellisz and Findlay 1986).

Bazaar trade in the Kyrgyz SSR as well as in other republics was restricted to foodstuffs, and the people who made their profit from other kinds of trade were treated as guilty of (business) fraud. Prior to perestroika, bazaars were managed by centralized institutions, and theoretically, only a very few agricultural products escaped official control. Selling luxury manufactured goods was absolutely forbidden and punished by imprisonment; however, people always found ways to evade the law. The practice of selling goods illicitly was termed 'speculation' and, under Soviet criminal law, was defined as 'one of the most dangerous economic crimes which affects the normal functioning of Soviet trade and genuine interests of buyers. It involves selling and buying goods with the purpose of making profit' (as quoted in Kaiser 1997).

Nevertheless, products which were not available in normal shops, such as fashionable clothes from the West, certain electronic goods or even common products in short supply, were frequently redistributed informally through a chain of people such as those who were working in commerce or representatives of the establishment, sportsmen, sailors, etc., that is, people who had the opportunity to travel freely to other countries and purchase luxury items.[3] With time, a certain 'profession' emerged related to informal trade – *fartsovshchik* – someone who was unofficially involved in redistributing foreign goods. The importance of the second economy increased during the Brezhnev era, when the general economic stagnation forced people to seek alternative sources of products and to increase their income (Kaiser 1997). In addition, Party members contributed significantly to the growth in the volume of the 'black market'. An example might be a Party member working as a director of a warehouse with electronic goods which were sold to people on the basis of allotment (since their availability was limited).[4] To get an attractive item such as a refrigerator, washing machine, TV set, etc., it was necessary to go on a long waiting list, or alternatively, to have the relevant personal contacts or pay slightly more to the director or other employees of the warehouse or shop than the actual price of the commodity. As regards bazaars (in Russian: *kolkhoznye rynki* – lit. 'collective farm markets'), as already mentioned, some surpluses of agricultural production could be sold on marketplaces.

The situation rapidly changed in the aftermath of market-oriented reforms introduced throughout the whole former USSR and Eastern Europe, including the newly-created Kyrgyzstan. Nevertheless, the degree to which former USSR republics and communist countries followed economic policy imposed by international financial organizations such as the International Monetary Fund (IMF) varied. From the very beginning Kyrgyzstan very rigidly applied the advice of the IMF and World Bank to reconstruct the 'market' according to the neoliberal principles aimed at deregulation of the state structures to release uncontrolled market forces. This offered the new country the possibility of joining the World Trade Organization (WTO) which in turn made Kyrgyzstan attractive from the point of view of the flexibility of trading and flowing goods, but on the other hand contributed to increasing instability in the labour market.

Routh indicates that 'withdrawing the state from the market fundamentally changed the power equilibrium in the market' which, when deregulated, gave businesses unrestricted freedom to establish their own rules, including those regarding employment (Routh 2011). As Portes and Benton point out, since creating regular 'formal' jobs is costly, it is more efficient to generate 'informal' jobs outside the industrial infrastructure (Portes and Benton 1984). To decrease operational costs, companies prefer to employ low-paid but also unprotected workers (flexible employment), which in fact means no union rights, no minimum wage, no social benefits, etc. (Routh 2011). I will return to this issue when discussing the Dordoy market and the *chelnok* business.

Consequences of labour market deregulation – emerging bazaar trade

To begin trading at a bazaar, no special qualifications are required; the start-up capital needed for getting into business can be relatively low. These factors make entering the bazaar trade easy for almost anyone. So, after the Soviet Union collapsed, as Olga's example shows, many people of various professions and levels of education went into bazaar trading because of a lack of other alternatives. Teachers, medical doctors, and engineers traded along with farmers and factory workers. Some people combined various activities, such as teaching at school in the morning and trading in the market in the afternoon. At the beginning, to start trading at a bazaar was very easy for Olga. She described how she used to buy the first Chinese goods in Bishkek from resident Chinese and then resold them in Russia and made a profit. From Russia she brought food products and sold them in Kyrgyzstan.[5]

At the same time as the spread of informal trading, the number of bazaars in Kyrgyzstan rapidly increased quadrupling from 1989 to 2005. The emerging free market also had an effect on the character of bazaars – not only in Kyrgyzstan but across the entire former Soviet Bloc. Apart from the 'classical' small local marketplaces of a more traditional character, large industrial-scale bazaars were established, as well as many places developed spontaneously, colloquially named *barakholovki* – these were set up sometimes in very unexpected places such as a corner of a square and so forth. Most former kolkhoz markets were privatized, and they functioned as a kind of intermediate form between an industrial-scale bazaar and a traditional market. By 2004, at least 214,000 out of 2.2 million economically active citizens of Kyrgyzstan were officially involved in the trade sector. The largest wholesale and retail bazaars in Kyrgyzstan created about 10,000 or more trading places, with an additional number of jobs provided in services (Spector 2008).[6]

The most important bazaar in Central Asia which opened at that time was Dordoy Bazaar in Bishkek called by some journalists 'a modern monument of the power of raw commerce' (Sershen 2007). The bazaar itself was established in 1992 in a suburb of Bishkek and then covered an area of 29 hectares. Currently the Dordoy is the biggest market in Central Asia and includes a number of smaller bazaars spread over 53 hectares. Traders bring goods from China, India, Turkey, the Middle East, Europe and elsewhere to sell there wholesale, then redistribute them to smaller, 'domestic' markets in Central Asia and other regions. The Dordoy is a gigantic, highly profitable trade machine which offers income for a multitude of people from Kyrgyzstan and the neighbouring countries. In 2012 there were 15,000 double-stacked shipping containers (stalls) and about 55,000 people are involved in the trade there.[7] According to World Bank research, the annual income of Dordoy amounts to $1 billion. To date, the monthly rent of the most expensive containers costs $2,000–$5,000, the cheapest $100–$150 (Shajkeeva 2012).

There are also other smaller 'industrial-scale bazaars' in Central Asia (the second largest bazaar in Kyrgyzstan is located in the southern town of Karasu), but the Dordoy is undoubtedly the hub of trade there, as well as a place of cross-cultural encounters where people of the region meet and exchange ideas and information. It is a place which, to a certain extent, can be seen as a symbol of the dissolved multicultural microcosms of the Soviet Union, without the ethnic divisions now created by the rigid boundaries of the new countries which artificially separate various ethnic groups and nations of the big melting pot of Central Asia.

At the beginning of the transformation, a common characteristic of all countries of the former Soviet Bloc was a lack of comprehensive trade regulations. Due to the scarcity of employment alternatives, many people began trading spontaneously. A lot of 'new traders' put their goods directly onto the street or on folding tables; only a few of them maintained proper stalls. Mostly they did not pay taxes or other dues for their activity. Over time, the bazaar trade was subjected to more and more legal regulations and the majority of street vendors were moved to designated marketplaces. At present, tradesmen have to pay a fee for a place to trade (which in the case of Kyrgyzstan is decided by the management of the particular bazaar or by the municipal council).

Another type of payment is a licence (Russian: *patent*) which is paid to the tax office as a form of the tax for business activity (but this is not a company registration since the licence can be bought for a limited period of time). The cost of the licence is dependent on the potential turnover of stock and is set by the tax inspectors. Usually, people try to show the lowest turnover possible. The tax inspectors are obliged to calculate the stock which belongs to the particular person in order to establish their potential income. This operation is related to a number of the controls on the marketplace. Everybody whom I interviewed paid the licence. To not pay is not affordable due to the frequency of inspections and penalties.

It should be noted that, initially, no business loans were available. People started trading mainly using their own resources, collecting money from family, selling property, etc. Not long afterwards, the growing demand for finance resulted in the development of the micro-credit system provided by many organizations and local institutions. Micro-credit enabled businesses to be started up by people who possessed no assets. Naturally, those with a certain amount of business capital or who were able to provide collateral could access other types of loans.[8]

Chelnok trade: from petty trader to businesswoman

The flourishing of bazaar trade was also associated with a new form of business which developed during the perestroika period – the trans-border (shuttle) trade

(Ozcan, 2006). Opening the borders, created relatively free movement of people and triggered cross-border merchandizing. Due to a shortage of some types of goods in various regions, it was profitable to buy certain products in one country and to sell them in another. The growth in cross-border trade in the initial stage of transformation was related to significant discrepancies in prices between the countries of the former Bloc. For example, different domestic/hardware goods were brought to Poland, mostly from the territory of the former Soviet countries where they were bought very cheaply. In Poland, traders purchased different products from textiles to electronic equipment, and subsequently re-sold them back in their home markets.

Traders involved in the shuttle trade are colloquially named *chelnoki*. They would travel from different countries of the former Soviet Bloc to India, the Arab Emirates, Iran, Italy, Pakistan, Syria, Thailand, Turkey or Central Europe in order to buy goods to be then sold in the domestic market. In the first phase of transition, the *chelnok* business typically involved just travelling with suitcases full of consumer goods, mainly food products, textiles and household goods (Esim 2002). There were special tourist companies which organized 'tourist trips' for people involved in trading. Although, formally, the companies arranged tours to visit different places, almost nobody was interested in visiting tourist attractions, and most clients were *chelnoki*.[9]

My key informant was Kazakh national Altynai, 38, who like Olga used to be *chelnok*, travelling to China to buy various products and reselling them at the marketplace in Almaty (Kazakhstan). Her story of becoming *chelnok* is similar to that of many people at that time. During the collapse of the Soviet Union between 1990 and 1991, she was at home looking after children. Later she started teaching at a school but the salary was low, so in 1992, she began trading products bought from China. She describes how in 1992 it was a really good business – a profit level of 100 per cent. Shortly afterwards the currency changed from roubles to national currency and trade stalled. Altynai and other traders had therefore to wait a very long time to be able to sell goods, but when finally she managed to sell all her stock she made a handsome profit. At that time, Altynai regularly travelled to China to buy food products and Chinese vodka which traders smuggled hidden among other goods. It should be underlined that the work of a *chelnok* was very difficult and exhausting due to many days of travelling by trains, cars or buses, in very uncomfortable conditions. Altynai said that she was going on 'tourist trips' to China of four to seven days long. Other people interviewed gave stays of similar duration or even longer for trips to more distant places.

When Altynai went to China she would buy goods and send them via a transport company. However, the trucks had to be changed at the border. For this reason, often women traders had to move the goods themselves from one car to another. In addition, traders lived under the constant threat of robbery. Sometimes people had to wait on the border for two or three days. Someone could not simply go to a hotel and sleep because the bus could be called to move at any time. Apart from these difficulties, bazaar trade had another unpleasant aspect. According to interlocutors, one of the main problems was racketeering at the marketplaces;

people had to pay so-called 'protection money' to extortion (mafia) groups. The so-called 'mafia' were mostly young men without particular occupation who during the political turmoil of 1990s were absorbed by various criminal groups which made illegal earnings from different types of business activities including bazaar trade. Nevertheless, Humphrey argues that despite the fact that most contemporary gangs emerged only in recent times, their criminal practices were transmitted from gang culture which developed in the Soviet period (2002).

At the time, a virtual absence of state institutions to protect citizens created favourable conditions for mushrooming criminal gangs. Most of them had close links with police and representatives of bazaar authorities. Usually each bazaar was 'guarded' by one particular group. Traders were forced to pay money and if they refused were intimidated, sometimes beaten; their goods were confiscated or destroyed. They could also be expelled from the bazaar. In time, rackets lost their importance and former racketeers were frequently getting jobs as guards employed by security companies protecting the bazaars. But in the period of renewed instability and political chaos, this phenomenon has re-emerged, but not on such a large scale as before.[10]

Another challenge for *chelnoki* during the cross-borders trips were the bribes paid to customs officers. Usually traders in the bus or train collected money and handed it to border guards to turn a blind eye to the smuggled goods which were hidden literally everywhere. For example, people who carried bottles of alcohol would fix them into their garments on their bodies putting on another layer of clothes to hide the illegal goods. Products on the train were hidden in various places; people even disassembled some parts of the compartments to put things there. Giving an account from the Polish–Ukrainian border, Polese describes how professional traders have a key to open most doors and a screwdriver to open walls and ceilings 'like a tin can' (2012). Bribery has been widespread on all the borders and these practices were triggered by circumstances related to illegal smuggling of large amounts of goods and closely related to the development of shuttle trade. For example, Altynai commented that 'at the beginning, Chinese customs officers did not take anything, but soon our people accustomed them to this practice'. It appeared that customs officers were not corrupted by 'nature' but rather the chaotic situation of the first years of transition created favourable conditions for such behaviour which to some extent continues to the present.

In Central Asia shuttle trade in the traditional form is still widespread: lugging heavy bags from one place to another. However, the nature of this phenomenon has changed over time and in many cases has evolved into professional trading. For example in Turkey, official revenues from suitcase trade were $8.84 billion in 1996 (Esim 2002). After the implementation of import taxes in the 1990s, there was a sharp drop in the volume of suitcase trade. 'By 1998, suitcase trade had come to an almost complete stop due to liquidity difficulties in Russia and the region. The suitcase trade has not recovered to previous levels, but it continues in much smaller volumes' (Esim 2002). Also, in many cases the *chelnok* trade has developed into a highly profitable business. People still travel but the scale and size of the trade is much bigger than in the case of the classical suitcase trade. It has become a wholesale business and traders offer goods to people who buy and redistribute the products to different parts of Russia and Central Asia. In fact, since the *chelnok* business developed in parallel to social and economic transformation, it is now a profession marked by something of a legendary reputation – an icon of the chaotic, market-oriented changes of the 1990s.[11]

Olga and Altynai had become 'big fish' of Dordoy – successful traders, despite the fact that they started from the lowest position in trading. Both of them used to go with suitcases for shopping tours to buy and re-sell products on the marketplaces. Olga, losing job and social status, plummeted into the chaos of the first stage of the changes, and spontaneously started trading to survive. Despite the fact that this profession now brings her reasonable income, Olga's situation is still not stable. She has not yet established a formal company, and despite the relatively large scale of her trade, most of her income is informal.[12] Nevertheless, she does not need to go on tiring trips with heavy suitcases. As she stated firmly:

> No more hassle with shuttle trade! I take a plane to India two or three times a month and buy clothes there. I send the goods through a cargo company and go back to Bishkek by plane. I have now developed my business and these days *chelnoki* from Uzbekistan buy goods from me.[13]

Is Olga happy about the fact that now she has a chance to run her own business, and so actively participate in the market economy which, in contrast to the socialist system, gives her an opportunity to take initiative and make money? At the end of interview, she said with deep conviction, 'I am a Soviet person!' to emphasize her negative attitude to capitalism, which she mostly associates with instability and uncertainty.[14]

Altynai's attitude is different. She was very young during the transformation, and like many young people at the time, her adult life began during the most difficult period. She neither analyses the current political and economic system nor expresses sentiment towards the Soviet period. Life is what it is, so she adjusted to the new conditions very quickly. She started living off informal trading due to a lack of other reasonable alternatives. After some time, she established a company, and so, theoretically, she legalized her activity; in practice, however, Altynai was still balancing between the informal and formal sectors to increase her profit. Presently, she is the owner of a few stands at a marketplace in Almaty where she set up a legal business to be able to sell the clothes produced by her small informal manufacture in Bishkek (Altynai employs a dozen women). Additionally, she buys some goods on the Dordoy market. According to her, corruption in Kyrgyzstan is so endemic that it is ineffective to have a legal company there. A person needs to pay a lot of money to various sorts of officials 'under the table' to be able to run a business. Someone has always got to know how to do things, who it is better to speak to, and so on. She further stated that despite some shortcomings of the same kind, the situation in Kazakhstan is much more stable and the law is more predictable. Besides, according to Altynai, in 2006 taxes in Kazakhstan were lower than in Kyrgyzstan. Even if a person has a trade licence in Kyrgyzstan, there are still a lot of problems with tax inspectors and police. She was aware that this kind of behaviour was technically evasion, but at the same time she considered it as a 'normal' way of coping with the imperfections of the state system. In fact, this attitude to the law is characteristic of almost all countries of the former USSR and Eastern Europe.

Frequently, people do not think that such 'little cheating' of the system is wrong because the state apparatus is perceived as something which works against the interests of ordinary people, mainly due to corruption, but also because of the uncertain regulatory framework.[15] Hence, tax evasion and other petty frauds are not seen in a negative light. Earning money from business is seen as a good, but since the environment is unstable, a person is constantly maneuvering between formality and informality. Frequently, the border between the two is rather blurred. Rasanayagam (2011) argues that, for example in Uzbekistan, 'informal economic activity is just one expression of a more general informalization of state, society and lifeworlds following the collapse of the Soviet Union' which has also affected people's attitudes to what they consider as immoral or dishonest, and what is just seen as finding a way to get something which is needed. In Kyrgyzstan, the situation is no different. Altynai does not like corruption in Kyrgyzstan, but on the other hand, she employs people informally to sew clothes for her. Finally, Altynai's behaviour can be seen in the category of rational practices developed in response to particular circumstances – in this case, the unstable economic and political situation in the country.

The majority of my respondents, including Olga, had previously worked as *chelnoki*, but at the time of research they were trading on a large scale, redistributing consumer goods to smaller traders. They were mainly women who went for shopping tours by plane and sent the purchased goods through a cargo company which took care of all import-related formalities. As was pointed out by the president of a non-governmental organization in Bishkek, the main dilemma is the issue of full formalization of their trading activities. All of them are still working according to trade licences, rarely establishing companies, and therefore negotiations with the authorities in terms of the size of their stock and taxes are a matter of much concern.[16] Consequently, the trading of goods is still partly channelled informally. Many of them, like Altynai and Olga, are manoeuvring between the formal and informal sectors.

However, despite the fact that many *chelnoki* developed their businesses and became professional merchants, there are still people who take part in this business in its original form. The third and final trader story in this chapter is the case of Gulnara – a 34-year-old Uzbek – who was still working as a *chelnok,* travelling between Uzbekistan and Kyrgyzstan (in 2006). She was actually one of the poor clients of the former *chelnoki* from Dordoy with whom I conducted an interview, and I met her while she was dealing with them. Her story illustrates the relationship between the classic *chelnok* trade and 'big business' at the Dordoy.

At the time of interview Gulnara had been working in the shuttle trade for almost three years. During the first stage of transition she was at university, and then she got a job as an accountant. But due to a low salary she gave up her profession and started a business. Later she went bankrupt and finally moved to the bazaar. She worked at a marketplace in Tashkent in Uzbekistan buying goods in Bishkek at the Dordoy market.[17] After the Andijan events in 2005 the situation on the border became very difficult.[18] Kyrgyz customs officers became very obstructive and sometimes traders had to wait for two or three days to get customs clearance. Every political event in the region has a large impact on cross-border trade. In 2010 in Kyrgyzstan the second power shift and subsequent ethnic conflict in the south also negatively affected the situation along the borders, and therefore trading.[19] The recently created customs union also raises a question about the future of the Dordoy and trading in Kyrgyzstan.[20]

Apart from Gulnara from Uzbekistan, all the women interviewed at the Dordoy market have a relatively high income and a comfortable financial situation. Over time some former *chelnoks* have become wealthy businessmen, running cafes, warehouses, luxury shops, etc., while others remain at the Dordoy. However, it should be borne in mind that none of the women interviewed initially chose to work as a trader at the bazaar – they were forced to do so by circumstances stemming from the chaotic reforms of the emerging free market, their choices spontaneous and a response to unemployment and poverty. They achieved relative success due to hard work and their ability to adjust very quickly to unstable and unpredictable conditions. In 2012, a friend of mine who has been working at the bazaar in Naryn in central Kyrgyzstan but is taking goods from the Dordoy, said:

> The labour market situation has not changed. Still, after graduation people take their diploma and move to the bazaar or to Russia. Some of them do not even try to search for a job due to the lack of relevant number of work places or very low salaries.

Be that as it may, not all people who work at the Dordoy are successful traders; the bulk of the bazaar's employees are people working for day rates or on a piece-rate basis, without benefits, under insecure and unsafe working conditions. It should also be noted that, instead of the classic stalls at the Dordoy, people now work in metal shipping containers, many stacked on top of each other. This makes their working conditions very oppressive – summer temperatures reach 40 degrees Celsius and winters see 15–20 degrees below zero. The majority of people work at the bazaar without any days off or holidays. Younger women report that they have had problems with raising children, who usually have to stay with their grandparents. Those people comprise a class of 'working poor' which emerged after the failed transition; due to a lack of other opportunities, they were absorbed by the informal economy. Many of them came to Bishkek from provincial areas to find income opportunities. They frequently squeeze into hastily constructed houses in the suburbs of the capital – the new slums of the new state, which are more and more reminiscent of some poor parts of Africa rather than of what was promised by the former president Akayev – the Switzerland of Central Asia.

Conclusion

There have been heated debates on the situation of the labour market in CIS countries, including Kyrgyzstan, since the beginning of the 1990s. The economic crisis triggered by the collapse of the USSR produced a rapid expansion of informal activities due to a rapid increase of unemployment. People were forced to seek alternative livelihoods. Despite the passage of 20 years, however, the bazaars are still the biggest 'employer' in the country, replacing offices, factories and *kolkhozes*, and the labour market cannot be considered stable. The development of *chelnok* trade into larger-size businesses (still partly informal) shows the size and the impact of the informal practices which frequently replaced legally structured businesses. Some traders look to the time of the Soviet Union as a period of wealth which is fully understandable if we reflect on the market reforms and transition as a process which destroyed the old structures but mostly failed to build new foundations.

Some success stories, such as those of the former *chelnoki* from the Dordoy market, also raise many doubts due to the fact that women's involvement in the suitcase trade was forced by circumstances rather than based on personal choice, and that their activity is still only semi-formal. This 'success' can be seen more as an escape from poverty than a conscious choice to attempt lucrative entrepreneurship. For others less lucky, working at the bazaar is almost the only option for survival.

Notes

1. It should be borne in mind that dissolution of USSR occurred in a very hasty and uneven way. In many cases, factories were closed very quickly and unexpectedly. In the case of Central Asia, many high-ranking officials were Russians, and during early transition, many of them moved from the former Central Asian republics to the newly created Russian Federation to eventually open their own businesses mostly linked with their previous occupation and based on networks from Soviet times. That is why they often took all documentation with them. Another explanation could be that despite a generally unstable situation, there were possibly some orders from Moscow to take all factory documents and to bring them to the centre.
2. All names have been changed in the text.
3. *De facto* even the position of shop assistant was considered good, since shop employees had access to different sorts of goods which were often sold informally, 'under the counter'.
4. This kind of 'attractive job' was mostly available to Party members.
5. In Kyrgyzstan there was scarcity of foodstuffs at that time due to a crisis in the aftermath of independence from the USSR. Many people reported that to get some products often they had to stay in long queues to shops, or pay much more at the 'black market'. So, it was an effective strategy to go to Russia with cheap Chinese clothes, sell them at profit then to buy food and afterwards to redistribute it in Kyrgyzstan.
6. It should be noted that, apart from providing employment in trading, market places also generate different forms of jobs including work in cafes, transport, currency exchange shops, manufacturing, making minor repairs, warehouses, etc., and even in the case of Central Asia, work for fortune-tellers, religious professionals, singers as well as jugglers. Thus bazaars are a source of income for people of various professions, not just traders.

132 *Anna Cieślewska*

7 Since Dordoy is a huge source of informal profit for many people including managers of the market place, the quoted official numbers may not be accurate. According to some estimates, the real number of containers is much higher (up to 40,000).
8 In 2011, according to the National Bank, more than 400 micro-credit organizations (MCOs) operated in the country, although most of the capital belongs to five or six organizations established by foreign donors. By the end of 2010, Kyrgyz MCOs had increased their loan portfolios by 25 per cent compared to June 2009. In 2010, they lent 15.44 billion KGS (US $340m) to more than 500,000 borrowers. However, due to the unstable economy and uncertain political environment as well as a lack of domestic resources, the interest rate is high (the annual interest rate at a private MCO is 28–30 per cent, twice as high as in neighbouring Kazakhstan (Osmonolieva 2011). In terms of bazaars, the most popular form of loan to start a business for the poorest people has been the 'group loan' for women. Usually, the number of women involved is from four to ten. Each member of the group is obliged to give a guarantee for another person, and no collateral is required, but 20 per cent of the loan value is mandatory (cash) savings (interview with the Micro Credit Company in Bishkek, July 2006).
9 Shuttle trade developed during perestroika across the whole former Soviet Bloc including Poland, Ukraine, Belarus, the countries of South Caucasus and others.
10 After 20 years of political instability and economic crisis in Kyrgyzstan, it is very difficult to estimate the extent of racketeering there. In fact, many people directly or indirectly contribute to different forms of racketeering, including employees of security services who often 'work' for various criminal groups apart from their official employment. This phenomenon has also been spreading in schools, where some student groups extort money from their colleagues (information obtained during an interview with representatives of the local NGO Nurlubek, November 2011).
11 In July 2009, in Yekaterinburg, near the main entrance to the largest market in the Urals, Taganskii riad , a monument to the *chelnok* business was erected, see http://www.lenta.ru/news/2009/07/20/chelnok/.
12 At the time of interview, she was working for a licence trying to show as small an income as possible.
13 India became a popular place to buy goods, mostly garments of the oriental style which recently have gained relative popularity in Central Asia.
14 There is a lot of debate about the interplay between money and morality in the post-Soviet space including Kyrgyzstan. Some scholars think that money was less important than material goods during communism and it rapidly changed after transition. Undoubtedly, to some extent this is true. However, some people have nostalgia for the old system not because they do not like money but because political changes and market reconstruction brought them only poverty and instability. Nowadays, people often struggle not to become wealthy but just to survive: to pay for basic things such as bills, food, medicines, etc. Even, if someone is a relatively successful businesswoman like Olga, they cannot feel comfortable due to the constant change of the Kyrgyz political and economic reality.
15 In many countries of the former Bloc, the law changes mean the legal system still suffers from a lack of a comprehensive regulatory framework, with acts of law often contradicting one another, or with the regulations being riddled with loopholes. Consequently, there are many problems in terms of the implementation and enforcement of the law, but there is also room to evade the law. As regards Kyrgyzstan, the power shift which took place three times during the last few years has also contributed to the legislative chaos.

16 Interview with the director of a non-governmental organization, Bishkek 2006.
17 The trade regime of Uzbekistan restricts import of many kinds of goods. For example, for a wide range of consumer goods importers need to pay excise duty, for some goods VAT. Furthermore, non-food items imported for commercial purposes from neighbouring countries without certificate of origin, but not necessarily made in these countries, are taxed with an additional 20 per cent tax. At the same time, the considerable flow of Chinese goods to Uzbekistan from Kyrgyzstan mainly through the Karasu bazaar (but also via Dordoy), remain unregistered by official statistics. This is mainly carried out by shuttle trade of different scales (Umurzakov and Burzhubaev 2010).
18 She refers to the massacre in Andijan in 2005.
19 The trade at Dordoy dropped by about 50 per cent at that time (Osmonolieva 2011).
20 The customs union aims at eliminating the obstacles to trade and investment that went up after the collapse of the Soviet Union. However, there are many doubts as to how it will affect poorer countries such as Kyrgyzstan, and there are also opinions that the Dordoy will stop functioning, since now it works as a big 'warehouse' for cheap goods to be transferred to other countries.

References

Esim, S. (2002) 'Women's Informal Employment in Transition Economies', United Nations Division for the Advancement of Women (DAW) Expert Group Meeting on 'Empowerment of women throughout the life cycle as a transformative strategy for poverty eradication', 26–29 November 2001, New Delhi, India. Online. Available (accessed 31 March 2013).
Granick, D. (1987) *Job Rights in the Soviet Union: Their Consequences*, Cambridge: Cambridge University Press.
Humphrey, C. (2002) *The Unmaking of Soviet Life: Everyday Economies after Socialism* Ithaca, NY: Cornell University Press.
Kaiser, M. (1997) 'Informal Trade Sector in Uzbekistan', Working Paper No. 281, Bielefeld 1997.
Kandyoti, D. (2006) 'The Informal Economy and Global Economic Restructuring: Approaches and Debates', Lecture at SOAS, Department of Development Studies, London.
Osmonolieva, A. (2011) 'Micro-credit Expands in Kyrgyzstan Micro-lending to Aid in Rebuilding the Country, Economists say', *Central Asia Online*. Online. Available <http://centralasiaonline.com> (accessed 11 July 2012).
Ozcan, G. (2006) Djamila's Journey from Kolkhoz to Bazaar: Female Entrepreneurs in Kyrgyzstan, in Welter, F. (ed.) *Female Entrepreneurship in Transition*. Aldershot: Ashgate, pp. 93–115.
Polese, A. (2012) 'Who has the right to forbid and who to trade? Making sense of illegality on the Polish–Ukrainian border', in Bruns, B. and Miggelbrink, J. (eds), *Subverting Borders: Doing Research on Smuggling and Small-Scale Trade*, Wiesbaden: VS Verlag für Sozialwissenschaften/Springer Fachmedien Wiesbaden, pp. 21–38.
Portes, A. and Benton, L. (1984) 'Industrial Development and Labor Reinterpretation', *Population and Development Review* 10(4): 589–611.
Rasanayagam, J. (2011) 'Informal Economy, Informal State: The Case of Uzbekistan', *International Journal of Sociology and Social Policy* 31(11/12): 681–96.
Routh, S. (2011) 'Building Informal Workers Agenda: Imagining "Informal Employment" in Conceptual Resolution of "Informality"', *Global Labour Journal* 2(3): 208–27.

Sershen D. (2007) '"Made in China" moves into Russia's backyard', *Christian Science Monitor*, 4 January. Online. Available: <http://www.csmonitor.com/2007/0104/p06s01-wosc.html> (accessed 31 March 2013).

Shajkeeva, A. (2012) 'Karman Dordoja bol'shoj', Online. Available: (accessed 31 December 2012).

Slay, B. and Bravi, A. (2011) 'Recent Trends in Remittances and Migration Flows in Europe and Central Asia: The Best Protection against Economic Crisis?'. Online. Available <http://europeandcis.undp.org> (accessed 31 March 2013).

Spector, R. A. (2008) 'Securing Property in Contemporary Kyrgyzstan', *Post-Soviet Affairs* 24(2): 149–76.

Umurzakov, K. and Burzhubaev, T. (2010) 'Kyrgyzstan: Aid for Trade Needs Assessment', United Nations Development Programme. Online. Available: <http://europeandcis.undp.org> (accessed 31 March 2013).

UNDP (1999) Jaroslaw Gorniak, 'Poverty in Transition' <http://www.undp.org/dpa/publications/choicesforpoor/ENGLISH/CHAP06.PDF#search=%22Jaroslaw%20Gorniak%2Bpoverty%20in%20transition%22> (accessed: August 2006).

Wellisz, S. and Findlay, R. (1986) 'Central Planning and the "Second Economy" in Soviet Type Systems', *Economic Journal* 96(383): 646–58.

No Author (2009) 'V Ekaterinburge otkryli pamjatnik chelnokam'. Online. Available: <http://www.lenta.ru/news/2009/07/20/chelnok/> (accessed 31 March 2013).

8 'Business as casual'

Shuttle trade on the Belarus–Lithuania border[1]

Olga Sasunkevich

Introduction

This chapter is based on the case of 'Elena', a composite pseudonym, representing the story of two female school teachers working together at one of the schools in the Belarusian border town A located 20 km from the Belarus–Lithuania border. Both women are not only involved together in petty trade activities across the border, they also share an extremely similar social portrait: both of them are in their forties but live with parents and have neither husbands nor children. They are also regular (Catholic) churchgoers. The case represents a story of women for whom cross-border petty trade is not a professional, but rather an additional and occasional economic practice in which people get involved not because of necessity but rather due to certain favourable circumstances determined by their personal and family stories as well as by the specificities of the border region. Analysing this case and supporting it by data from my research in the border town A which took place in 2010–2012,[2] I attempt to demonstrate the multiplicity of cross-border petty trade and of factors which make this activity a widespread practice of everyday life in the borderland region.

According to the definition of international petty trading given by Allan Williams and Vladimir Baláž, it presents 'a form of arbitrage ... understood as the exploitation of differences in prices and exchange rates over time and space via circulation activities' (Williams and Baláž 2002: 323). The authors also underline that since international petty traders usually have limited capital, they tend to exploit the differences in prices between countries over relatively short distances (ibid.). Therefore, the geographical proximity of an international border is significant for petty trade. In Belarus, however, the latter statement is complicated by the fact that three of its five state borders (the Belarus–Lithuania border is one of them) have been the borders of the Schengen Area since 2007. This external circumstance makes a border an additional obstacle to petty trade. Nevertheless, post-Soviet border regions still remain a space where this kind of trade has not only kept its popularity but has even intensified in the recent years. Therefore, in this chapter I try to understand which particular resources border regions provide for people, how they differ from those in hinterlands and in which particular circumstances 'the border may be used as an economic resource by inhabitants living nearby' (Bruns and Miggelbrink 2012: 11).

Since the collapse of the Soviet Union petty trade (also known as shuttle trade, or *chelnochnaia torgovlia*) has become an important economic activity in post-Soviet states. However, the motivation to undertake this activity has changed during the last 20 years. Survival, which has been often considered as a leading motive for the involvement into petty trade, has ceased playing such a significant or at least a primary role in this regard. I argue that nowadays people would rather start shuttle trade when they have certain opportunities to do this, i.e. pull factors might better explain people's motivation to be engaged into this activity. This shift from 'trading for necessity' to 'trading for "advantage"' (Stammler-Gossman 2012: 234) is not a particular Belarusian phenomenon. The same tendency, for instance, is identified in prosperous Russian border regions (Murmansk region and St. Petersburg) which border Finland (ibid.).

Thus this chapter aims to shed light on the particular everyday practices of shuttle trade in the border regions. The aim of the chapter is to demonstrate how informal petty economy works on the border, which resources it needs and which particular favourable circumstances it exploits in the border region. I also seek to explain what motivates people to become involved in shuttle trade and why survival or economic necessity cannot provide us with the exhaustive interpretation of the persistent existence of petty trade on borders. Moreover, considering petty trade as 'the normality of life in the border area' (see Müller and Miggelbrink in this volume) I try to elaborate on the social meaning of shuttle trade in border regions.

Beyond survival: informal economy and petty trade practices after socialism

Although the roots of shuttle trade lie within the history of socialism, real flourishing of petty trading practices began in the period of post-socialist transformations. A significant body of scholarly work on this issue which was published in the 1990s–early 2000s dealt with empirical data gathered in the first 5–6 years after the collapse of the socialist bloc and the disintegration of the Soviet Union (Iglicka and Sword 1999; Irek 1998; Morokvasic 2003; Sik and Wallace 1999). However, nowadays, after more than 20 years of political and economic change in the region petty trade has survived the period of transformations and become an activity embedded in economic and social structures of post-socialism. The resurgence of scholarly interest and the increasing literature on the issue published in recent years indicates this conspicuously (see, for example, Bruns 2010; Olimpieva *et al*. 2007; Stammler-Gossmann 2012; Wagner 2011; Wagner and Łukowski 2010). However, an important question still remains – how can we explain this persistence of petty trade in East Europe and in particular in its border regions?[3]

Many studies of the earlier periods of shuttle trade regard it as a survival strategy during times of economic and social transformations (Andreeva 2003; Iglicka 1999; Konstantinov *et al*. 1998; Sword 1998). This explanation has been criticized for its insufficient interpretation of the persistent character of shuttle trade in post-Soviet countries (see, for example, Klimova 2006; Williams and Baláž 2002). Svetlana Klimova even suggests that the 'story of survival' might be a kind of narrative required for the legitimization of shuttle trade by people involved in this activity (Klimova 2006: 31–2), especially taking into consideration the extremely low or even stigmatized social status of such trading after socialism (Andreeva 2003; Wallace *et al.* 1999; Williams and Baláž: 2002; Zhurzhenko 2008). Nevertheless, even recent studies of the cross-border petty trade still consider survival as a leading motive for people's involvement in this activity (Polese 2006; Wagner 2011). In his comprehensive research on petty smuggling on the Polish–Russian border, for example, Mathias Wagner stresses this point several times, citing poverty and the lack of labour opportunities as reasons why petty trade in the region is not only widespread but also highly tolerated by the local society (Wagner 2011: 23, 315, 317). Although Wagner also analyses social implications of the petty trade and its embeddedness in the everyday life of the society in a provincial Polish town on the border, his interpretation of people's motives for involvement in petty trade remains primarily centred on economic rationality lying behind their choice. Income and self-sufficiency in the inferior social and economic conditions are considered as a primary reason for people becoming involved into shuttle trade.

Acknowledging the importance of economic factors in prompting people to start petty trade, I, nevertheless, argue that scholarly perspectives could be broadened and include other explanations. Having much in common, the practices of shuttle trade on different borders remain contextually determined to a certain extent. That is why the situation on the Russian side of the Russian–Finnish border, for example, is rather different from that described by Wagner in relation to the border between Russia and Poland. As Anna Stammler-Gossman maintains, shuttle trade for highly industrialized and compactly populated areas of Murmansk region and St. Petersburg

> is no longer merely a survival niche for those marginalized by society and neither is it about a scarcity of basic goods and services. . . . Nowadays, northern cross-border petty trade is a dynamic sector that is driven more by trading for 'advantage' rather than by trading for necessity. Shuttle trading activities may even be associated with higher incomes that often exceed those in the formal sector. (Stammler-Gossman 2012: 234)

Investigating the shuttle trade on the Belarusian side of the border between Belarus and Lithuania, I also argue that survival does not explain the whole range of petty trading activities. I was pushed to consider this issue by the following striking examples that appeared during my own fieldwork. Talking to some people involved in petty trade activities, I noticed that many of them indeed mentioned profit as a primary justification for carrying goods across the border. However, what confused me was the way they calculated their profit. Often my respondents either could not say explicitly what exactly they took into consideration to establish the prices they sold their goods at or they referred only to the actual revenue they gained without taking into account expenses accompanying their trips to carry commodities across the border. Another example I observed and which did not make any sense to me at first was the relations between the traders and the driver of a local bus from Vilnius to A. According to some internal agreement, most passengers did not buy their tickets at the ticket office but paid the driver directly although he was not allowed to sell tickets on the bus. Confusingly, passengers not only paid the same price they could have paid at the cash desk but also the whole procedure to arrange this seemed rather inconvenient for them. First, they had to come to the platform the bus departed from in order to occupy a place on the bus and to leave their bags there. Then they had to go out of the bus station and to wait until the bus picked them up not far away from it. Otherwise, there was a risk that leaving the station the bus could have been checked by a station inspector and the driver could have been penalized if it had appeared that the passengers had not had tickets. Thus the whole situation did not make much sense for traders from the point of view of either profit or convenience; therefore, I supposed that some other factors lay behind it. Hence these two examples need some theoretical explanations to shed light on mutual relations between economic and social aspects of shuttle trade. The first question is how to explain the lack of calculation in petty trade if profit is considered as its leading motive. The second is whether the solidarity between the traders and the driver and among the traders themselves has only economic rationality or other social reasons lie at the core of its interpretation.

Following Adrian Smith's ideas on the nature of informality after socialism, I suggest that we should consider informal economic practices, in particular petty trade, as 'complex cultural and socioeconomic phenomena' (Smith 2010: 47). Smith and Stenning argue that informal activities in postsocialism 'are best seen as practices because they are part of a regular set of activities undertaken and used by individuals to try to sustain livelihoods but also to sustain a sociality to economic life which requires mutual, reciprocal and embedded forms of economic activity' (Smith and Stenning 2006: 192). Understanding informal economic activities in this way, we can examine 'different, and at times divergent, forces' which constitute them (ibid: 193). Considering the issue of survival, Smith underlines that it can barely explain the fact that in Slovakia, for instance, where his research took place, people involved in the so-called 'dacha economy' were 'not the poorest and the most excluded, but those who have access to the resources necessary to sustain a relatively inefficient form of food production' (Smith 2010: 52). Therefore, the argument is that informal economic activities do not occur as only the result of economic necessity but for other, more complicated, reasons (Smith and Stenning 2006: 196). Smith suggests that in order to understand them we should reconsider informal economy as a practice of everyday life with a 'range of economic and resource activities' attributed to it (Smith 2010: 53).

To grasp the multiplicity and heterogeneity of informal economic activities after socialism, some scholars apply Michel de Certeau's ideas on the practice of everyday life, in particular his distinction between strategies and tactics as modes of everyday practice (Round *et al.* 2010: 1200). From this perspective multiple informal economic activities can be regarded as 'spaces of resistance and coping tactics' in response to different types of marginalization (ibid: 1198). This marginalization does not unavoidably mean low income and the necessity of survival (ibid: 1200); people may feel disappointed by the lack of consumer variety, high taxes, a border regime. Most important is that, as opposed to strategies, 'tactics are a negotiation of the space enveloped by the strategies of the powerful' (ibid.). This distinction has another important dimension: enabled in the space of the other, tactics, according to de Certeau, have a rather spontaneous character: they depend on time ('always on the watch for opportunities that must be seized "on the wing"') and on circumstances (where '[p]eople have to make do with what they have') (de Certeau 1988: xix, 18). In other words, tactics are enabled at appropriate moments when people 'are able to combine heterogeneous elements' and to turn them into 'opportunities' (de Certeau 1988: xix). Therefore, according to de Certeau, these 'victories of the "weak" over the strong' (as he explains the social meaning of tactics) have nothing like a strategy (or pure economic rationality) behind them; they are rather 'ways of operating', 'clever tricks, knowing how to get away with things, "hunter's cunning", manoeuvres, polymorphic simulations, joyful discoveries, poetic as well as war like' (ibid.).

Considering informal economy and petty trade as a part of people's common everyday activity in this way, I argue that a 'casual' petty trade which is the central focus of this chapter emerges on the intersection of certain dissatisfaction, economic interests, favourable circumstances and appropriate time to be involved in it. In the following sections I try to illustrate how all of these factors work together in a particular case. However, one more comment that should be made before I proceed to the analysis of the case is the social logic of petty trade. Round *et al.* argue that there is a need to explore 'decommodified' spaces of non-capitalist/non-market relations in informal economic activities (in particular, in domestic food production) 'beyond the economic rationales . . . to examine the plurality of practices in operation within and around them' (Round *et al.* 2010: 1201). Their approach corresponds to de Certeau's argument according to which diverse everyday operations including subversive economic practices form a particular logic or 'a "popular" *ratio*' (de Certeau 1988: xv) that the social consists of after all. Therefore, sociality is always presented in economic operations which 'derive their meaning and their *efficacy* from the same cultural logic that informs social life in general' (White 1994: 157). In contrast to neoclassical economists who admit the existence of mutual commitments in 'real' markets but consider them as 'imperfections in ideal model' or to new institutional economists who tend to treat mutuality as a part of transactional costs aimed after all at economic efficacy, Stephen Gudeman argues that 'all economies are both embedded and disembedded. Economy contains two value realms, mutuality and market, or community and impersonal trade' which, according to Gudeman, are always 'dialectically connected' (Gudeman 2009: 18–19). Thus to understand particular economic activities and the motives attached to them we need to take into consideration a particular social, cultural and geographical context in which these practices emerge. In other words, 'the economic . . . cannot be simply conjectured to be separate from the society it takes place; this economic practice is a subset of the society in which it occurs' (Williams and Marcelli 2010: 230). Therefore, analysing the results of interviews and of the fieldwork I also try to understand how both economic and social aspects interplay in the case of cross-border petty trade and what this complicated interaction can tell us about economic and social relations after socialism.

Space as a weapon of the weak: resources of the Belarus–Lithuania borderland

Writing on the spaces of economic practice in post-socialism Smith and Stenning suggest that we should address adequately 'multiple geographies within which such practices are constituted, enabled and constrained' (Smith and Stenning 2006: 191). This takes place on a variety of scales or spaces in which economic relationships are reconstructed and reproduced (ibid: 203). In other words, economic practices are shaped and determined by a particular space which, following de Certeau, could be understood as 'a practiced place', a locus transformed into a space by operations of social agents (de Certeau 1988: 117). Therefore, to practice a place means to operate it through particular tactics. In other words, to operate a place means to manipulate it through manoeuvres and tricks gaining opportunities from it. I suggest that in considering a borderland as such a particular place it is important to understand how this place becomes a space, or how it is experienced and operated by its inhabitants in order to provide the 'victories of the "weak"'. I argue that first of all a particular space, whether a family, a community or a region, supplies people with particular resources which can be unavailable to those who do not belong to it. Following the logic of de Certeau on the combination of heterogeneous elements and turning them into an advantage, different aspects of a space should coincide and intersect at a certain moment in order to make it favourable for an agent. In what follows I will demonstrate how this coincidence takes place and is practised in the particular case.

Having emerged at the intersection of the personal, family and community scales, three factors make shuttle trade available to Elena – the Polish ethnicity of her family, Elena's belonging to the Roman Catholic Church, and the existence of a certain knowledge of how petty trade functions rooted both in her family experience and in the experience of a broader milieu of Elena's friends, neighbours and colleagues. At the same time all three factors are determined by the history of the region to which a town A belongs and are activated by the current situation in which the town exists. Thus the public and the private (space), the history and the present (time) interact and through this interaction Elena's petty trade is being brought into life.

First of all, history matters here. Most of the town's inhabitants are Catholics and the influence of the Roman Catholic Church as well as of Poland's history is important. Town A had been part of Poland before 1939 when as the result of the Soviet invasion it was incorporated into the USSR. After World War II many Poles left A according to the agreement on repatriation between Poland and the Soviet Union. However, the ethnic Poles did not emigrate from the town entirely.

Many of them stayed. The situation when a part of the family emigrated and a part remained in the town was common in the region. This was the case of Elena's mother's family. Elena's aunt left A in 1946 and since then has resided in Poland. However, Elena's family have always kept connections with their Polish relatives. These connections were important for petty trade because during socialism Poland was a country where shuttle trade was advanced (Williams and Baláž 2002: 326). At the same time many citizens of A travelled to Poland during the Soviet period. Many of my respondents as well as other people in the town share this experience. On the one hand, in the forefront of those trips were visits to relatives. On the other hand, the economic aspect also mattered. The small provincial Soviet town was poorly provided with consumer goods especially those of Western origin. However, gold (more precisely gold jewellery), coffee, flax linen, and some technical equipment were accessible to people, although with certain restrictions. These goods were transported into Poland and sold in order to receive some local currency which was either unavailable or strictly limited for citizens of the Soviet Union. Then this currency was spent on clothes and textiles imported into Poland from other socialist countries, in particular from Hungary and Yugoslavia. These commodities were easily sold in A upon return.

Thus the roots of cross-border petty trade in the town lie in its Soviet past. The knowledge of shuttle trade is shared by many in A and is a part of the intergenerational and intergroup experience of people in the town (people from different social strata were involved in this trade in the 1980s). At the same time shuttle trade in A in the Soviet period was directed towards the border with Poland while the internal Soviet Belarus–Lithuania border did not have any significance in this regard. There was only an administrative boundary between the two Soviet republics, completely porous for people in the region; therefore, trade did not make much sense since everyone was able to travel to Lithuania, in particular to Vilnius, and to bring whatever they needed. Consequently, Vilnius was an essential part of people's everyday life. Elena recalls:

> I remember being young we did not know what Minsk was – because it was far away [120 km], but Vilnius – it is 50 km away, when it was visa-free, border-free. Yes, we were more regularly in Vilnius. I remember it like today: Mama receives an advance payment or a monthly wage, at 7.30 goes to Vilnius, and at 10.30 she is already back, hands full of foodstuffs. . . . Everything was bought in Vilnius. Even flowers. When one needed flowers for 1 September [the beginning of the school year in the USSR], one went to Vilnius and brought them.

Moreover, Vilnius was the main destination for local migration from the region:

> Many people moved from here to Vilnius when they had an opportunity. That's it, the relatives, here in every family, ask any person, everyone has a relative in Vilnius. Especially those from villages. There were fewer people in town who left, but villages . . . From villages young people moved to Vilnius at that time. Vilnius, Vilnius, it was the closest to us.

The past of the Belarus–Lithuania border region represented in these extracts has important resource consequences for shuttle trade. First, there is an established tradition of consumption in the town oriented towards Lithuanian goods which are regarded as cheaper and of a better quality than those in Belarus. This tradition appeared in Soviet times but was not interrupted by the border's appearance. On the contrary, it became a stimulus for the development of cross-border trade between Belarus and Lithuania afterwards. In some sense today the lack of proper consumer supply in the provincial Belarusian town as well as the dissatisfaction of people with the prices is a kind of marginalization which many in A experience and try to cope with. Therefore, the demand for goods from Lithuania is high in the town and is mostly satisfied through informal networks. The latter makes shuttle trade not only more or less profitable (although in a rather special sense which was mentioned above) but also easily implemented. Second, another important resource inherited from Soviet times is the previous knowledge of Vilnius and of its trade destinations (open air markets, in particular) gained as a result of everyday consumption practices in the region during Soviet period. This knowledge is shared by many in A and has an intergenerational dimension as in the case of my youngest respondent, for instance, who was born almost before the disintegration of the Soviet Union but 'inherited' this knowledge from her mother who is also involved in shuttle trade. Third, the practice of local migration from A to Vilnius led to the establishment of an extensive social network between the two places. Besides circulation of information, this network has an outstanding structural meaning for the trade since most of those who have relatives in Vilnius, or, in other words, are included in this network, can apply for multiple-entry visas to cross the border regularly.

Elena herself, however, is not a part of this network since her family does not have any relatives in Lithuania, but only in Poland. This to some extent explains the fact that during a long period (more than 10 years) Elena had hardly visited Lithuania and had resumed her trips only very recently before I met her for the first time. This case demonstrates what we can understand by a pertinent moment or *utilization of time* upon which tactics operate (de Certeau 1988: 38–9). As I mentioned already, Elena shares some family and community knowledge about how to set up petty trade business. She also gained some experience carrying goods across the Belarus–Lithuania border in the early 1990s when the border appeared. Moreover, she is surrounded by people who are well aware of how to handle a successful trade business (her colleague, for instance, who operates an advanced and almost legal business based on the principles of cross-border petty trade). The question is which element of the puzzle is missing here; what precisely prevented Elena turning these diverse aspects of her experience into practice or 'a way of operating'?

In his research on the Polish–Russian border Wagner suggests that to understand entirely the social implications of shuttle trade we need to consider not only why people start this activity but also why they do not (Wagner 2011: 23). According to Wagner, the main reason for involvement in petty trade or cross-border smuggling in a Polish provincial town where his research took place is unemployment and poverty. However, he argues that although cross-border trade is widely distributed among the disadvantaged in the region, not all of them consider the trade as a way out of their unfavourable situation. Wagner concludes that the main factors which prevent the poor or unemployed from involvement in trade are their professional socialization, the lack of necessary financial and social resources, and the low status of the trade in the local society (Wagner 2011: 114). Nevertheless, I argue that in the case of Elena the situation is to some extent different. Professional identity of a teacher is indeed important for her; however, in her narrative she never stresses discomfort in combining teaching with shuttle trade. Neither does she seek to justify her choice for the interviewer.[4] Elena also has important resources such as her knowledge, network and experience which she has been able to make use of for the current activity. The trade is indeed still considered as a dubious practice by some in the region, but since Elena does not identify herself with traders entirely, she does not consider this as a particular problem for herself. Foremost, she is a teacher with some occasional involvement in informal trade.

The only barrier she specifies in her interview is the border regime which according to Elena prevented her from visiting Lithuania until recently. However, she barely recalls which particular regulations she could not cope with. Simultaneously Elena notes that she applied for a single-entry national visa to Lithuania at least twice before the Schengen Agreement but she used those visas for vacations on the Baltic Sea coast. Therefore, I suggest that during that period Elena actually did not have a strong necessity to be involved into shuttle trade. Otherwise, she would have found a way to get a visa and to include the visa expenses in the commodities' price, taking into consideration that until the border between Belarus and Lithuania gained the status of a Schengen border, the whole procedure of application for a Lithuanian national visa was neither very expensive ($5) nor complicated. Therefore, I hypothesize that the lack of motivation or necessity kept Elena from getting involved in shuttle trade.

Nonetheless, what has changed recently is not a sudden economic necessity as one might suppose. An appropriate moment, an opportunity, prompted Elena to turn back to petty trade. Paradoxically enough, this opportunity for Elena was brought by the Schengen Agreement which was supposed to toughen border-crossing rules between the European Union and non-EU countries. However, peculiarities of local history and Elena's family circumstances combined with Schengen to weaken the border in this particular case. For a long time the Catholic Church in A had provided its members with Polish visas to visit holy places in Poland. Nevertheless, as Elena states, there were not so many of those who wanted to go to Poland but 'now there is no end of them', she says. The reason for this sudden interest in pilgrimage is that since 2007 a multi-entry visa to Poland has allowed people to cross the Belarus–Lithuania border as well, and people can use this opportunity for petty trade activities. And this is how *Elena* regained the opportunity to visit Vilnius and to venture into petty trade.

Thus the case of Elena demonstrates that people do not always intentionally initiate informal activities themselves but rather try not to miss their chance to do this if it accidentally appears. Another respondent who does not imagine the prosperity of her family without her trade would have probably never started it if she had not worked at a sports organization which provided her with a Schengen visa very recently. In other words, petty trade is not always a particular strategy, or 'the calculus of force-relationships' which 'assumes a place that can be circumscribed as *proper*' (de Certeau 1988: xix); it is rather based on 'a *logic of operation of actions relative to types of situation*' (de Certeau 1988: 21, emphasis added).

But this *logic of operation* can be enabled only in certain circumstances. The reason why the combination of different factors results in shuttle trade lies in the fact that this activity is well-known in the border region and the border itself is considered in its economical aspect first of all. In this sense we observe not just a particular coincidence of factors but precisely 'a "popular" *ratio*, a way of thinking invested in a way of acting' (de Certeau 1988: xv). Therefore, to have an opportunity and not to use the border for gaining at least tiny economic revenue is often considered by locals as puzzling behaviour. One of the dialogues between two local women noted during my fieldwork trip was as follows: 'Do you carry something? – Of course, why else would one go there.' Hence to use the border in this way is regarded as a type of social convention in the region. Following de Certeau, I suggest then that not only economic rationality lies behind this convention, but rather a kind of social solidarity (de Certeau 1988: 25). In the following section I develop this idea.

Market and mutuality: balancing between solidarity and economic rationality

The start of a regular trip from Vilnius to A on a local bus may seem for an external observer as total chaos. People (mostly women) come to the bus, then they leave the bus and disappear, then they come to the bus again but this time from outside of the bus station. Then someone collects money from most of the passengers and gives it to the driver; afterwards the passengers start exchanging things (food and clothes) with each other in order to repack and to hide them. People are rather nervous at this moment since the bus is small and the distance from the border is rather short, only 30 km, therefore the time to get ready for border control is limited. Some slight conflicts among women may appear but they are quickly and easily solved. When the process of exchange and hiding is done, the bus becomes relatively calm. The people have a bite of some food which they have bought in Vilnius. They share the food with each other and occasionally some of them even have a drink. Meanwhile the bus leaves Vilnius and gradually approaches a border crossing point. A little tension starts growing. Everyone is speaking about the border. Women are trying to work out which customs officers are on duty at the moment and whether the border crossing will be peaceful or if something will happen. They are sharing their stories on how and who was caught by officers in the morning on the way to Vilnius. Simultaneously some of them are trying to distribute some additional jeans among passengers they do not know, and I also offer help. Fortunately, we pass the border without any incidents. When the bus leaves the crossing point, the reverse exchange of goods takes place; everyone takes back what she has given. After that, a relaxed time begins. The women do not talk about the border anymore; they are back to their daily problems: the wedding of someone's son, a home loan, prices, currency exchange rates and so on. After the bus comes to A, everyone leaves it and goes in their own directions.

Such a regular bus carries three types of passengers. The majority are women like Elena who make their trips from time to time in order to provide themselves with cheaper goods from Lithuania but at the same time to earn some money selling some commodities to friends, neighbours and colleagues. Another group – a smaller one – is made up of women who work on a more professional level: they carry jeans and other clothes across the border for an entrepreneur from Minsk and are paid for this. The third group is the tiniest: it consists of occasional passengers who are rare guests on this bus. Nevertheless, all three groups of passengers and the driver express their solidarity with each other at the particular moment of the trip and especially at the border crossing. It is at this particular moment mutual and economic realms of the petty trade intersect.

Writing on petty trade on the border between Turkey and Bulgaria, Henrik Egbert argues that almost everything that happens at the moment of the border crossing among, on the one hand, traders themselves, and, on the other hand, traders and other involved agents (customs officials, a travel agent who accompanies such trips and negotiates with border controllers on behalf of traders) is a matter of rational choice (Egbert 2006: 355, 356). Egbert considers petty trade in the framework of New Institutional Economics and argues that 'it is a rational behaviour when individuals rely on social capital (acquaintances, relatives, etc.) on the bus because it reduces the risk of suffering from opportunistic behaviour' (Egbert 2006: 356). At the same time Egbert himself gives an example of social solidarity among traders describing a situation when one of them was forced to pay import duties (while the rest of the group was able to cross the border without paying) and received voluntary compensation from other traders afterwards.[5] However, Egbert still tries to find a rational explanation and argues that such 'solidarity' might be forced by a tour guide who could oblige other traders to pay this compensation in order to keep her reputation of being able to protect every trader (Egbert 2006: 356).

I partially agree with Egbert on the point that social solidarity among traders on the Belarus–Lithuania border is to some extent economically rational. The main aim of commodities exchange is to carry goods across the border. According to recent customs regulations on the borders of Belarus, a person travelling across the border regularly (at least once every five days) cannot import a significant quantity of identical goods to Belarus. These regulations mainly target the inhabitants of border regions and are aimed at preventing intensive informal cross-border petty trade. However, as many people in the town of A say, these regulations are rather fuzzy, and their implementation pretty much depends on the discretion of customs officers. This ambiguity of law enforcement was also proved by one high-rank customs official who told me that in the case of petty trade, customs officers working at crossing points are authorized to decide for themselves whether a person is carrying goods for commercial reasons or not.[6] Besides, I noted several times that traders themselves are not entirely sure what rights they have and which quantity of different goods they are actually allowed to carry.[7] Therefore, to avoid additional problems even in the situation when nothing illegal is carried, passengers exchange their goods among each other in order to mix them and to escape suspicion during the border control. Thus the social network appearing as a result of this exchange determined, paraphrasing Mauss, by the 'obligation to take'[8] becomes part of the traders' regular activity. Traders know that they can always rely on someone the day they carry something illegal. It is especially true in relation to those women who carry cigarettes across the border. Taking clothes on the way back from Vilnius, they expect to some extent that another time someone will take a couple of cigarette boxes on their way from A to Vilnius. In other words, constant reciprocity takes place, and effective trade to a large extent depends on it.

Economic rationality, however, does not explain the entire situation as in the case of unofficial paying of the bus driver which does not have any evident economic sense and, moreover, causes additional inconvenience for traders. Such paying may be considered, first, as a supplementary reward to a driver for his patience during the processes of hiding and exchange but also as a prepayment for possible problems which crossing the border with traders on board may occasionally cause for him.[9] However, I also suggest that this unofficial paying may simply express solidarity with a person from the same town who is also given the opportunity to earn some additional money. It is worth mentioning that most women know the driver well and address him by his first name. The money from passengers is gathered very carefully, and most people themselves express the wish 'to pass it to Kolia'. At this moment the driver shares the experience of being involved in informal activity, and through this experience most people in the bus are symbolically united. In this sense the situation recalls that described by Jenny White in Turkish society where the economy (labour, trade) is not only based on social relations but also fosters them. She argues that 'among the small-scale commodity producers in Istanbul, money is not fetishized as a commodity that breeds money . . . , nor is money as capital. . . . Rather, money is embodied in social life itself, as part of a system of reciprocal exchange' (White 1994: 157). In other words, money establishes social bonds between people playing sometimes the same role as a gift in traditional societies.[10] By giving money to a bus driver, traders recognize him as a part of their group involving him in a system of reciprocal relations.

The social bonds arising as a result of such exchanges which take place in the bus may extend the external space of trade as in the case of the group of 'professional' traders who work together for a long time and whose relations exceed those characterizing co-workers:

Researcher: 'And which relations do you have with your colleagues, with this group of people you have mentioned above, with these women? Are you friends in your regular life or it is only trade that connects you?'
Katerina: 'Well, in regular life there are birthdays, anniversaries; there was one in September, in October one celebrated their fiftieth, now in April another one will celebrate her 55th, this one who I mentioned trades at Gariunai [a large open air market in Vilnius]. Her daughter is in Sweden, so she will come, and she will reserve somewhere in a Russian restaurant. I had an anniversary, we all together, all our company celebrated.'

At the same time even the economic rationality of trade can be represented in terms of decent social relations: 'monetary relations may be represented *as* bonds of kinship and friendship' (White 1994: 157). As Elena, for example, explains, she mostly carries goods for sale when someone gives her a particular order, and to satisfy this order is considered as a part of local social rules. Elena herself regards this as a way in which her trade is not simply oriented to her own profit but is rather aimed at doing a *favour* to her friends and colleagues:

Elena: 'I bring stuff both for myself, and for others. Clothes generally. What is needed. Sometimes this, sometimes jeans, sometimes that, to order, the girls [*devchata*] ask. Only to order. When you go, they know already that you are going, and one asks for this, another asks for that, you know, teacher's wage; everyone wants something cheaper but, however, quality . . . '
Researcher: 'But you sell a little more expensive then . . . '
Elena: 'Well, yes, already to earn for myself. But at the same time it's good both for me and for those who buy because we don't have such prices anyway.'

In other words, Elena's activity arises at the intersection of market, or economic, reasoning ('to earn for myself') and mutuality, or social relations (to satisfy the demands of friends and colleagues). Moreover, as another of my informants states, one of the most complicated issues is to 'cross the line' between these two realms, to overcome the expectations of community members that you will bring them orders from Lithuania for free and to start selling these orders to them. Therefore, 'the naked economic aspects of the relation (buying, selling, money, profit) become euphemized as personal relations of loyalty, trust, and membership in a group . . . as friends or symbolic kin' (White 1994: 98). In this sense shuttle trade goes beyond an economic motivation and can be to a certain extent compared to the diversionary practice of *la perruque* which, according to de Certeau, 'is free, creative, and precisely not directed toward profit' but allows workers to confirm their social solidarity with 'other worker or . . . family' (de Certeau 1988: 25). What this solidarity might say about the post-socialist societies in which such practices are embedded is a question which needs some further consideration.

Conclusions

'Business as casual', the metaphor opening the title of this chapter, has an ambiguous meaning here. It describes shuttle trade on the border between Belarus and Lithuania as not only a part of everyday life but also as an irregular, to some extent spontaneous and unplanned *diversionary* tactic existing notwithstanding toughening rules of border crossings and goods transportation. Considering the case of such a trade through the story of Elena, I have tried to overcome the problem of prevailing macro-scale survey research on informal economy after socialism which often fails to articulate connections between scales and economic formations, such as state and household (Smith and Stenning 2006: 204). In a more nuanced way I attempted to understand how petty trade on borders occurred and which social relations it simultaneously requires and brings into existence. Rather than being a strategy of survival, 'casual' shuttle trade, I suggest, should be interpreted as a tactic, a way of operating, a practice of everyday life which appears at the intersection of favourable coincidences, economic interests and social tolerance of trade in the border region. In the logic of de Certeau which I sought to follow, this practice becomes a part of people's social life and either requires or even stimulates social solidarity in the local community.

However, one last question I would like to briefly touch upon here is what conclusions on post-socialist transformation in Belarus one can possibly make from this case? Leaving apart the methodological problem of the extrapolation of micro studies on the entire society, we can suggest, reformulating Gudeman, that since economic practices where market realm has not '*colonized* and *debased* the mutual one' (Gudeman 2009: 19, original emphasis) (as this case demonstrates) still exist, then market rationality has not expanded in this society so extensively. On the local scale of a small provincial town traditional social relations still play an important role in how everyday life is organized. Town A is a tiny place where individualism and rationality of urban life are dominated by the relations of kinship and mutual aid. Social networks have a crucial meaning for the everyday life in the town. I experienced this extensively trying to find respondents for my research and feeling a constant resistance within the field until a couple of important contacts inside the network of traders were established. However, I would argue that this personalized nature of social life (Lonkila 1997: 1) extends boundaries of a local community and confronts Belarusian society in general. The importance of informal exchange of 'favours, goods or important information' which, according to scholars, is inherited from socialism (Lonkila 1997: 3), continues to be a significant part of social life in Belarus especially taking into consideration that since the USSR's collapse Belarus's economy on the macro level remains mainly unreformed and barely 'marketized' (Havlik 2009: 214). Nevertheless, should we understand this 'lack' of economic rationality and importance of informal exchanges only as the consequence of failing economic reforms or, in other words, as a blocking element in the transition to capitalism? Following Smith and Stenning, I would suggest that more nuanced explanations shedding light on the meaning of informal activities within and outside global capitalism are needed.

Notes

1 I would like to thank the editors of this volume for their valuable comments on the first drafts of the chapter and theoretical suggestions which prompted me to reinterpret my empirical material. I am also grateful to the participants of the workshop *Infringing the Border* which took place in the frame of 15th Berlin Roundtable *Borders and Borderlands* (28–31 March 2012) for their comments on my paper where the case of *Elena* was also discussed.
2 The research was funded by German Research Foundation (DFG) (IRTG 1540 'Baltic Borderlands: Shifting Boundaries of Mind and Culture in the Borderlands of the Baltic

Sea Region' (University of Greifswald, Germany) and is a part of the work on the PhD-dissertation 'From Political Borders to Social Boundaries: the History of Shuttle Trade on the Belarus–Lithuania border (1990–2011)'.
3 It should be noted that most of the recent literature dealing with petty trade after socialism concerns border regions, in particular the external borders of the European Union.
4 For more on moral justificatiions of shuttle trade see, for example, Polese 2006 and Sasunkevich 2010.
5 Egbert argues that this compensation 'can only be rational if the traders expect reciprocity in case they are in a similar situation. However, since the traders in a bus do not establish a permanent trading group that will travel together again in future, it seems to be irrational to compensate someone with whom they will not travel again and from whom they cannot expect reciprocal behavior' (Egbert 2006: 356).
6 Such ambiguity creates multiple possibilities for corruption. Corruption among customs and border officers in the case of shuttle trade is described by many authors (see, for example, Egbert 2006; Polese 2006; Wagner 2011). However, most of my respondents kept silent on this issue in their interviews, although in non-taped conversations some cases were mentioned.
7 Egbert argues that corruption on the border may also be provoked by the lack of information among traders for whom 'it was nearly impossible to get details about import law and regulations'. That is why, Egbert suggests, 'it became a rational decision for the trader to look for an alternative institution that would reduce information costs and would allow an untaxed import of goods' (Egbert 2006: 354). However, in the case I describe here the 'alternative institution' of commodities exchange is not a matter of rational choice but rather a consequence of spontaneity of the shuttle trade activity when possible risks are not entirely taken into account. Sometimes women in the bus take part in the exchange without any visible necessity, just because everyone else around does it.
8 The citation from Mauss is taken from de Certeau: 'It is no doubt related to the *potlatch* described by Mauss, an interplay of voluntary allowances that counts on reciprocity and organizes a social network articulated by the "obligation to give"' (de Certeau 1988: 27).
9 After all, a driver is responsible for the bus: if something illegal or suspicious is found and no one will take responsibility, the driver will be accountable. Therefore, non-local drivers who drive transit buses (Kaunas–Minsk, Vilnius–Minsk) sometimes even refuse to take people from town A on board in order to avoid additional problems.
10 According to of the position of Parry and Bloch which White relates in her book, 'where the economy is not seen as a separate and amoral domain, monetary relations are not likely to be represented as the antithesis of bonds of kinship and friendship. In such societies, money may be appropriate as a gift' (White 1994: 157). It is worth mentioning that in Belarusian society money may still serve as a birthday or wedding present.

References

Andreeva, T. (2003) 'Chelnochnyi biznes kak strategiia domohoziaistva: Analiz rezultatov empiricheskogo issledovaniia', In *Gendernye otnosheniia v sovremennoi Rossii: issledovaniia 1990-h godov*, L. Popkova and I. Tartakovskaja (eds), Samara: Samarskii Universitet: 121–42.

Bruns, B. (2010) *Grenze als Ressource: Die soziale Organisation von Schmuggel am Rande der Europäischen Union*, Wiesbaden: VS Verlag.

Bruns, B. and Miggelbrink, J. (2012) 'Introduction', In *Subverting Borders: Doing Research on Smuggling and Small-Scale Trade*, B. Bruns and J. Miggelbrink (eds), Wiesbaden: VS Verlag: 11–19.

de Certeau, M. (1988) *The Practice of Everyday Life*, Berkeley, Los Angeles; London: University of California Press.

Egbert, H. (2006) 'Cross-Border Small-Scale Trading in South-Eastern Europe: Do Embeddedness and Social Capital Explain Enough?', *International Journal of Urban and Regional Research* 30(2): 346–61.

Gudeman, S. (2009) 'Necessity or Contingency: Mutuality and Market', In *Market and Society: the Great Transformation Today*, C. Hann and K. Hart (eds), Cambridge: Cambridge University Press, pp. 17–37.

Havlik, P. (2009) 'Belarus between Russian and the European Union: Some Reflections on the Belarusian "Economic Miracle" and Future Prospects', In *Belarus: External Pressure, Internal Change*, H.-G. Heinrich and L. Lobova (eds), Frankfurt-am-Main: Peter Lang.

Iglicka, K. (1999) 'The Economics of Petty Trade on the Eastern Polish Border', In *The Challenge of East–West Migration for Poland*, K. Iglicka and K. Sword (eds), London: Macmillan, pp. 120–43.

Iglicka, K. and Sword, K. (1999) 'Introduction', In *The Challenge of East–West Migration for Poland*, K. Iglicka and K. Sword (eds), London: Macmillan, pp. 1–14.

Irek, M. (1998) *Der Smugglerzug: Warschau–Berlin–Warschau: Materialien einer Feldforschung*, Berlin: Das Arabische Buch.

Klimova, S. (2006) 'Chelnoki: begstvo ot nuzhdy ili pogonia za shansom', *Sotsial'naia real'nost'* 2: 26–41.

Konstantinov, Y., Kressel, G. M. and Thuen, T. (1998) 'Outclassed by Former Outcasts: Petty-Trading in Varna', *American Ethnologist* 25(4): 729–45.

Lonkila, M. (1997) 'Informal Exchange Relations in Post-Soviet Russia: a Comparative Perspective', *Sociological Research Online*, 2(2). Online. Available: <http://socresonline.org.uk/2/2/9.html> (accessed 31 March 2013).

Morokvasic, M. (2003) 'Transnational Mobility and Gender: a View from Post-Wall Europe', In *Crossing Borders and Shifting Boundaries: Vol. 1: Gender on the Move*, M. Morokvasic, U. Frel and K. Shinozaki (eds), Leske, Budrich: Opladen, pp. 101–33.

Olimpieva, I., Pachenkov, O., Ejova, L. and Gordy, E. (2007) 'Informal Economies of St. Petersburg: Ethnographic Findings on the Cross-Border Trade', Jefferson Institute.

Polese, A. (2006) 'Border-Crossing as a Strategy of Daily Survival: The Odessa–Chisinau Elektrichka', *Anthropology of East Europe Review* 24(1): 28–37.

Round, J., Williams, C.C., and Rodgers, P. (2010) 'The Role of Domestic Food Production in Everyday Life in Post-Soviet Ukraine', *Annals of Association of American Geographers*, 100(5): 1197–1211.

Sasunkevich, O. (2010) '"Pride Identity" as a Strategy of Self-Representation in the Situation of a Research Interview: The Case of Belarusian Women Involved in Market Trade', *Anthropology of East Europe Review* 28(1): 138–64.

Sik, E. and Wallace, C. (1999) 'The Development of Open-air Markets in East-Central Europe', *International Journal of Urban and Regional Development* 23(4): 697–714.

Smith, A. (2010) 'Informal Work in the Diverse Economies of "Post-Socialist" Europe', In *Informal Economy in Developed Nations*, C. C. Williams and P. Joassart (eds), London, New York: Routledge, pp. 47–65.

Smith, A. and Stenning, A. (2006) 'Beyond Household Economies: Articulations and Spaces of Economic Practice in Postsocialism', *Progress in Human Geography* 30(2): 190–213.

Stammler-Gossman, A. (2012) '"Winter-tyres-for-a-flower-bed": Shuttle Trade on the Finish-Russian Border', In *Subverting Borders: Doing Research on Smuggling and Small-Scale Trade,* B. Bruns and J. Miggelbrink (eds), Wiesbaden: VS Verlag, pp. 233–55.

Sword, K. (1999) 'Cross-Border "Suitcase Trade" and the Role of Foreigners in Polish Informal Markets', In *The Challenge of East–West Migration for Poland*, K. Iglicka and K. Sword (eds), London: Macmillan, pp. 145–67.

Wagner, M. (2011) *Die Schmugglergesselschaft. Införmele Ökonomien an der Ostgrenze der Europäischen Union: Eine Ethnographie*, Bielefeld: transcript Verlag,

Wagner, M. and Łukowski, W. (eds) (2010) *Alltag im Grenzland: Schmuggel als ökonomische Strategie im Osten Europas*, Wiesbaden: VS Verlag.

Wallace, C. with Shmulyar, O. and Bedzir, V. (1999) 'Investing in Social Capital: The Case of Small-Scale, Cross-Border Traders in Post-Communist Central Europe', *International Journal of Urban and Regional Development*, 23(4): 754–70.

White, J. B. (1994) *Money Makes Us Relatives: Women's Labor in Urban Turkey*, Austin: University of Texas Press.

Williams, A. and Baláž, V. (2002) 'International Petty Trading: Changing Practices in Trans-Carpathian Ukraine', *International Journal of Urban and Regional Research* 26(2): 323–42.

Williams, C. C. and Marcelli, Enrico (2009) 'Conclusions', In *Informal Work in Developed Nations,* E. Marcelli, C. C. Williams and P. Joassart (eds), London and New York: Routledge, pp. 220–32.

Zhurzhenko, T. (2008) *Gendernye rynki Ukrainy: politicheskaia ekonomiia natsional'nogo stroitel'stva*, Vilnius: Izdatel'stvo Evropeiskogo Gumanitarnogo Universiteta.

9 'The glove compartment half-full of letters' – informality and cross-border trade at the edge of the Schengen Area

Kristine Müller and Judith Miggelbrink

Introduction

This is the story of Konstantin,[1] a Ukrainian entrepreneur who trades groceries and is involved in what can be called 'informal cross-border trade'. He is also a representative character insofar as we take him and his stories about the border as typical of small-scale cross-border trading along the Polish–Ukrainian border that became a Schengen border in 2007. By telling his story we want to reveal how the restrictions, opportunities and unpredictable nature of this 'new' border are negotiated to earn a living and how economic activities that are part of a widespread economic practice are embedded in perceptions of 'informality', 'the border', 'the economy', and 'the state'.

Before telling Konstantin's story, some remarks are necessary to at least roughly sketch the conceptual narrative within which we would like to tell it. A first preliminary remark concerns the question of 'identity'. Although we address Konstantin as a Ukrainian citizen, an entrepreneur, a trader, a third-country national, etc.,[2] and thereby refer to the categorical orders within which he moves, these categorizations should not be regarded as taken-for-granted – this would mean simply to reproduce them as seemingly stable and irreducible structures of the social world (Bourdieu 1974: 27f, 1999: 222f). Rather, we regard them as produced as well as productive elements of social practices. Some of these categorizations, like 'third-country national' are part of border(ing) politics and relatively new categories implemented by the European Union's politics of inclusion and exclusion by which individuals are positioned and placed – regardless of their own ambitions or self-descriptions. Especially with regard to (state) borders as a spatial means of power technologies, categories are an important instrument to sort people and qualify them as unwanted or welcome travellers. Other identifications, such as 'entrepreneur', are closely related to self-understanding and everyday practices of attribution. It may serve as a marker of one's occupation but may also draw a line between small-scale trade as a regular job and 'smugglers' although the actual activities may be the same. And yet other identities are deeply inscribed in state–society relations. The obedient subject on the one side, and the person who challenges the state, tricks it and tries to subvert it on the other, are two possible though contrary incorporations of these relations. As regards borders, the latter is epitomized by the (idealized) figure of the smuggler as a hero: 'the ordinary person' tricking the state power embodied/incorporated by border guards and customs control (see Paul *et al.* 2002). Beyond its often emphasized that economic necessity, informal economic practices in general as well as cross-border trade in particular may thus also be seen as activities reacting to an 'unfair' or 'incapable' state that provokes a circumvention of its laws and rules.

Although some of the categories mentioned are powerful, they do not entirely determine the subject. Moreover, to understand 'how subjects "become" (that is, how they shift and create new identities for themselves despite the seemingly hegemonic power of dominant discourses and governmental practices)' (Gibson 2001: 641), requires further theoretical effort, as Gibson states, referring to authors like Judith Butler and William Connolly. Our chapter does not take up their theoretical strands of reasoning in detail, however, categories and ascriptions that arose in Konstantin's story are understood as potential prefigurations in processes through which subjectivities are built performatively.

A second preliminary note concerns the 'circumstances' under which informal cross-border activities take place. From the theoretical perspective of practices taken here, structures are not understood as supra-subjectively existing elements of the social world but as emergent property thereof deriving from its practices (Reckwitz 2000: 289 *et passim*). Nevertheless, some more structural remarks could help to contextualise his story. Moreover, even though we regard structures as emerging phenomena they may be perceived as 'hard' structural settings or conditions to which one has to adjust (as Konstantin stresses several times).

Konstantin's story exemplifies the situation of small-scale traders at the Polish–Ukrainian border insofar as people on both sides of the border have been confronted with a similar situation of economic transformation in which economic practices beyond the boundaries of formality and legality have gained a substantial meaning (see Smith and Stenning 2006; Round and Williams 2010; Bruns *et al.* 2011). While being at least partially informal and illegal, cross-border trade has also been widely accepted as an unavoidable and legitimate way to cope with precarious situations, at least within the local context of transformation societies (see Bruns and Zichner 2010). Among informal practices, cross-border trade has some specific characteristics as it works through various scales from the local to the national and the supranational with diverging constraints, norms, rules and expectations. Moreover, traders are challenged by two different national contexts, and their economic performance depends mainly on coping tactics and strategies developed for and adjusted to the respective conditions. These have changed dramatically since Poland implemented the Treaty of Schengen and its subsequent regulations, transforming the border between both states into a strictly regulated place: a border between the EU's 'area of freedom, security and justice' (European Communities 1997: 7) on the one side and a 'neighbouring state' on the other. This has produced an even wider gap between those who are inside enjoying European citizenship and those who are outside (Balibar 2009) and are subjected to the 'assemblage' of the border (Walters 2002: 563). Although new visa politics – the core of a growing ensemble of filtering mechanisms – have impeded cross-border flows of people remarkably, informal cross-border trade is still regarded as part of the normality of life in the border area. Nevertheless, functionality and legitimacy of cross-border trade and informal practice in general have become subject to changes as they are questioned more and more due to EU policies aiming at creating a 'secure' environment. Consequently, not only border crossing itself has become more intricate and expensive, but cross-border trade is increasingly being criminalized, thus requiring new adaptations of practices (see Belina and Miggelbrink 2013).

Methodological remarks

In order to reveal the experiences of Konstantin and his fellow entrepreneurs in dealing with formal regulations and informality within their border related activities, the stories of local inhabitants were recorded and analysed using the method of group discussions.[3] In their shared experiences, collective schemes of orientation came to the fore[4] (see also Müller 2013). These contain the actors' practical knowledge as regards coping with old and new challenges of crossing the border, including their perceptions on the legitimacy of informality. By analysing these orientations, the approaches and meanings of informal cross-border practices could be revealed. As a composite of Konstantin's and partly others' experiences in the ways of dealing with the effects of the new Schengen border regime, the story highlights the currently challenged role of informality in this context.

Informality and borders: embedding the case

The characteristics of cross-border small-scale trade that are usually emphasized are their traits of informality and illegality. Indeed, making profit at the border largely depends on strategies to circumvent rules of trade and procedures of control. The peculiarity of cross-border small-scale trade thus results from its relation to the state, in particular to the law, that regulates the sphere of the (il)legal and the (in)formal. This means that the informal or/and illegal character of cross-border small-scale trade is an effect of how state sovereignty is exerted through a set of laws, regulations, technologies and procedures of implementation that form the 'border'. Although there is no clear distinction between what is (in)formal and (il)legal, it has been argued that illegality refers to actions outside the law, whereas actions outside state regulation are addressed as informal (Ledeneva 2006; Round et al. 2008). A similar distinction can also be drawn according to the treatment of actions, as a criminal act or as infringement.

These differentiations are mirrored by small-scale traders when they (at least implicitly) distinguish between their ways to circumvent regulations on the one hand, and clearly regarded criminal acts on the other hand, the latter mainly equated with human trafficking or large-scale smuggling. Even in the sphere of everyday life where judgements and moral concerns are negotiated according to shifting contexts, there lies only a narrow ridge between practices that do not (completely) follow the rules but are 'somehow' acceptable and practices that are perceived as unacceptable. From a formal/legal point of view, economic practices across the border are informal if they exceed the officially allowed amount of duty-free goods, if taxation is avoided or if traders set goods apart for further trading but do not declare them accordingly (Bruns *et al.* 2011: 668).

Besides a more formal distinction along the axis of formality and legality, cross-border economic practices are seen in the light of their social acceptability which, of course, is always a contextual acceptability. For many members of the transformation societies, informal structures are the basis to withstand the ongoing challenges. Studies show that for solving everyday problems, people only rarely fall back on formal institutions.[5] The decision on what counts as legitimate rather depends on a strong obligation to fairness, which is measured and mostly adhered to within close networks of neighbours, friends and acquaintances (Hendley 2009: 2, see also Ledeneva 2006). If informal or illegal practices are somehow justified despite their formal and juridical meaning, perceptions of informality and illegality depend on judgements that are deeply rooted in everyday justifications of practices. The shared consciousness of this local knowledge and informal norms of how to cope with life is not necessarily restricted to traders but stretches across a broader community and may even include those people who execute border controls on the ground. Although they act in the name of the state, strategies of circumventing it may be regarded as acceptable if the state is perceived as not being able to guarantee a minimum of income and welfare. Even though this does not always result in complicity, cognizance (and at times aiming at a share of profit) is a possible and even welcome strategy. The peculiarity of small-scale cross-border trade compared to other informal activities, thus, derives from the literal embodiment of the state at border crossing points:

> Unlike many other informal economic practices, the state is immediately present – as the border is the incarnation of state. Informal practices have to be carried out literally in front of the executive power of the state. And unlike many other informal practices, small-scale trade and smuggling do not take place in '"floating mists" that grow in . . . poorly regulated spaces' (Round *et al.* 2008: 173) but in spaces that claim to be highly regulated. (Bruns *et al.* 2011: 668)

The highly regulated and controlled area of the border thus embodies the implementation of state sovereignty. Nevertheless, the capacity of traders and smugglers to substantially influence the border regime could be expected to be rather limited due to the highly institutionalized social space.

Konstantin: being an economic actor at the Polish–Ukrainian border

We meet Konstantin in one of our group discussions along the eastern EU border in the neighbouring region of western Ukraine. We all sit around a table in a small upper-floor hotel suite in a rural town some 30 kilometres from Lviv. The border to Poland is not far away, and for the handful of people we invited, it is always present. Konstantin works in a company trading groceries between Poland and Ukraine. Cross-border trade is one of his daily issues.

The socio-economic life of Konstantin and other inhabitants of this region is characterized in large part by the marginal geographical location. The challenges related to this situation become visible in the labour market and infrastructure. It is not surprising that everyday life in these places is closely linked to the border and to its meaning as a resource. The border between Poland and Ukraine divides two states that were part of the same political block over the last centuries; they have followed similar routes of political, economic and social transformations since the 1990s. Still, differences in living conditions also exist between these border regions. Significant disparities in prices in combination with relatively 'open' borders led to the emergence of lively cross-border trading activities in the 1990s, carried out by Poles as well as Ukrainians. The borders thus functioned as a centralizing force by enabling and encouraging nearby inhabitants such as Konstantin to profit from the advantages of cross-border trade (see also Wust and Haase 2002: 24).

At the border crossing point in Shegyni in western Ukraine, some 2,000–3,000 Ukrainian citizens visited the Polish side per day[6] – at least during the years before the introduction of the Schengen border regime. When asked about their motives for the transnational journey, the plan to purchase goods on the Polish side amounted to about 70–90 per cent of the answers. An additional 7 per cent of Ukrainian border crossers named job-related activities as the main reason. Groceries and building materials were the favoured products to bring back from Poland. For trading in Poland, tobacco and alcohol were best.

Such cross-border trading activities have helped to secure the livelihood of many neighbouring inhabitants over the past decades. This has happened to various degrees and purposes which are generally difficult to quantify but ample evidence exists for similar borders in Eastern Europe (for an example concerning the Polish–Russian border see Bruns 2010: 191). Some have developed strategies to continually smuggle and/or trade various goods back and forth, and thus fully depend on this form of income generation. Others – such as Konstantin – have shifted only a part of their economic focus onto informal cross-border trading and smuggling. This is only at first sight linked to a lesser significance; the role of informal trade for their economic wellbeing is still indispensable. Engaging in any economic business in Ukraine is a risky undertaking. It is difficult to rely on official structures and rules; laws are weak and are frequently changed, there is no way of relying on incomes and plans. Therefore, many turned to at least supplementing their formal businesses with additional, informal small-scale cross-border trade. It has helped them to compensate for ever increasing income gaps.

The Schengen border regime, introduced at the Polish–Ukrainian border crossing points in December 2007, brought an end to this advantageous situation, especially for the non-EU citizens of the border population. The Schengen regulations impose a rigid structure on border-related economic activities, one which affects people wishing to cross the border in a variety of ways and on different levels.

Next to the reduction of mobility, social encounters and economic opportunities, the introduction of a new system of formal rules on the Polish side of the border crossing points also changes patterns of formality and informality, legitimacy and illegitimacy within the local contexts. When actors along the border, confronted with the new regulations, continue or change their behaviour, in instances where local entrepreneurs continue or adapt their economic strategies – these are the moments in which some effects of the EU border regime on the long-lived legitimacy of informal cross-border trade can be observed.

On 'making the border'

Konstantin's cross-border activities always involve informalities to ease the passage. 'For the customs control,' he tells us, 'our colleagues carry letters from the Polish consulate as well as from our government, stating that they are honourable businessmen and that they should receive special support. To cut it short: they have their glove compartments half-full with letters. It's actually not that great,' he adds. 'But basically, this is the common way.' Crossing the border is never a comfortable task. Long waiting times and inefficient control procedures turn the trip into a lengthy and arduous procedure. 'You have to know a way to help yourself; after all you need to move on. So you "make yourself a border"', Konstantin explains:

> I have this acquaintance. I tell her that I will go through customs today. She asks me about the licence number of the car, and that's it. Later that day, I will quickly be checked and let through. 'Please continue directly through the customs corridor' – and everything is fine. And if you don't have any acquaintance, it works as well. You just put 50–100 Grivna between the pages of the passport.

Waiting at the border control points can be tiring, especially when there is a change of shifts. Therefore, the effect of such letters is warmly welcomed by border crossers. It is an advantage that Konstantin can rely on. As a business person he can use contacts in the government, and even get letters signed from the customs officers on both sides of the border. Especially for people crossing the border on a daily basis, the letters provide a very important instrument. When crossing the border only every now and then, one can just as well use the more spontaneous technique of handing over some banknotes for 'making the border'.

Smuggling products across the border is widely considered a normal activity. In his little town, Konstantin tells us, almost everyone once started as a 'slider',[7] and earned their first car this way. After the border was opened at the beginning of the 1990s, people started smuggling vodka and cigarettes. 'This border area practically lived from the phenomenon that people were almost like relatives with the Polish neighbours, going back and forth across the border. It was their job to go to Poland.' This lively exchange with the Polish side has always been there. In most cases, it was built up step by step. People went back and forth to look for potential earnings, after a while they took some cigarettes along, and eventually also a type of sausage in demand. Prices were good, and they knew the custom officers from their home villages and towns. They never had to wait for long.

'This system works'

As Konstantin goes on with his stories, he underlines that, in his understanding, the system in Ukraine just works as it is, with bribe money and everything else. It is a fact that one has to include into calculations when acting in this context. Not only in the interactions at the border control points, but within the preparations of the customs procedures, one has to be prepared for a lot of effort and costs. Laws are frequently changed, 'hundreds' of declarations and forms are needed, sometimes covering similar or equal aspects. You need to pay for all these forms and certificates – thus producing more profit for the administrative offices. In the EU it would be impossible to impose such extra costs – but, as Konstantin proclaims, 'this is the logic of the Ukrainian market'. He describes the way the Ukrainian state institutions and public companies work as 'very interesting'. His remark better not to get involved with them almost sounds like a warning. 'These companies order something, receive the delivery, but then they are bankrupt and never pay. And of course the state approves it.' Foreign business partners should familiarize themselves with the institutional conditions in Ukraine. To illustrate this point, Konstantin brings up the example of a German business partner, who is well versed in dealing with Ukrainian institutional settings. 'He knows our mentality, our character. That is why his company was able to be a leading player in the market. You know, we are made of a different material, and some are surprised about that. But the people that I work with, they do not wonder anymore, they understand that it is the system. And this system works. And you cannot escape it.'

Konstantin continues with another example of informal adaptations of behaviour at the border. When crossing the border with goods, traders are already prepared for the different ways of regulation and practice on both sides of the border: 'When I buy some goods in Poland, I set up two versions of accompanying documents, one for Poland, and one for our own customs officers.' The Polish officers would not care very much about what is exported, but for the Ukrainians one has to think of some deception. If everything went according to the law, things would be all right. For instance, the sales tax would be reimbursed to the traders. But the way it works at the moment, trading conditions are out of balance. One reason for this is the fact that many used the sales tax regulations for their own profit, Konstantin explains. They filled in documents to receive reimbursements, even if they did not have any goods to declare: 'Only the papers travel. They travel just until the customs. Well, maybe not even to the official customs office. They travel no further than to the home of a customs officer.'

Many ways of deception exist in this field of cross-border trade, also for import and price development. It is a bit awkward to talk about all these things, Konstantin observes, but then again there is nothing secret about these issues, they are all over the media. Some people make up a whole series of schemes and strategies; others even devise their own laws. A certain supervisory board chairman once used his position and contacts to enact a law for facilitating the import of cacao:

> The law was enacted, just for one week, it was only valid for one week. It was about the termination of import taxes for the import of cacao to the Ukraine. If I remember right, he gathered about 40 trucks at the border, then enacted the law, and shortly after that he withdrew it again. And his competitors were pretty much taken for a ride, since after him withdrawing the law, the import taxes went up to 30 per cent again. He imported his goods, and was lucky; his sweets were 1 or 2 per cent cheaper in production. So he pretty easily made profit. That's the way it is done. It's just one out of many examples.

The example shows how economy and state jurisdiction are interwoven, a partly informal liaison that is used and misused on various levels of society. Also for Konstantin, informal contacts, not only with the customs but also to the government officials, are of the highest importance for successful cross-border trade. Actually, the formal regulation of customs procedures was probably not much different from regulations elsewhere in Europe, Konstantin reasons. There was just this peculiarity that all problematic aspects of controls and handling at the border were negotiated in various ways. That was just the common way:

> If it doesn't work fast in the official way, you quickly work it out unofficially. The typical system of a bureaucratic state. There is no need to cover this up. There is both the legal economy and the shadow economy. They both function and do not disturb one another.

Challenges to persistence?

The Ukrainian system, of course, is not an island. The conditions Konstantin describes also interplay with the behaviour of people from divergent backgrounds, with different routines and experiences; people that happen to get involved in interactions in the Ukrainian context. Konstantin reflects that for foreign tourists, the situation at the Ukrainian border controls is not easy. Often they have to wait for many hours. It would be better if they adapted to the conditions and included those bribes into their budget plans straight from the beginning. Some, he reminds himself, have already done that. 'An impossible situation,' states Konstantin, 'especially now, when so many people will come for the 2012 European Football Championship.' Once, a coach from Germany crossed the border, and the tour guide refused to pay the bribe money. After many phone calls and with a high amount of insistency, the bus was let through without any payments. But not all manage to succeed and to muster the necessary endurance. And that is taken advantage of. It is almost like a bad virus, Konstantin concludes, it rests in everyone, but all hope they will be cured. 'Maybe something will change at the border, when all the new delegations arrive.'

Transborder seminars on border regulations were soon expected to take place, for discussions about new developments of the border control systems, now that the Schengen regulations have started to be implemented. Highly ranked international entrepreneurs from both sides of the border would get invited to such meetings. Some of these people do not even have to go to the consulate to get visas; they work for Mercedes or similar companies, and that is all that is necessary to have a smooth cross-border passage. These large companies have contacts in the government and are able to take part in the decision-making processes. Then again, Konstantin complains, some of these meetings are not that effectively focused on policy structures and changes anyway. A participant of such a meeting once told him that all he had learned at the meeting were new strategies of deception at the control points. 'That's also of course some quite useful information,' Konstantin has to admit.

As opposed to such high-ranking economists, Konstantin's own formerly privileged treatment at the border has been challenged. In earlier days, the interactions and relations with Polish border guards and officers had always been good and easy for entrepreneurs like him. However, that has changed with Poland joining the EU and implementing the Schengen regulations. A new and even stronger dividing line has emerged between EU-domestics and non-domestics. Suddenly, every Ukrainian crossing the border is perceived as a potential smuggler or dangerous intruder.

> I have to tell you that the situation at the border between Poland and Ukraine has changed a lot. If you, eh, drive to Rawarusk and observe everything, you will notice what is going on. There are 10 Polish cars and one Ukrainian. It has become very problematic for Ukrainians to bring cigarettes through the customs because they are checked very thoroughly. Their cars are taken apart. Do you understand? But the Poles, they do it. They do it because they are domestics. The custom officers are also domestics. And the smugglers are domestics, too. They all have a wonderful life over there.

This is a very dramatic transformation, especially for people just wanting to attend a soccer match on the other side of the border. Everyone is checked in such a thorough way on the Polish side, Konstantin can only call it humiliating.

> Somehow, you are treated as if you were a second-class person. You are treated that way, even if you have money or if you are well-dressed and drive a decent car. I find that very exhausting, personally.

Konstantin describes how bad the conditions have become at the Polish consulate. Long waiting queues, people almost have to stay overnight. And you get treated equally, he complains, even as an entrepreneur you have to take a number and wait. Before, it was not even necessary to deal with these visa-processing steps personally – you would just get things done via an agency. Organizing a cross-border trip was always very easy. Now it has become difficult, as personal visits to the consulate are required, and month-long waiting times for processing the documents are nothing unusual. It is something one has to take into account when doing business these days, especially with partners abroad. You have to be careful with making appointments for meetings, and need to start paperwork sufficiently ahead of time.

These are experiences that run against the former routines, when being an entrepreneur was a distinct and meaningful category granting (and guaranteeing) privileges and preferential/favourable treatment in cross-border mobility. Cross-border trade was always something both national populations were involved in, and the categories for smooth interactions at the border ran along the lines of the type of business people engaged in. Entrepreneurs were treated better than smugglers. After the introduction of Schengen, such privileges had to make way for differentiated patterns of treatment between EU and non-EU citizenship. 'Not even the deputy badge works any longer,' Konstantin protests. 'It used to work for 20 years. By car, by train, everywhere the red passes and red licence plates did their job. When I tried to use this strategy some days ago, the Polish custom officer said "of course you will be let through as a member of parliament.". But then I got processed as the very last person!'

The new behaviour of Polish guards also shakes the foundations of trust in the success of informal practices at parts of the cross-border passage. The procedures at the border are full of uncertainties these days; you do not know what will happen. 'Actually,' Konstantin realizes, 'when you cross the border in an honest way, it is easier to pass the Polish side of controls. When you cross like you always used to do – then our side is easier.' This statement shows that while facing the challenges of rising formalization and legalization of border-related interactions on the Polish side, Konstantin remains caught in the normality of informal practices within most of his societal contexts. He himself does not see much urgency to change: 'In fact, we can live quite well in this chaos, we have got used to it.' Many constantly blame the government. But then again, it is the population itself that elected those officials; these are people who have grown up in the same country, as he underlines. Probably nothing will change, until different, new people are there. The specifications of this state of controls are deeply rooted in the mentality, there is not much you can do about that, Konstantin observes. It may change when the children have grown up and studied in the West and then returned home. 'Sooner or later, we will make it. I can see it with my son. Yesterday, I put my little grandson on the front passenger seat in the car. My son said I could get arrested for that. It's the psychology. He came to visit back here, and he abides by the law. But here, we don't do it.' Legislation is not perfect, Konstantin states, but it would help a lot if people adhered to it. Unfortunately, there are so many people who ignore the law – so in the end you are forced to join in. After all, they all depend on one another: 'Whoever wants to abide by the law has already lost.'

Conclusion

Cross-border trade at the Polish–Ukrainian border has always been a meaningful resource for local inhabitants. Throughout his trading experiences, Konstantin, a Ukrainian entrepreneur, has been privileged when crossing the border. Also today, he is still able to use informal ways to 'make the border'. His stories reveal the diverse ways of using informal strategies, contacts and networks as well as local knowledge to cross the border swiftly and unproblematically, be it letters in the glove compartment, easier procedures or bribe money for border guards. The normality of informality constitutes a main orientation of actors in the field of cross-border trade at the external EU border. This persistence of informality is supported by a generally high and widespread legitimacy of informal activities in the Ukrainian economic context; and therefore the ongoing pressure to act this way. Konstantin feels forced into informal behaviour, since the more powerful enterprises, state enterprises, also ignore the official law (otherwise you have already lost) and also by the ongoing successful experiences of informal economic activities – at least for border crossers like him having the necessary contacts, social capital, practical knowledge.

Informality as normality is only beginning to be challenged by changes in the behaviour of the Polish border guards and customs officers. An apparently growing reward for formal procedures and legal interactions on the Polish side brings about some uncertainty for Ukrainian traders and entrepreneurs. Some former privileges have disappeared, and informality seems to be slowly losing in legitimacy in some places. For people like Konstantin, these changes bring about a loss of trust and confidence in their own economic activities. Since the beginning of the implementation of Schengen regulations, he has therefore slightly rearranged his cross-border trade in the way that he himself does not cross the border that often anymore having partly externalized transport.

Generally though, and speaking for the Ukrainian economic context, Konstantin rarely questions his position towards informality/illegality. He observes some slight changes in the next generation, but does not actively and determinately consider altering his own behaviour. The adaptations of practices that do occur do so only indirectly, as the consequence of slight insecurities about the success of 'making the border' at the Polish side of border crossing points. Konstantin and his fellow border crossers cannot fully trust the functioning of informal strategies any longer. He has to take longer waiting times or non-privileged treatment into account, and in consequence increasingly tries to avoid crossing the border.

Notes

1 The name has been changed in order to anonymize our informant.
2 The term 'third-country national(s)' is commonly used when discussing issues within the context of international relations and referring to people who do not come from or possess citizenship of one of the two or more countries that signed the agreement in question. With regard to the European Union (as in this paper), it denotes a person from outside the European Union including Switzerland or, as it is applied mainly in the context of migration and asylum policy, a person from outside the Schengen Area.
3 Implicit, practical knowledge is rarely shared openly, but is transferred within communities of interpretation who, in their everyday life, imitate each other's actions, repeat,

correct and supplement each other in their resolution of problems (see also Hörning 2001, Polanyi 1985). The approach adopted in this study was to reveal aspects of local practical knowledge by arranging group discussions of these communities of interpretation. The transcripts were then analysed with the Documentary Method (Bohnsack 1999), immersing oneself into the discourses of the actors, recognizing and reconstructing their orientations along with their dialogues. For a more detailed description of methods applied in the project see Bruns *et al.* (2011: 670f).

4 Everyday practices entail a continuous reflection on an implicit, intersubjective level (Hörning 2001: 162), one which includes constantly renewing practical knowledge. While experiences are made, practical knowledge is gained from coping in certain situations, and the involved inventiveness to confront all kinds of challenges. A common level of exchange exists in these experiences, a latent collective sense or spirit of common ways of communication and action (Schatzki 1996: 188, as quoted in Hörning 2001: 164). On that level, collective schemes of knowledge and interpretation emerge, ones that help actors to orient themselves in concrete situations and interactions. As such, the collective orientations contain rules of action as well as the knowledge of when to stick to these rules and how to develop possible adaptations, in case the routines no longer function.

5 Based on a study on trust in informal structures in contemporary Russia, Hendley cites the former experience of a lack of trust in Soviet state institutions as a background for the ongoing legitimacy of informal strategies. Unwritten laws or everyday routines would therefore constitute parts of perception of legality that were at least as meaningful as formal laws (Hendley 2009: 1).

6 Urząd Statystyczny w Rzeszowie (2008: 24): Polish-Ukrainian Border Area Profile, Rzeszów.

7 In Ukraine, the term 'slider' (orig. 'chovniki') describes the travelling merchants or hawkers, who regularly trade small quantities of goods across the state borders.

References

Balibar, E. (2009) 'Europe as Borderland', *Environment and Planning D: Society and Space* 27: 190–215.

Belina, B. and Miggelbrink, J. (2013) 'Risk as a technology of power. FRONTEX as an example of the de-politicisation of EU migration regimes', in Müller-Mahn, D. (ed.) *The Spatial Dimension of Risk. How Geography Shapes the Emergence of Riskscapes*, London: Routledge, pp. 124–36.

Bohnsack, R. (1999) *Rekonstruktive Sozialforschung: Einführung in die Methodologie und Praxis qualitativer Forschung*, Opladen, Leske & Budrich.

Bourdieu, P. (1974) *Soziologie der symbolischen Formen*, Frankfurt a.M., Suhrkamp.

—— (1999) *Language and Symbolic Power*, 5th ed., Cambridge MA: Harvard University Press.

Bruns, B. (2010) *Grenze als Ressource: Die soziale Organisation von Schmuggel am Rande der Europäischen Union*, Wiesbaden: VS Verlag für Sozialwissenschaften.

Bruns, B., Miggelbrink, J. and Müller, K. (2011) 'Smuggling and Small-scale Trade as Part of Informal Economic Practices: Empirical Findings from the Eastern External EU Border', *International Journal of Sociology and Social Policy* 31(11/12): 664–80.

Bruns, B. and Zichner, H. (2010) 'Moral an der Grenze? Theoretische Überlegungen und empirische Befunde zur Moral im Alltag an der östlichen Außengrenze der Europäischen Union', *Geographische Revue* (1): 21–36.

European Communities (1997) *Treaty of Amsterdam amending the Treaty on European Union, the Treaties establishing the European Communities and certain related acts* (97/C 340/01). Online. Available: <http://www.europarl.europa.eu/topics/treaty/pdf/amst-en.pdf> (accessed 20 March 2012).

Gibson, K. (2001) 'Regional Subjection and Becoming', *Environment and Planning D: Society and Space* 19: 639–67.

Hendley, K. (2009) 'Legal Consciousness in Post-soviet Russia. A Preliminary Study,' NCEEER Working Paper, University of Wisconsin, Madison.

Hörning, K.H. (2001) *Experten des Alltags. Die Wiederentdeckung des praktischen Wissens*, Weilerswist, Velbrück Wissenschaft.

Ledeneva, A. (2006) 'Informelle Netzwerke in post-kommunistischen Ökonomien: eine "topographische" Karte', in Bittner, R., Hackenbroich, W., and Vöckler, K. (eds), *Transiträume*, Berlin: Jovis, pp. 300–39.

Müller, K. (2013) 'Yet another layer of peripheralization. Dealing with the consequences of the Schengen treaty at the edges of the EU territory', in Fischer-Tahir, A. and Naumann, M. (eds), *Peripheralization: The Making of Spatial Dependencies and Social Injustice*, Wiesbaden: Springer VS, pp. 187–206.

Paul, B., Lindenberg, M. and Schmidt-Semisch, H. (2002) 'Der Schmuggler', in Horn, E., Kaufmann, S. and Bröckling, U. (eds), *Grenzverletzer. Von Schmugglern, Spionen und anderen subversiven Gestalten*. Berlin, Kulturverlag Kadmos, pp. 98–114.

Polanyi, M. (1985) *Implizites Wissen*, Frankfurt a.M.: Suhrkamp.

Reckwitz, A. (2000) *Die Transformation der Kulturtheorien. Zur Entwicklung eines Theorieprogramms*, Weilerswist: Velbrück.

Round, J. and Williams, C. C. (2010) 'Coping with the Social Costs of "Transition": Everyday Life in Post-Soviet Russia and Ukraine', *European Urban and Regional Studies* 17(2): 183–96.

Round, J., Williams, C. C. and Rodgers, P. (2008) 'Everyday Tactics and Spaces of Power: the Role of Informal Economies in Post-Soviet Ukraine', *Social & Cultural Geography* 9(2): 171–85.

Schatzki, T. R. (1996) *Social Practices: A Wittgensteinian Approach to Human Activity and the Social*, New York: Cambridge University Press.

Smith, A. and Stenning, A. (2006) 'Beyond Household Economies: Articulations and Spaces of Economic Practice in Post-socialism', *Progress in Human Geography* 30(2): 190–213.

Urząd Statystyczny W Rzeszowie (2008): Polish–Ukrainian Border Area Profile, Rzeszów. Online. Available: <http://www.stat.gov.pl/cps/rde/xbcr/rzesz/ASSETS_charakterystyka_pogranicza_pl.pdf> (accessed 5 March 2013).

Walters, W. (2002) 'Mapping Schengenland: Denaturalizing the Border', *Environment and Planning D: Society and Space* 20(5): 561–80.

Wust, A. and Haase, A. (2002) 'Europas neue Peripherie? Die Regionen beiderseits der polnischen Ostgrenze', *WeltTrends* 34: 11–30.

10 Informal economy writ large and small

From Azerbaijani herb traders to Moscow shop owners[1]

Lale Yalçın-Heckmann

Introduction

This chapter examines the life-world and career of an Azerbaijani trader in Moscow and his strategies of managing kinship obligations, sociality and economy in the informal and transnational space between Moscow and rural Azerbaijan. More generally it examines the relationship between the traders from a village in west Azerbaijan and their kin and economic partners in the home village and other locations. Many Soviet citizens especially in the last decades of the Soviet Union travelled to cities and markets in the most distant corners of Russia, and sold vegetables like tomatoes, cucumbers, pomegranates, melons and apricots, which in those days they transported by train or airplane. This was done partly with state support, within the informality of the second economy, or at least with state authorities' tolerance (Humphrey 2002: 63). Hence, it is tempting to see continuities between the former and the contemporary semi-formal market economic and transnational relations and networks. However, 20 years after the dissolution of the Soviet Union, it is equally important to focus on new and emerging structures and relations around contemporary post-socialist markets as well as provide some kind of periodization of these changes. The Azerbaijani traders who came to Russia to sell primarily agricultural produce in early 2000 were mostly young and middle-aged men, some from the villages and some from towns, mostly from Gəncə, Qazax, Tovuz, Şəmkir, Göyçay, the western and north-western *rayon*s (districts) in Azerbaijan. They had to leave their families behind and take risks, endure hardships and were subjected to humiliation as many of them were educated and over-qualified for carrying out such manual, risky and lower status jobs. 'It is *rəzillik* (drudgery and degradation)', they used to say. Not only did they take risks of having to deal with the various forms of mafia and mafia-like state and municipal authorities in Azerbaijan, on the road to and in Russia, by going away from their home villages, they also gave up the possibility of cultivating the privatized land shares (*pay torpağı*) which they had received after the 1996 agrarian reforms (see Yalçın-Heckmann 2010). The decollectivization and agrarian reforms have led to new forms of ownership, use and management of agrarian land, and in certain cases created new partnerships between the traders abroad and cultivators in the Azerbaijani countryside (ibid.). These new economic activities also led to re-structuring of the existing kin and other relationships in the rural locality, sometimes causing much anxiety and conflict, sometimes helping to establish new dependencies between different generations.

The background to the migration for trade is implicated by the radical privatization of agrarian land in Azerbaijan. Unlike other former Soviet states such as Ukraine where previous work in the collective or state farm has been the main criterion for entitlements to privatized agrarian land (Kaneff and Yalçın-Heckmann 2003) or in Russia, Uzbekistan and Turkmenistan where former collectives and state enterprises have continued to function under different forms and the privatized individual land shares still remain within the structure of the collective (see Gambold Miller and Heady 2003; Lerman 1998; Lerman and Brooks 1998; Trevisani 2010), in Azerbaijan state agrarian enterprises have almost all been dissolved and rural residents have been given individual land shares, the average size varying according to the region, type of agriculture and soil quality (i.e. with irrigation or not) and the size of the specific enterprise. Furthermore, the fact that rural residents all received land shares without having to pay anything, contrasted to the situation of urban Azerbaijanis, many living in the big city of Baku, having lost their jobs and without any alternative source of livelihood like land in the early 2000s. So, the question at the beginning of this millennium was why the Azerbaijani village men and women were willing to leave uncultivated the land they received through privatization and migrate in order to trade under insecure and often risky and dangerous conditions abroad; I have addressed the early phase of this phenomenon elsewhere (Yalçın-Heckmann 2010).

Petty trade (in Azerbaijani, *al-ver*),[2] that is small-scale trade which is also dependent on informal networks, has, on the whole, negative connotations – partly a remnant of the Soviet ideology, rejecting the capitalist type of profit and earnings through the market as anti-social and anti-moral (see also Heyat 2002a, Kaneff 2002, Pachenkov and Berman 2007: 216–217). Informality here is used in the classical sense after Keith Hart (1973). Economic activities are informal as they are not in the state sector and are unaccounted for, beyond taxation, registration and regulation, as they would be also in the private economy. Although a large section of the adult population has been involved in petty trade, the attitudes towards it continue to be ambivalent, class-specific and often contrasting to the more desirable type of trade activity, as in trade as *biznesmen* and not *al-verci* (petty trader). By exploring the biography of a rural but not agriculturalist family in rural Şəmkir, I shall raise a series of questions concerning the reasons for economic choices, and the issue of determination and agency in the emerging economic relations.

How, for instance, should we understand the agency of traders and producers in these economic relations; is this one of mutual interest between producers and traders, of survival or of surplus accumulation? Not only are the interdependencies between the producers and traders significant: through migration for petty trade, existing dependencies between the generations and siblings are challenged and transformed, and the relations between the village and the city production systems are effected. Through such trade and migration new niches for absorbing unemployment but also for siphoning off the incoming surplus are being created within

Azerbaijan's micro and macro-economic structures. This chapter, therefore, aims to show the mechanisms and career possibilities within the different degrees of informal trade, from tomatoes and fresh herbs to cheap clothes and explore some kinship and generational aspects of the new economies in Azerbaijan.

Although the questions addressed in this chapter partly deal with the relationship between agrarian economy, petty trade and migration in general,[3] it also looks at the post-socialist system of land ownership and labour in the countryside, agrarian production and the market mechanism. The reasons for this focus are several: in countries like Azerbaijan post-socialist economic discourse is dominated by macro-economic concerns and interests. The income from oil production and gains from oil export dominates most of the national and international reports and discussions (see Cornell 2011). Agricultural production continues to be marginal for the national economy (see Temel *et al.* 2002, Cornell 2011: 244), so is petty trade within the economic discourses and policies in Azerbaijan, especially petty trade among the Azerbaijani abroad (in Russia, other former Soviet countries and Turkey). Yet given the fact that migration of Azerbaijanis to other countries falls between a conservative estimate of two million and a higher-end estimate of three million (out of a population of nine million), that such a high number of Azerbaijani people live and work abroad, the denial of the economic, social and political significance and consequences of petty trade abroad for Azerbaijan in general is puzzling to say the least.

In some ways, the examination of the exact workings of petty trade and informal economy is difficult to carry out: It needs multi-sited research and analysis of short-term mobility of people and goods in a complex pattern. Moreover these types of trade links and enterprises are usually short lived and the turnover is high. There is no visa requirement between Azerbaijan and Russia and many people travel frequently as tourists without acquiring a work permit, hence short-term travel arrangements involve mainly covering the costs of travel but hardly any bureaucracy.

My discussion of informality, petty trade and market is inspired by Stephen Gudeman's revisit of the debate about the market as a place and as a principle (see Gudeman 2001, 2008). Gudeman identifies the economy as having two realms: one community and the other market. He explains this distinction as follows: 'The market realm revolves about short-term material relationships that are undertaken *for the sake of* achieving a project or securing a good. In the communal realm, material goods are exchanged through relationships kept *for their own sake*' (2001: 10, emphasis in the original). He underlines the interplay and interaction between community and market: 'The two realms of market and community complement one another, conjoin, and are separated in acts, institutions, and sectors. No trade or market system exists without the support of communal agreements, such as shared languages, mutual ways of interacting, and implicit understandings. Communities also are inside markets, as households, corporations, unions, guilds, and oligopolies, and contain them as nation-states that provide a legal structure for contracts and material infrastructure' (ibid: 11).[4]

In this chapter I expand on the idea of kinds of entanglements between the community and the market. I especially consider how this entanglement applies to petty trade on the one hand and informality on the other. Furthermore, this chapter traces how the community can remain inside markets once they go beyond the sphere of the nation-state and the community and market interaction is constituted within transnational space. Theoretical works on transnational space point to the processual aspects of creating this space for maintaining meanings and links across national boundaries (Glick-Schiller *et al.* 1992; Pries 2008). Ruth Mandel underlines how this transnational space is criss-crossed with multiple trajectories of movement, how the transnational space could be appropriated as 'cosmopolitan' by the dominant majority society and how the same society's discourse can ignore the existing transnationalism of German-Turks in her case as marginal (2008: 1–22). Nevertheless, as a critique to transnational theory, Pnina Werbner warns against assumptions in 'transnational theory of uninterrupted, continuing, intimate, taken-for-granted sociality across homeland and diaspora' (Werbner forthcoming). I follow her critical conceptualization of the transnational space between Azerbaijan and Russia, and propose that it is shaped by contested, ambivalent and competitive meanings for community, petty trade, informality and market. The 'illusion of simultaneity' of shared socialities and cultural intimacies and 'rupture' felt in visits to home and in relations with age-peers and kin as suggested by Werbner play both an important role in this case; simultaneity of shared informality and trust is imagined and discursively addressed both by migrants and kin left behind, but at the same time rupture is inevitable given the differential access to economic sources and opportunities in markets in Russia and Azerbaijan.

Post-socialist markets, informality, degrees of licit and legal transactions

The meanings and workings of the new post-socialist markets have been the subject of numerous anthropological studies, starting with the collection edited by Ruth Mandel and Caroline Humphrey (2002). These ethnographies deal with the morality, the ambiguities of and confrontations in these markets, the attitudes of the people involved in these trade relations and the gendered aspects of petty trade and new business relations. The editors stress the shock effect of the way the market has been introduced in the former socialist countries, as a doctrine, and accompanied by 'rapid privatization, the freeing of prices, withdrawal of subsidies, and free trade, as distinct from state-supported and more regulated varieties of capitalism' (Humphrey and Mandel 2002: 2). They also emphasize that

> this version of 'the market' did not land on unoccupied ground', but that 'including even remote areas of the former Soviet Union, the 'market' was introduced into societies where there were already a variety of entrepreneurial or profit-oriented practices of one kind or another. Some of these were legal and had had a long-standing existence within the overarching state-run economy, as in Hungary.... Others were illegal, like the underground workshops and racketeering activities that operated in Russia. (ibid.)

This historical and theoretical background to post-socialist and contemporary markets addresses dichotomies of formality–informality, legality–illegality, licit–illicit from a diachronic perspective. It draws attention to the historical links and possible explanations through the framework of historical causality. Nevertheless, there remains an unaddressed synchronic dimension of informality in markets which is constituted in the transnational space between Russia and Azerbaijan, between Russian 'rules and regulations' (read: market) and Azerbaijani 'socialities and networks' (read: community). Informality appears in both types of trade discussed: tomatoes and kitchen herbs (*göy-göyerti*). Yet the first one is perceived as adhering more to Russian (market) rules and regulations, than in the case of Azerbaijani *göy* trade and 'market-cum-community'. The latter, as we shall see, is strongly integrated into the village production system and implies intense, informal, even if risky and contested links to the 'community'. By describing the Azerbaijani markets, market, trust and sociality relationships, and how a young trader and his kin and other networks are involved in tomato and *göy* trade, I illustrate how tensions and competing legitimacy discourses are contained and travel in the transnational space, which is shaped between Azerbaijani rural producers and Russian consumers.

Azerbaijani traders in Russian markets

Azerbaijani traders in Russian cities like Moscow and St. Petersburg have been the object of various sociological studies since the late 1990s (see Brednikova and Patchenkov 1999, 2002; also Volkov 1999). The focus of these studies has been more on understanding the functioning and organization of Azerbaijani trade and traders within the city's local markets, to question the role of ethnicity as a principle of organization and solidarity and whether one could talk about an ethnic economy. In their work on Azerbaijani migrants in Russia Brednikova and Patchenkov hardly pay attention to the historical dimensions and continuities of the tension of transnational space and networks nor do they make any attempt to reckon for the economic and social background and the other side of this story of economic migration, that is, to rural economic and social conditions prevailing in Azerbaijan.

My take on Azerbaijani traders in Moscow's markets diverges from concerns with their ethnic identity and ethnic economy and highlights the experiences of a few young men and their families I know in the transnational space. The ethnographic material I present here is primarily based on a visit in summer 2002 where I shared the life of a family group, several households and closely known family members of my host family in Azerbaijan. I was also able to meet and talk to some of the younger villagers from Azerbaijan, who were also involved in various kinds of trade activities in and around Moscow.

First I describe two market settings: one was a market where traders brought fresh fruit and vegetables for wholesale – products from former Soviet countries and from Russia, some from the regions surrounding Moscow but also from as far away places as Uzbekistan. The second market setting is the illegal market of

Azerbaijani kitchen herbs, *göy*. My purpose is to illustrate and discuss the shades of legality and licit-ness as they are experienced and reshaped through the actions, strategies and relations between the 'main actors' I deal with here. The first is Hikmət, the younger son of a family I have now known for over a decade. This is a family with transnational networks and acts within the transnational space, even if the local connections are to rural Şəmkir, urban Gəncə and Baku and finally Moscow and its rural outskirts.

The second person is Elşən, Hikmət's partner in the tomato trade, also from the village, but from a different neighbourhood of the village. This neighbourhood has large household plots from Soviet times, has been the residence of kolkhoz (collective farm) and sovkhoz (state farm) workers and also of settlers from various deportations of Azerbaijanis from Armenia (the first one was in 1948, the last in 1988, see Yalçın-Heckmann 2010). Elşən has his father and five brothers in the village and had already some trade experience from the late 1980s when he sold cheap watered-down wine in Siberia with his maternal uncle. After independence he tried some trade business in Russia a few more times. He cooperated closely with his brothers in trade and cultivation and was planning at the time to build two more houses for his younger brothers who were to get married. He and Hikmət were not related to one another before their partnership in early 2000, neither were they friends. In 2002 they cooperated for the first time in the tomato trade and had already transported four truckloads of tomatoes. I observed the sale of the last load in Moscow. Elşən had organized the purchase of the tomatoes in the village and loaded it on a truck together with three others. He then travelled separately to Moscow, to meet the truck with Hikmət and then to sell the tomatoes at this wholesale market.

The third person is Məcid, Hikmət's wife's brother. He had been working in Moscow since the late 1990s and then settled there and is a few years older than Hikmət. Məcid first came without kin but following a friend who was already a trader, then came his mother, his mother's brothers' sons, his other sister, sister's husband and his brothers. He worked first in the bazaars selling herbs like his mother but already by 2002 he had accumulated enough to buy a van with Hikmət and work as a small scale manager-trader rather than seller-trader like Hikmət. Məcid had a sales-stall for vegetables at the exit of a Moscow underground station, for which he bought the produce at the wholesale market but had employed a Russian woman as salesperson. Məcid, unlike Hikmət was from the city of Gəncə and had almost all his close family members in Moscow: in addition to his wife and child, his mother, both his sisters (one of them is Hikmət's wife), his sisters' husbands and several uncles (mother's brothers).

The fourth person, another young man at the time, is Anar, Hikmət's older brother in the village. Anar and Hikmət got married in the same year and Anar stayed in the village, taking care of the ageing parents and the parental house. Hikmət had a higher educational degree at a technical college; Anar finished high school alone. Both of them had been drafted to military service during the Karabakh war and never managed to find an appropriate job in the village, like many other educated and aspiring young men of their generation.

Legal trade, informal entanglements and the race against time: tomato sales in a Moscow market

From field notes (July 2002):

On my second day in Moscow, when I got up about eight in the morning, other women in the flat were still sleeping. Hikmət had already left at about 4:30 in the morning to go to the XY *baza* (wholesale market) to sell tomatoes. His partner Elşən, who had been staying the night at Hikmət's wife's sister's flat, not far away from where we were, had also left for the *baza*. This was their second day of tomato sales. According to Elşən, they had sold about 100 *yeşik* (cases) of tomatoes on the first day, but Hikmət corrected this to have been less, something like 87. The truck had brought 1,050 *yeşik* which belonged to a group of traders including Hikmət and Elşən (Hikmət and Elşən and two more partners they had in the village had 600, the rest belonged to other traders from the same neighbourhood of the village).

I went to the *baza* together with Hikmət's wife's brother Məcid. (Məcid and Hikmət bought the van together for their trade business and Məcid alone drives it, as Hikmət does not have a driving licence.) At the entrance to the *baza* we paid the guard 10 Roubles[5] and got in. When we arrived at the place where the truck arriving from Dagestan had parked, we saw Hikmət and Elşən frantically busy unloading the cases of tomatoes, desperately sorting out the rotten tomatoes, arranging them into new cases and trying to sell them as fast as they could, a race against time. On that day they had been working nearly eight hours literally non-stop and were exhausted. In the *baza*, there were Russians and people from other places. It is a vegetable and fruit wholesale market. Next to us, a truck selling cucumbers from Byelorussia arrived. As the season of *parnik pomidor*, i.e. glasshouse tomatoes (and cucumbers), comes to an end, the sale of open tomatoes and cucumbers begins. Hikmət wants to move into that business next, as he wants to buy tomatoes and cucumbers grown in the open and around Moscow. There was another group of Azerbaijani men also with tomatoes, a couple of trucks away, almost all their tomatoes were rotten and the men were also trying to sort out the good ones. This was a problem for Hikmət's cases too. When a few tomatoes get rotten in the case, the juice affects and rots the others immediately, he was saying. Some of his cases were actually dripping juice. Hikmət says that they are still beginners, many of their cases got rotten on the way, because apparently they have not been properly arranged and the paper between the layers was too thick. He estimated to have lost up to 170 of their 600 cases. The reason according to Hikmət is that his own elder brother Anar in the village, together with Elşən's brothers and father and another partner from the neighbourhood were overseeing this job, they apparently did not know much about proper packaging or did not pay enough attention to it. The other two partners' cases (for the tomato load from the village) were in better shape, apparently because they have been doing this trade before and have more experience with it. (In the village other traders were telling me that to lose 50–100 cases out of some 1,000 total would be normal.)

The price for the place to park the truck and sell the tomatoes was said to be 5,000 Roubles the first day and additional 400 Roubles every extra day. The price for the *kamaz* (truck) driver was $6,000.[6] But what the driver gets when he comes late because of a puncture or delays at the border is unclear. Hikmət seemed to imply that he will not be paid less, but he did not believe the driver either, that he had a puncture. The driver took nine days to arrive, which is absolutely the highest possible number of days carrying fresh tomatoes in a simple closed truck without any air-conditioning for that distance.

The prices were about 350 Roubles (c. €11) per *yeşik* (case containing some 15–16 kg) on that second day. They said that there were not many tomatoes on the market that day, but it was unfortunate that they had to throw away so many. Məcid was helping a bit too, but he is not involved in this trade directly. I later went with Məcid to see and talk to the Turks (from Turkey) who were also selling tomatoes. They were placed closer to the entrance, selling the produce in smaller and expensive carton cases, neatly piled up and displayed from the trucks. Even if the tomatoes looked better than Hikmət's the Turks had hardly any customers. They were selling it for about 30 Roubles per kg (ca. €1). I greeted one of the truck sellers and asked where they are from. The tomatoes are from Antakya [in southern Turkey near the border with Syria] they said, and were first transported overland and then with the ship from Samsun to Sochi and then again by trucks. The trucks have however air-conditioning and the journey takes ten days.

On the third day Hikmət and Elşən were to finish the sale of tomatoes. They left again early in the morning and got back around 10 a.m. with the money from the sales. That afternoon the money was to be sent to Azerbaijan by plane. So we all came to the airport.

Hikmət left the van to talk to some friends he saw and after having disappeared for a while came back and wanted to have the money he had given me to take back, telling me to wrap it up in a piece of inconspicuous paper. He then took the parcel along to give it discreetly to a stewardess waiting at the gate of the airport. Stewardesses are couriers of money to Azerbaijan. They take 800 Roubles (c. €26 Euro) per $1,000 (c. 31,500 Roubles) (i.e. for the $2,300 sent that day, they took some 1,840 Roubles). Hikmət says he knows all the stewardesses especially those from Gəncə, where he went to study at the agricultural institute. He got to know them because of a student friend of his, who became a stewardess and then introduced him to the others. Due to his good relations with them, he claims to pay them less than the normal rate. The women take the money to the airport in Gəncə and they give it to Şamil, Hikmət's partner from the village for fresh herb trade in Azerbaijan. Şamil is supposed to wait outside the airport, so that the personal transfer of money from the stewardess to Şamil will not be seen by third parties (i.e. by customs officers and the police, who otherwise will all ask for a bribe).

Upon giving the money to the stewardess Hikmət said that all producers in the village neighbourhood are waiting for the money (*hamı pulu gözleyir*). This way money is transported safely, avoiding declaration at the airport but also robbers and customs officials, who would all otherwise try to get shares from the sum.

Income, costs and organisation of tomato trade:

In three and a half days the tomatoes were sold. Hikmət and Elşən estimate a loss (*ziyan*) of $1,500 altogether. From this fifth truck load that year they estimated to have lost about 170 *yeşik*. On the first day one *yeşik* was sold for as much as 400 Roubles (c. €13), but then on the last day, Thursday, it was sold for 300 (c. €10) at most, going down to 270 Roubles (c. €9) even. On the third day in order to sort out the rotten tomatoes they employed two Russian women who worked for them the whole day, into the night, and then Mecid drove them home after work. They paid them 150 Roubles (c. €5) each and the women worked without having a break or food the whole day. Hikmət and Elşən would have been lost without them, they said afterwards. Hikmət does the sale, but actually it is Elşən who understands the produce and knows how to sort out the tomatoes. He has been doing this alone the first two days, but not fast enough, or the work load was too much. The truck then left on the fourth day, when all the cases were sold.

Partners in trade:

The truck had brought the tomatoes of three parties from the village: One party is that of Hikmət and Elşən, and there are two more parties (i.e. several men as partners). Although Hikmət and Elşən are 'the only official' partners in the tomato trade, there are others who expect shares as partners too. These are: 1) Şamil (Hikmət's partner in herbs' trade) 2) Vilayet (someone living in the particular neighbourhood and who helped with buying and loading the tomatoes there). Hikmət is supposed to give his brother Anar a share too, so he himself counts as two persons. They were partners for 600 *yeşik* tomatoes and from this amount they lost 170, so more than one quarter. Hikmət and Elşən were responsible for the sale in Moscow, whereas the other partners [including Anar and Elşən's father and brothers] were responsible for the purchase and putting the tomatoes in cases. Hikmət feels he has done his own share well enough, but that those who loaded the truck and prepared the cases had not done their jobs well enough. At the end, there were more tomatoes rotten in their cases then in those of the other two men. According to Elşən, the *yeşik*s are loaded in producers' gardens and marked with their names. If the tomatoes from this specific producer are not good, they do not buy from these again.

Analysis: economy and market

What conclusive points could possibly be deduced from the ethnography of the first type of market, social and economic relations above? In 2002 in the particular village neighbourhood, tomatoes were being produced increasingly for the markets in Russia, especially for big Russian cities like Moscow and St. Petersburg, because the prices were lucrative and there was demand for early tomatoes grown in glasshouses in Azerbaijan, before the tomatoes grown outside become available in Russia in mid-summer. Therefore, those who looked for access to these markets seemed to be increasing in numbers in the early 2000s. On the other hand, the demand fluctuated and was difficult to estimate because this niche was being discovered not only by small producers like those in the neighbourhood and traders like Hikmət and Elşən, but also by big and efficient traders like vegetable trading firms from Turkey and other countries. Although the produce of these rival traders was relatively expensive and thus less competitive at the beginning, in the long run, traders like Hikmət and co. were bound to lose to large-scale traders with better means of transport and storage capacities. Hikmət and his partners were forced to sell as fast as possible because of the costs and time pressure (rent, tomatoes spoilage, etc.).

From this perspective the trade was only marginally profitable due to a lack of skills (e.g. lack of know-how, the preparation of the cases in the village was poor), high risks (no written contracts, no possibility to seek justice within legal frameworks and dangerous trade atmosphere due to mafia networks for extorting money and intimidating the traders), small scale (small amounts brought for sale at a high rate of loss), small amount of capital (all small traders, many of whom were also producers, thus with limited amount of capital) and too many intermediaries (payment for entering the wholesale market in addition to payment for a pitch, payment for the transport of money, bribes for the customs at borders). The informality and small scale of this market niche was doomed to have a limited existence and to give way to professionalization once more small traders entered and became rivals, either forcing one another to seek other kinds of trade or to leave the market to better equipped larger producers and stronger traders. Indeed the market since those early 2000s seems to have become an established one; the informality and simplicity of trade and trade organization have given way to more formalized companies (even if still middle-sized companies) with professional cooled trucks in Azerbaijan.[7] These changes came however from many directions; Russia introduced stricter rules of residence and work in Russia for those permanent and temporary economic migrants since the early 2000s; Azerbaijan demonstrated high economic growth in late 2000, improving relatively the conditions for the rural producers such that now there is more capital and interest for professional trade and better infrastructure (even if the customs and trade terms remain non-transparent). Small traders like Hikmət moved on to new trades and economic activities, once the competition became too harsh and unprofitable and probably there was no more interest to expand after having established better economic livelihoods and political integration in Russia.[8]

Analysis: market and community

Following Gudeman's notions of the market and community, what kinds of communities existed and were being reproduced in these markets? More specifically, who became partner with whom and traded with whom? What were the advantages and liabilities in forming trade partnerships among people from the same village? To what degree does the community shape the sociality and informality in this transnational space? In 2002 Hikmət and his partner Elşən had, to begin with, complementary qualities for a successful partnership in tomato trade: Hikmət was from the village, but had been resident in Moscow for a few years then, spoke decent Russian, had a relatively large kin (through marriage) network, was sociable and knew how to deal with different types of people (in Azerbaijani, one said he was *dil tapan*, literally, 'communication finder', someone who knows how to communicate with different kinds of people). These personal qualities qualified him as a potentially suitable trading partner for someone who had the necessary links to the producers in the village neighbourhood. Elşən fulfilled this latter role: he had, unlike Hikmət, a large group of close kinsmen, who were all involved in agriculture, but they were also skilled craftsmen and worked as renovators for rich villagers' houses in order to earn supplementary cash income. Elşən's own larger household (he lived with his parents, his wife and three small children) and his larger kin group (he said that he shared the budget with the households of his four married brothers) were ideal for establishing links to the producers in the particular village neighbourhood (they were mostly their neighbours, co-producers and some kin) and buying and packing the tomatoes, chores all accomplished still in the locality.

After this stage, however, his skills were of less use. He did not know the Russian language well enough and is not apparently clever enough to resist the money demands of the customs and security people at the border of Azerbaijan and Dagestan;[9] that is why the truck was delayed so long, and the tomatoes started rotting on the road. Elşən was completely dependent on Hikmet's connections and company all the time he was in Moscow. Hikmət organized for him to stay with his own relatives without any costs for him; Elşən stayed over a month. Nevertheless, the partnership broke up after the last truck load of tomatoes. What was missing between the two was trust for a longer and sustainable trade relationship.

Trust itself was a scarcity throughout the whole process. The scarcity of trust was found at all stages of the trade: to find a trustworthy driver from Dagestan was difficult. One had to rely on recommendations but had limited choice because the drivers had to be from Dagestan due to the convenient proximity to the village and the Russian traffic plates these trucks carry. If they were to take other trucks, from Iran or Turkey (in those days in Azerbaijan there were not that many new trucks that were capable of surviving the bad roads), the non-Russian traffic plate would have provoked even more bribes and payments to customs and security officers, said Hikmət.

Trust was also needed to work together with those bargaining the prices with the producers, with those actually making the purchases, packing the cases, and loading the truck. Here Hikmət had to trust not only Elşən but also the latter's brothers and father as well as the other partners in the neighbourhood. He complained that the partners in the neighbourhood were not competent, even if Elşən was. Elşən had to rely on Hikmət for carrying out all the deals and sales in Moscow and did not trust him fully whether he was counting and keeping the money properly. Hikmət's family and his relatives through marriage (especially the female members of this group) were, for Elşən, spending too much on (according to him) unnecessary consumer goods. The fact that Hikmət's wife kept the money at home made his suspicions stronger. So, the partnership between the two young men ended after a single season and both sides seemed to think that they would get along better with their own kinsmen.

After this episode Hikmət started cooperating with his own brother Anar in the village, who in fact knew nothing about agricultural production, or about trade. Relying on kinsmen as partners is the local ideal in the village (see also Yalçın-Heckmann 2010). Kinsmen could be a potential source of cash and labour; through cultivating relations of generalized and delayed exchange. These relations resemble more those of the community than of the market; one could ideally accumulate capital and resist the pressure of immediate return and distribution of the gains. However, kinship and friendship, which ideally provide trust in relations, are also a source of pressure on others in demanding support in trade and financial assistance. This was the case of Feridun, who supported his friend who came to Moscow after him and became his partner. If the partnership does not work out, usually the friendship ends as well.

Finally, how does this trade have an effect on the community relations and property regimes in the village and the neighbourhood? As the lucrative tomato trade to Russia's markets became known as a risky but 'licit' way of making good money, the tomato growers increasingly concentrated their production to their household plots. Those with means to expand the production started renting land for glasshouse cultivation of tomatoes. This is a labour intensive and costly horticulture. It could be carried out only on those plots given to households as household plots (*heyət yanı*) because these plots can be irrigated. The privatized and distributed land shares (*pay*) are mostly far away from irrigation canals and few households have the financial means to afford irrigation money anyway. So those households engaging in tomato production, especially those with the intention of getting involved in its trade directly, would invest cash and labour in cultivating tomato on household plots and either leaving the *pay* shares uncultivated or renting these out to others who want to cultivate corn and wheat on them. As most of the households carry out the horticultural activities for growing tomatoes as members of the household and kin group as labourers, cultivating additional land would be impossible without hiring additional labour.

Other than this constraint of household size on shaping the extent of tomato cultivation, the other factor in tomato produce is the financial input necessary for early cultivation. Glasshouses have become widespread in this village since the late 1980s and early 1990s. In those years the villagers still had state support for agricultural inputs, if not they were still able to 'organize' it themselves through the sovkhoz or kolkhoz. Until 1994 there was also free natural gas delivered to village households and the glasshouses used gas for heating. Later on when the free gas was turned off, some households managed to keep heating by using oil. These days very few households could afford such expenses and for them the glasshouses are for growing early tomatoes, but not as early as the ones grown in heated glasshouses.[10] So those who have the heating and a large labour force would in this case have the best chances of carrying out successful cash crop production.

'Illegal' trade and informality: Azerbaijani herbs in a Moscow market

Tomato trade took place during the daytime and in the legal wholesale market, even if there were some 'additional' fees to be paid to various functionaries and protectors. The second type of market which was thought to bring lucrative profits was the Azerbaijani illegal market for fresh kitchen herbs (*göy*) in Moscow.

Excerpts from field notes (July 2002):

The market is at a quite central location in the city. Hikmət claims that his mother-in-law Nadirə was one of the first persons to introduce the sale of *göy* in Moscow shortly after 1991. Following her there came many women, especially teachers from Gəncə. At the height of the fresh herb season about eight tons of *göy* from the village neighbourhood (possibly an exaggeration and pertaining to an area larger than the neighbourhood, but nonetheless about 60 per cent of the c. 7,000 inhabitants are involved in cultivation) are brought daily to Moscow and about two tons to St. Petersburg. Hikmət says '*hamı burayla dolanır*', (lit. the village neighbourhood survives on sales in Moscow and St. Petersburg). There are about 40 traders of *göy* from the region. 25 of them are women (these are from Gəncə) and the rest are men. The women are mostly teachers. Upon my inquiry, Hikmət explained that the teachers give a share (*pay*) to the school director, who hires a substitute (hence probably takes money for 'subletting' these teaching hours to someone else too) to teach this person's hours and lets the teacher be absent for some months. The husbands of these teachers are their partners in Azerbaijan; i.e. they buy the produce from the villagers and send it to Moscow. Presently the *göy* business is very profitable, according to Hikmət, 'there is not a single box of *göy* left in Azerbaijan', ('*Azerbaycan'da bir karopka (коробка) göy kalmayır*'). But he says, one is legally allowed to take only one *bağ* (bundle) along which is about 50 kg, when one leaves Azerbaijan; the customs 'does not allow it' ('*koymuyor*'). So the rest, that is the major portion of *göy*, has to be passed through the customs by giving bribes. *Göy* is sold to Russia from the village neighbourhood from about mid-September to the end of May. There was of course still some *göy* coming in July, but the season from this neighbourhood was over, the *göy* now coming was from villages in Gəncə district. When *göy* trade comes to an end, the season for tomatoes which are grown in glasshouses begin.

Hikmət believes that some people have made very good money with the *göy* business; for instance, there is Besti, a teacher from Gəncə who is supposed to have earned $30,000 in 1996. The people who earn this money do not invest in production but build houses or renovate their houses. Some also become quite obnoxious and pompous, says Hikmət, playing the rich: in Azerbaijani one says to such people '*tosbağa çanağından çıkıb çanağından beğenmir*', which means something like: 'these are people who come from a modest background but got rich and look down upon their origins'.

On my last evening at Hikmət's, we made plans to go to the *göy* fresh herbs wholesale market with Hikmət and Mecid. Hikmət was not working then (July) but he had been selling herbs there from mid-October until the end of May. We were to go about 10 p.m., as the market operates at night. Mecid would come and take us there, but Hikmət did not want to go inside because he did not want to be seen by, and have to chat with, many people he knows there. Another reason is that he had said he would be in Azerbaijan during summer; this is what people do in order not to pay the price of the stall at the market during summer months. Mecid had to keep to this story too, so when people were asking him about Hikmət, Mecid gave evasive answers. Only Mecid's cousin Ramil knew about Hikmət and he came around with us. He still works and sells *göy* there.

The market was an amazing place. It is right in the centre of the city. Within its compound there were hundreds of people walking around looking at and choosing products, chatting and bargaining, sitting in the cafeteria or selling vegetables and herbs directly from the back of small trucks and cars as well as from the market stalls. Mecid showed the stall and the specific place from which Hikmət commonly trades. Becoming quite fascinated with the business of the place, I asked Mecid and Ramil whether it would be alright to take pictures. They said yes but that I should do it discreetly. However at night the camera goes with the flash light of course, so after I took two pictures from a platform looking down on the stalls someone came and held my arm and said something to me in Russian. I replied in Azerbaijani and Mecid and Ramil immediately interfered, saying that I am with them that I am a friend interested in the place they work. This was the *çaycı*, tea seller, I was told later. I thought that the intervention was over and wanted to go down among the sales people to look at the prices and the goods. As we went down, two other young men came and demanded my film from me. Mecid and Ramil were quite composed and calm and said that I am their guest and have been taking their pictures all day long and that there is nothing wrong with my being there. As the men insisted somewhat Mecid said I had been taking pictures of everything and anything, also of Kremlin; the response was: 'she should take pictures of Kremlin but not of the market!' I mumbled something like 'I am here with permission and would not give my film', supposedly referring to some licit right to be there, which was quite ironic of course. The men seemed somewhat convinced but continued to threaten us, saying that if anything comes out of these pictures then Mecid and Ramil would be 'in it': '*sizden sorarık!*'. Without haste but not wanting to stay there anymore we left the place. Ramil came with us to the car, where Hikmət had been waiting for us. I got quite worried for them – whether the men would do anything to them or harass them. Only then did it become clear to me what was meant by illegal market. The men were in fact only the underdogs of the '*reykits*' (racketeer), who are in charge of the whole place. The market functions formally during the day; night sales are not allowed and take place under the control of the Azerbaijani mafia. The mafia pays the head of the militia who in return pays up to the *mergorod*, mayoralty, of the city. That is why there was no control or payment as we entered the place. This market is allegedly under the control of a mafia from Nakhchivan, the former autonomous region annexed to Azerbaijan. Mecid thinks that this mafia is still better than the Russians; if it had been the Russians they would have broken my camera and would have heard no arguments or pleas from us! Hikmət says he pays $4,000 for the stall place he has for selling his herbs during the main herbs season. Daily he estimates that the mafia collects $5,000 from the sellers. They also control the transfer of money. The way he sent the money from tomatoes through the stewardesses does not work here. Everyone has to give the money to them, they organize the transport and charge accordingly (500 Roubles per $1,000) a bit less than the stewardesses. The procedure works according to the rules however, says Hikmət: '*qaydasıyla*', i.e. they do not cheat, but this is also the way they control who is earning how much money. For Hikmət this is '*korkulu iş*' ('a fearful job'); that is why Mecid quit. Once the *reykits* had beaten up a man who did not want to give the money demanded from him, and they killed another one who had talked about the place. One has no right to resist their demands, and they could come any day and demand higher payments or kick one out. But it is the best way available to them for making some money even if not becoming rich. The tomato business was legal in comparison to *göy*, but is more difficult and risky, because they get rotten easily. *Göy* becomes rotten too sometimes, for instance in winter they lost the whole produce at least twice because of fog, when the plane could not land and went somewhere else, and the whole produce was lost.

What kind of concluding remarks can we draw from this ethnography of the illegal market? Young men like Hikmət or his wife's brother Mecid engaged in this trade because of its profitability and promise of earning good money fast. However, they knew that their gains were strictly controlled by the mafia networks (who also fought among themselves for profits and control) and hence even if they were to work harder, sell more and at better prices, they would then have to give higher payments to the mafia. So the fulfilment of the dream of making sufficient gains and accumulating capital, a dream which was commonly articulated as returning to Azerbaijan with enough money to start up a shop or a small business, was delayed continuously. It still looks like such men would in fact settle in Russia, especially if their families have joined them and if they earn enough to lead a life as the new lower class with risky existence and hardly any secure legal status in Russian cities. This is what has happened with his brother-in-law Mecid. Furthermore, Hikmət and Mecid have both moved on to expanding and increasing the scale of their businesses; they moved on to trade with fabrics and ready-made clothes and have opened up shops in the outskirts of Moscow. This means that Hikmət has become an employer for trainees from the village who want to earn some money in Russia, but is no longer dependent on local agricultural production for his business. Interestingly this seems to strain his relationships with his hometown and household members even more; his brother Anar has been working as Hikmət's help in his shops several times in the last few years, but the demand came more from Anar to earn some money, than from Hikmət, who in an early phase of his trade would have needed and been more dependent on his brother as trustworthy kin.

The question of why this specific product, *göy*, is chosen for trade can also be answered with its high profitability. A bundle (*bağ*) of *göy* was sold in 2002 at ten times higher than the price than in local markets, and the bundles in Moscow were much smaller. The other reason given by villagers was the high demand in Russian cities for the good quality fresh herbs from this region, believed to be the highest quality anywhere.

As for the question of community relations for organizing the access to this market, one obvious point was the then essential dependency on, and informality of, Azerbaijani networks. Without the contacts to the local producers and salesmen and women in Moscow's markets, there was hardly any entry possible to the market. The bundle of relations was spread along local, friendship, and kinship ties and they were all usual and useful links for establishing the contacts within the chain between the producers and the customers. It was mostly young and middle-aged men who carried out the trade on the market, but also women as in the case of teachers from Gəncə. Traders needed some language skills, although within the 'illegal' herb market one could in fact function without Russian, if one was well connected with those already working there. There were, however, some drawbacks to this trade, as expressed by villagers: although 24 per cent of the households of the sample surveyed in the village (2001–2002) had at least one household member working abroad (mostly in Russia, and almost all as traders, *al-verci*) (Yalçın-Heckmann 2010), the trading activity was nevertheless socially looked down upon. People referred to their kinsmen abroad as being engaged in trade (*ticarat*) but not *al-ver* (petty trade) (see also Heyat 2002b). Even if everyone knew that the majority of those absent were working in such markets or as street-sellers, it was almost taboo to refer to this activity as such.[11] Only in jokes or as a verbal challenge would one mention this in public. The other drawback was of course the illegality involved in it; that the salespeople were all dependent on payments and agreements with the mafia. As Hikmət indicated, it was a fearful job, and his wife said that she could not sleep at night and waited for him when

Informal economy in Azerbaijan 181

he went out at night to work on the market during these winter months. The other difficulty was of course the bitter cold and snow one had to put up with standing outside in Moscow's winter nights.

Although it was mostly men involved in this trade, as in the case of women teachers from Gəncə, female presences and activity was also tolerated. In fact, Hikmət seemed to think that women were better sellers; they bargained better and were tough with selling on credit. Furthermore, mafia men – since they were all Azerbaijani – shared the gendered behaviour codes with the traders and did not hassle women as often as they did men. Women, however, faced more risk than men of losing their sexual reputation. On the whole, women who were and are involved in petty trade, be it within Azerbaijan or in Russia, still risk being the target of gossip, of accusations of intimacy with men and of neglecting their own families, children and household. Hikmət, for instance, said that he would never allow his wife or other female members of his family in Moscow to work on the market. They did, however, carry out some of the chores related to *göy* trade, such as making smaller bundles of *göy* at home after the parcels arrive from the airport and before Hikmət took them to the market.

Trade activities in Moscow have general implications for relationships in the transnational space between the generations and kin households in the village. When men go abroad alone, their wives and children need the support of the parental generation, and they either live together with their parents-in-law or the women go to their own parental households, especially if they have small children. Hence the parental generation has to support socially and morally and sometimes even financially the family members left behind. This causes strains on inner household and inter-generational relations, even if the prospect of money (incidentally, US dollars, and not Russian Roubles) coming from abroad is an incentive for fulfilling this obligation, and families of migrants left in the village are on the whole considered to have easy access and supply of foreign currency. In the early 2000s when the news came about a migrant abroad returning home, the question raised immediately was: how much money did the person bring along? Again, upon such news or the expectation that the migrant person might be coming himself or sending money with a third person, new plans for expenditure would be prepared: the shop keeper would be getting ready to collect from the relatives of the migrant person the money lent, or the debts paid back, the relatives of the migrant would plan time for carrying out a circumcision ceremony or a wedding, the parents of the migrant would consider the possibility of finally going to the doctor, getting treatment and being able to pay for it. Hence the remittance arriving from abroad was seen as a money pool to answer the demands of more than one person and where relationships between the sender and the receivers had to be kept alive and renewed constantly, often causing conflicts within the transnational space.

What determined the success or failure of trade with fresh herbs or tomatoes such that the trade could grow and expand in the village and the market? The primary factor was having the necessary support of networks both in the village, place of production, and in Moscow, the marketplace. These networks required social as well as trading skills, i.e. skills in bargaining, establishing trust, but also being cunning when necessary, hence attending both moral values and informal strategies. The second factor for success was having protection from the mafia, and hence being ready to get involved in payments or other obligations towards one of the mafia groups. Hikmət had the protection of a mafia boss from his district, and relied on this protection for any problem he might ultimately have with other Azerbaijani mafia groups in Azerbaijan and in Russia. He was not directly in contact with them, but knew the connections and had some distant kin who had been related to this mafia boss. Even such knowledge could be of use in times of trouble; that is why he and Mecid were not too worried about the problem I unintentionally had caused for them by wanting to take pictures of the market.

One further factor of success in this trade seemed to be the necessary flexibility of crossing borders between legal and illegal trade and between moral and immoral rules of trading behaviour. Hikmət's mother, for instance, would have been appalled if she had known that Hikmət had been cheating with the scale he used at his stall. She, coming from a public sector employment background and with former communist party membership, shared some of the prejudices about petty trade (*al-ver*) as an undesirable and morally low activity, as well as wanting to keep her reputation as a respectable elderly women in the village (*aqsaqqal* is the term given to elderly men and women of high social esteem). Hikmət believed, however, as he told me, that there was no way he would have made enough money to cover his costs, if he were not to cheat with the scale. This thin boundary between legal and illegal spheres of social and economic action caused and still causes anxiety about keeping one's reputation back in the village context. The community of Azerbaijanis, of friends and acquaintances in and around the markets in Russia keeps the traders under the social control of gossip and moral evaluation. Stories of treachery, of corruption, of fraud, as well as improper behaviour, of love affairs with Russian women are ample and reach the village with speed. These gossip stories counterbalance the reputation as successful traders, as 'those who made it'. Success is often displayed with fancy and big houses built in the village, but increasingly flats bought in Baku. The village as a social context where the traders come back to be with their friends and families, to celebrate festivities and build houses is the crucial framework of social reference and status as long as parental generation is there to play the part of thankful receivers of support through remittances and cautious observers of migrants' reputation and social standing.

Concluding remarks

What effects did the trade with fresh herbs have on the agricultural economy, market and property regimes in the Azerbaijani village? Similar to the tomato cultivation, *göy* was cultivated on household plots, because it needed irrigation. Household labour was crucial; however, it was less intensive than the case of tomatoes. In the specific village neighbourhood, *göy* was produced primarily for the markets in Moscow and St. Petersburg. The best quality *göy* was sold to traders who came and bought daily from the producer village households. The rest of the *göy* went to local markets, either to the weekly village market, to daily district market or to weekly market in the city of Gəncə. The price offered and bargained for with the daily buyers (*al-verci*) determined the upper limit for the prices on local markets. *Göy*-producing households were dependent on the purchasing traders, as they could not sell all their produce at the local markets and did not have the means to transport their herbs to another lucrative market in Baku, for instance. Furthermore, all of this produce trade was organized along informal networks, which required skills in using economic strategies and maintaining social relations.

Beyond the village, the trade of food provided employment and income for a large sector of people, not only in the village. The airport workers, customs' officers and security personnel, as well as schools where Gəncə's teachers worked were all implicated in this 'illegal' trade to some extent and made earnings from it. On the other hand, the ironic aspect of this trade was that it offered a threshold to criminalization, of accepting criminal behaviour for making earnings, even if the earnings were for socially and morally acceptable 'licit' goals, such as wanting to pay the costly medical treatment of one's mother or other close relative. This was the reason given by another friend of Hikmət who found the income from fresh herbs too low and changed to trading stolen car parts which was then apparently more lucrative, although much more risky in terms of payments to the mafia and the police. Young men like Hikmət did not seem to be too far away from crossing the borders of illegal and legal trade, and even to getting directly involved in mafia groups, as this had been the case of several young men from the village, who had made careers in Russia as *reykit*s (racketeer) and of whom some were killed in mafia fights.

Finally, at the time of infrastructural and economic difficulties in the countryside in the early 2000s could the village producers have survived, if they had not sold their herbs and tomatoes to Russia? Probably not. The system of agricultural production for markets abroad caused intensified production on household plots, and correlated to the neglect of privatized land shares and their cultivation (Yalçın-Heckmann 2010). The other consequence of this vegetable trade with Russia was of course the systemic reproduction of corruption, of 'criminalization' of agricultural trade and of illegal siphoning of surplus in the Azerbaijani and Russian economies.

Notes

1 The research for this chapter has been financed by the Max Planck Institute for Social Anthropology (Halle/Saale, Germany) from 2000–2009, and the research visit to Azerbaijan in 2011 by the University of Pardubice, Czech Republic. The author would like to thank these institutions for their generous support.
2 Petty trade (*al-ver*) can be contrasted to trade (*ticarat*); the latter refers to more formal even if small-scale trade, e.g. where people sell and buy in shops and act within regulated conditions.
3 Labour migration to developed Western countries has been from early on associated with shortages in employment and rural income in less developed countries (see Lee 1996). Nevertheless, the case I discuss here deals with a specific type of migration:

a) it is unaccounted for and not formally guided by state structures, b) it involves often short-term and fairly ad hoc planning and back and forth movement of people. For a comparative analysis of South Caucasian migration flows, see Dermendzhieva 2011.
4 Gudeman's concepts and the description of the interplay between community and market has been criticized by Johan Rasanayagam (2003), where he draws attention to the difficulty of keeping the realms clearly separate from one another, when applied to socialist and post-socialist societies like Uzbekistan. Rasanayagam prefers to use the concept of 'economic spheres' in order to show the fuzziness and flexibility of the economic processes between the state, society and the market.
5 Currency rates are given for 2002. 1 Russian Rouble was equal to €0.03. 10 Roubles = €0.32.
6 Exchange rates in 2002: 5,000 Roubles = €160 Euro, 400 Roubles = €13 Euro, $6,000 = €6,050.
7 A recent report on Şəmkir's tomato producers in glasshouses indicates that tomato production and sale in Moscow's markets is still highly important for the local economy. See Azadlıq Radiosu, 'Əlləri mazutlu Şəmkir "parnik"çiləri', Online Radio Broadcast, 9 March 2013 (www.azadliq.org, accessed 11 March 2013).
8 Hikmət applied for Russian citizenship in order to ease his trade and economic activities in Russia, even if he continues to invest in housing in Azerbaijan (by buying himself a half finished flat in Baku) as well as expanding his business in Moscow and surroundings.
9 He travelled with the truck for the first four transports he did with Hikmət. In this last one he took the plane and explained his reason to me that he was sick of being racially hassled on the road by customs and policemen: 'Qara milləti incidirlər yolda' (they harass the 'black people' on the road).
10 See the report of Azadlıq Radiosu, mentioned in note 7 above.
11 On one occasion, my host family, a couple of guests and I were sitting outside in the garden and chatting about many topics, when I did some filming of the conversation around the table. Later on as I was showing the film to Hikmət's mother, my hostess, she was surprised and then nearly upset about the fact that her mundane chat about Hikmət's trade activities in Moscow, that he was planning to buy cucumbers from a region close to the city, was mentioned on record. It was for her unsuitable to record such 'empty talk' on film, and hence publicly register the *al-verci* activities of Hikmət.

References

Azadlıq Radiosu 'Əlləri mazutlu Şəmkir "parnik" çiləri . . .', Radio Broadcast, 9 March 2013. Online. Available: (accessed 11 March 2013).
Brednikova, O. and Patchenkov, O. (1999) 'Economic Migrants from Azerbaijan in St. Petersburg: The Problems of Social Adaptation and Integration', *Caucasian Regional Studies* 4(1).
—— (2002) 'Migrants – "Caucasians" in St. Petersburg: Life in Tension', *Anthropology and Archeology of Eurasia* 41(2): 43–89.
Cornell, S. (2011) *Azerbaijan since Independence*, Armonk, NY: Sharpe Publishers.
Dermendzhieva, Z. (2011) 'Emigration from the South Caucasus: Who Goes Abroad and What are the Economic Implications?' *Post-communist Economies*, 23(3): 377–98.
Gambold Miller, L.L. and Heady, P. (2003) 'Cooperation, Power, and Community: Economy and Ideology in the Russian Countryside', in Hann C. and the Property Relations Group (eds), *The Postsocialist Agrarian Question: Property Relations and the Rural Condition*, Münster: LIT Publishers, pp. 257–92.

Glick-Schiller, N., Basch, L. and Blanc-Szanton, C. (1992) *Towards a Transnational Perspective on Migration: Race, Class, Ethnicity, and Nationalism Reconsidered*, New York, NY: New York Academy of Sciences.

Gudeman, S. (2001) *The Anthropology of Economy: Community, Market, and Culture*, Malden, MA and Oxford: Blackwell Publishers.

—— (2008) *Economy's Tension: The Dialectics of Community and Market*, New York and Oxford: Berghahn Books.

Hart, K. (1973) 'Informal Income Opportunities and Urban Employment in Ghana', *Journal of Modern African Studies*, 11(1): 61–89.

—— (2000) *The Memory Bank: Money in an Unequal World*, London: Profile Books.

Heyat, F. (2002a) *Azeri Women in Transition: Women in Soviet and Post-Soviet Azerbaijan*, London: Routledge Curzon.

—— (2002b) 'Women and the Culture of Entrepreneurship in Soviet and Post-Soviet Azerbaijan', in Mandel, R. and Humphrey, C. (eds), *Markets and Moralities: Ethnographies of Postsocialism*, Oxford and New York: Berg Publishers, pp. 19–31.

Humphrey, C. (2002) *The Unmaking of Soviet Life: Everyday Economies after Socialism*, Ithaca and London: Cornell University Press.

Humphrey, C. and Mandel, R. (2002) 'The Markets in Everyday Life: Ethnographies of postsocialism', in Mandel, R. and Humphrey, C. (eds), *Markets and Moralities: Ethnographies of Postsocialism*, Oxford and New York: Berg Publishers, pp. 1–16.

Kaneff, D. (2002) 'The Shame and Pride of Market Activity: Morality, Identity and Trading in Postsocialist Rural Bulgaria', in Mandel, R. and Humphrey, C. (eds), *Markets and Moralities: Ethnographies of Postsocialism*, Oxford and New York: Berg Publishers, pp. 33–51.

Kaneff, D. and Yalçın-Heckmann L. (2003) 'Retreat to the Cooperative or to the Household? Agricultural Privatisation in Ukraine and Azerbaijan', in Hann C. and the Property Relations Group (eds), *The Postsocialist Agrarian Question: Property Relations and the Rural Condition*, Münster: LIT Verlag, pp. 219–55.

Lee, E. (1996) [1965] 'A Theory of Migration', in Cohen, R. (ed.), *Theories of Migration*, Cheltenham, UK: Edward Elgar, pp. 47–57.

Lerman, Z. (1998) 'Land Reform in Uzbekistan' in Wegren, S. (ed.), *Land Reform in the Former Soviet Union and Eastern Europe*, London: Routledge, pp. 136–61.

Lerman, Z. and Brooks, K. (1998) 'Land Reform in Turkmenistan', in Wegren, S. (ed.), *and Reform in the Former Soviet Union and Eastern Europe*, London: Routledge, pp. 162–85.

Mandel, R. (2008) *Cosmopolitan Anxieties: Turkish Challenges to Citizenship and Belonging in Germany*, Durham NC and London: Duke University Press.

Pachenkov, O. and Berman, D. (2007) 'Spaces of Conflict and Camaraderie. The Contradictory Logics of a Postsocialist Flea Market', in Cross, J. and Morales, A. (eds), *Street Entrepreneurs: People, Place and Politics in Local and Global Perspective*, London and New York: Routledge, pp. 201–22.

Pries, Ludger (ed.) (2008) *Rethinking Transnationalism: The Meso-link of Organizations*, Abingdon and New York: Routledge.

Rasanayagam, J. (2003) 'Market, State and Community in Uzbekistan: Reworking the Concept of the Informal Economy', MPI for Social Anthropology Working Paper No. 59. Halle/Saale.

Temel, T., Janssen, W. and Karimov, F. (2002) *The Agricultural Innovation System of Azerbaijan: An Assessment of Institutional Linkages*, ISNAR Country Report 64, The Hague: International Service for National Agricultural Research.

Trevisani, T. (2010) *Land and Power in Khorezm: Farmers, Communities, and the State in Uzbekistan's Decollectivisation*, Berlin: LIT Publishers.

Volkov, V. (1999) 'Violent Entrepreneurship in Post-Communist Russia', *Europe–Asia Studies* 51(5): 741–54.

Werbner, P. (forthcoming) 'Migration and Transnational Studies: Between Simultaneity and Rupture', in Qayson, A. and Daswani, G. (eds), *Blackwell Reader in Migration and Transnational Studies* Oxford: Blackwell.

Yalçın-Heckmann, L. (2010) The Return of Private Property: Rural life after Agrarian Reforms in the Republic of Azerbaijan. Berlin: LIT Publishers.

Index

affective labour 68–9, 73, 78
Azerbaijan: food traders 165–186

bazaars *see* marketplaces
Belarus: cross-border trade 135–151
blat xv, 7, 26, 91–2, 111, 114
borderland spaces 140, 153
bribery 12, 26–7, 41, 86, 90, 94–5, 111–12, 127, 158, 177
Burawoy, Michael 41, 52

care *see* childcare
carer 67–8, 71, 73, 76, 81; familial carer *see* informal carer; informal carer 71, 81; paid carer 68, 80; professional carer 80
Carothers, Thomas 6
Castells, Manuel 3
Certeau, Michel de 8, 13, 138–40, 144, 147–8
chelnoki see shuttle traders
childcare 11–12, 67–73, 75, 77, 79–82; childcare market 67, 70–1, 81; childcare services 68–70, 73, 79–82; class identity 8, 11–12, 36, 52–3, 63, 69, 73, 76–7
cleaner 68, 74–7
cleaning 69, 72, 74–8, 81; *see also* domestic services
community exchange, 29–30
construction work 43
contraband 113; *see also* smuggling
corruption 6, 26–7, 86, 93, 128
criminality 37–8, 51, 94, 127, 179, 183
cross-border arbitrage 13, 126, 135, 141
cross-border trade *see* shuttle traders
customs and excise 93–4, 127, 153, 156, 158–9, 173, 175, 177

democratization 6
development 6, 32, 86–7
diverse economies 21–34
do-it-yourself 11, 30, 51, 53
domestic 68–9; domestic employee *see* domestic worker; domestic services 27–8, 69–70, 72–3, 77–81; domestic work *see* domestic services; domestic worker 68, 72, 76–7
double book-keeping 3, 96
dual economy thesis 3–6, 21–22

early retirement 68–9, 75
economic rationality 11, 73, 115, 137–139, 144–8; *see also* moral economy/ rationality
emigration 40, 140–1
entrepreneurialism 9, 11, 63, 85, 87, 97, 104, 152, 160, 170, 180
envelope wage 25, 71–2, 95
EU accession 39–40
European identity 42

favours 26–7, 147; *see also* reimbursed favours
financial crisis (2008–) 1, 37, 40, 71
firma babochka (butterfly firm) 89
formal employment, paid 24–5, 51–62, 69, 71, 74–5, 78; unpaid 28–9
formalization thesis 3, 10, 21, 129, 174

Gibson-Graham *see* diverse economies
gifts 27, 32, 108, 111
globalization 4, 53
governmentality 9, 41; *see also* entrepreneurialism
Gudeman, Stephen 139, 148, 167, 175, 184
gypsy cabs *see* taxis

Hart, Keith 3, 55
Harvey, David 41
healthcare 21–34
health insurance 44, 74
household labour, paid 27–8, 30–1

illegality 86, 153–5, 179; *see also* criminality
illicit xvi, 12, 13, 51, 86, 103, 113–5, 123, 169, *see also* illegality

Index

IMF 3, 123
import duties *see* customs and excise
informal employment 25–6, 56–8, 60, 68–9, 75–6
internships 28
'invisible' citizens 37

Kideckel, David 9, 38, 41–2, 46
kinship relations 12, 30, 52, 109–10, 141, 170, 175–6, 180–1
kompromat xv, 12, 85, 89–90, 99
Kyrgyzstan: bazaars 121–134

Labour sharing 106
Ledeneva, Alena 6, 26, 91
licit *see* illicit
Lithuania: informal trades 35–50

marginality thesis 114, 139
market hegemony 32, 148
marketplaces 124–5, 127–8, 130–1, 142, 170–3, 177–9
Mauss, Marcel 111, 146, 149
memory 13
microcredit 125
migration, international 122, 166–7; rural-urban 38–9, 130, 141
modernization paradigm 6, 9
money laundering 89
moonlighting 4, 8, 51–2, 62, 75, 77, 79, 105–6
moral economy/rationality 63, 73, 78
mutual aid 12, 63, 108
mutualism *see* symbiosis
mutuality *see* reciprocity

nanny 67–8, 70–3, 75, 78–82
neocapitalism *see* Kideckel
neoliberalism 4, 38, 41–2, 64, 87, 123

Orange Revolution 93

pensioners 1, 9, 12, 37, 77, 85, 86, 108
personhood 41
petty trade 13, 14, 135–146, 166–7, 180
Portes, Alejandro 4, 124
portfolio (or patchwork) employment 59–60, 69, 71, 75, 81
poverty 12, 39, 46, 51, 54, 64, 69, 72, 75, 77, 103, 121, 130–1, 137–8, 142–3
precarious work 54
profit motive 137–8

quantitative approaches to informality 2

reciprocity 31, 57, 61, 107, 109, 138–9, 145–7
reimbursed favours 26

remittances 172–3, 179, 181
Romania: childcare 67–84
Russia: blue-collar work 51–66

Schengen Area 13, 135, 143, 152–3, 156, 160–1
Scott, James C. 8
self-employment 61–2, 71, 105
self-provisioning 30–1, 51, 57
shock therapy 1, 4, 168
shuttle traders 122, 125–8, 129–30, 135–8, 141–2, 144–8, 153–62
Slovakia: transit and trucking 102–118
small plot agriculture 3, 138, 165–6, 176, 182
smuggling 12, 94, 113, 126–7, 146, 152–3, 157
social capital 53–4
socialist era, 6–7, 40, 79, 103, 107, 122–3, 140–1, 165
social network relations 7, 11, 53–4, 57, 68, 109, 116, 142, 146
solidarity, 13, 40, 42, 51–2, 60–1, 63, 68, 99, 138, 144–8, 169; *see also* reciprocity
state withdrawal 8–9, 26, 41, 86, 92, 155
structuralist thesis 4, 8, 124
subsistence agriculture 3, 70–2
symbiosis 4, 8

tax evasion and avoidance 6, 26, 40, 63, 79, 89–90, 95–6, 106, 113, 128–9, 155
taxis 60, 85, 107–109, 112, 115
total social organization of labour 22–4
transition, critique of category of 1, 6, 32, 99
transnational space 168–70
trust 12, 37, 39, 51, 57–8, 60, 63, 68, 69, 72, 77, 81–2, 99, 106–7, 109–110, 113, 147, 161–2, 168–9, 175–6

Ukraine: cross-border trading 152–164
Ukraine: healthcare sector 21–34
Ukraine: SME entrepreneurs 85–101
undeclared work 25–6, 68, 69–72, 74–8, 81
unions 46
unpaid work 29–31

Verdery, Katherine 4, 41
volunteering 28

working-class solidarity 52
working poor, *see* poverty
World Bank 3, 123

Yanukovych, Viktor 89

Lightning Source UK Ltd.
Milton Keynes UK
UKOW06n1425240415

250218UK00001B/44/P